Jill Foulston, a former commissioning editor of the Virago Modern Classics, has also published *The Virago Book of Food: The Joy of Eating*. She lives in London and Italy.

Also by Jill Foulston

The Virago Book of Food: The Joy of Eating (editor)

THE
VIRAGO BOOK
OF
THE JOY
OF
SHOPPING

EDITED BY JILL FOULSTON

virago

VIRAGO

First published in Great Britain in 2007 by Virago Press
This paperback edition published in 2010 by Virago Press

A CIP catalogue record for this book
is available from the British Library.

ISBN 978-1-84408-274-2

Typeset in Goudy by M Rules
Printed and bound in Great Britain by
Clays Ltd, St Ives plc

Papers used by Virago are natural, renewable and
recyclable products sourced from well-managed forests and certified
in accordance with the rules of the Forest Stewardship Council.

Virago Press
An imprint of
Little, Brown Book Group
100 Victoria Embankment
London EC4Y 0DY

An Hachette UK Company
www.hachette.co.uk

www.virago.co.uk

*The women reigned supreme. They had taken the shops by storm,
camping there, as in a conquered country, like an invading
horde, surrounded by the ravaged merchandise . . .*
THE LADIES' PARADISE
EMILE ZOLA

*The awful prevalence of the vice of shopping among women
is one of those signs of the times which lead the thoughtful patriot
almost to despair of the future of our country. Few people
have any idea of the extent to which our women are
addicted to this purse-destroying vice.*
NEW YORK TIMES, 1881

*What lack ye? What lack ye?
Madam, will you buy?*
17TH-CENTURY MARKET CRY

CONTENTS

INTRODUCTION

What is shopping?

Is it the furtive click-click at your desk while the rest of the department is in a meeting? The one-stop jaunt to Peter Jones at the weekend? The crushing ooze of streets at Christmas? Bargaining in the souk on holiday?

Finding the right thing, putting up with the wrong thing. Women have been doing it for centuries with mixed emotions of glee, satisfaction and frustration. We've never had so much choice, and yet how we shop has changed enormously. In a curious way, the boom in online purchasing has returned us full circle to the earliest days of shopping – which was done in or from the home, at one's desk. In the Middle Ages, estates and families were as self-sufficient as possible, and shopping was done mostly by servants or men, often at annual fairs. For the most part, women were not allowed out on the streets unaccompanied, so the medieval housewife, Margaret Paston, wrote from Norwich to her husband John, on business in London, to ask him to buy fabric for 'your child's gowns'. She knew where to find the best price and selection, and directed him there; she also specified just how much he should spend on cloth for her hood.

It was not until the seventeenth century that shops became fixed features in towns and cities and spending in them a normal thing for someone with the money to do so. Aphra Behn makes use of the imagery of exchange, setting parts of her 1677 play *The debauchee, or, The credulous cuckold* in a shop. However, many things – certainly clothing – continued to be made at home, or by the local craftsperson, rather than bought from a distant or unknown supplier. In 1798, Jane Austen complained of her new gown: 'I wish such things were to be bought ready-made'. She would have had to wait until after the First World War in order to take her dress off the peg.

Consumer complaint, though, is nothing new. In 1737 Elizabeth Purefoy chastised her suppliers, complaining of spoiled 'mackerell . . . what fish you sent last week stank and could not be eat so I desire you would not send any more fish until further orders'. And Sara Hutchinson, Wordsworth's sister-in-law, turned sulky when her commissions were delayed: 'I had desired you to send two Gentleman's hats fashionable & hansome . . . a chip hat also for myself but as it is so late in the season it is of little consequence – you need not trouble your-self – the other hats you must forward immediately'.

Whereas shopping was once specialised – any given trip might have included a visit to the draper, confectioner, greengrocer, chemist, the tea or coffee merchant, and so on – the emergence of the mid-nineteenth-century department store set the trend for one-stop shopping, concentrating a vast range of merchandise within a single building. It was the French who invented the idea of one shop divided into departments selling different sorts of goods: the first, Bon Marché, was established as a department store by 1852. In America, the general store was the homely rural parallel, stocking everything from briny pickles and frilly lace to axes – a fact that astonished Laura Ingalls Wilder, who 'could have looked for weeks and not seen all the things that were in that store. She had not known there were so many things in the world.'

With the explosion of department stores, women gained a

new freedom to roam the city unaccompanied and to exercise personal choice. It was also a time of increasingly sophisticated marketing ploys, with department stores offering women respite from their busy, anxious lives in the form of soda water, pink teas, animals and manicures. Women were inclined to couch their shopping experiences in words such as 'shimmer', 'glow', 'magic' and 'light' – the same images that later inspired the architects of countless city and suburban malls in the United States.

Today's discount departments, multiples or chains and no-frills warehouse stores (Costco, Asda, IKEA, Wal*Mart, and the like) have once more changed the urban landscape, diminishing the individuality of the shopping street. No longer is there a greengrocer on every corner, a cobbler down the alleyway or an unusual clothing or gift shop along the High. Instead, it's the same string of chains everywhere you go, the same selection of merchandise. Where once we were spoiled and surprised by the unique, now we are seduced by price and range – that is, a range chosen for us by the shop or company that will pay the highest rent because they can order the greatest volume from suppliers. The journalist Joanna Robertson has reluctantly watched the gradual disappearance of the traditional shops of Rome, and here writes about one of the surviving sweet shops in the city's historic centre, La Confetteria Moriondo e Gariglio. Yet although there are supermarkets all over Europe, you still find the indomitable grocers in most small towns, and they'll soon learn your name, your children's names, and your usual order (cheerfully delivered, if you like), much as they might have done in past centuries.

Shopping has often been about socialising. Before the widespread adoption of the automobile, the pedlar was an important figure in rural communities, bringing goods and news, sometimes even healing, to isolated country people. Peddler Jenny, Mari Tomasi's memorable Syrian immigrant, bargains: 'You buy one spool of black tread, one white, and one blue. I make four cents profit and I talk to you all you want . . . All right?' even as she complains that the women in town now have cars. Simone de Beauvoir (*The Second Sex*) could in 1949 call buying 'a discovery, almost an invention' and the woman who does it 'queen; the world is at her feet with its riches and its traps for her to grab herself some loot. She tastes a fleeting triumph when she empties the bag of provisions onto her table.' Her shoppers 'are members of a community which – for a moment – is opposed to the society of men as the essential to the inessential'. De Beauvoir shared the ethos of Gordon Selfridge, who had founded the landmark London department store forty years earlier, asking: 'You know why they come here? It's so much brighter than their own homes. This is not a shop – it's a community centre.'

This sense of community is something that some smaller shops still try to foster, as the manager of an Oxford charity shop acknowledges: 'Quite a few come in every day in their lunch break for something to do. Others come in because they're lonely; there are quite a few about. OAPs come in for a chat, have twenty minutes' browse . . .' In the United States, the shopping mall was once a meeting place for the disenfranchised (women, the elderly, ethnic minorities, the lonely) as well as the affluent. Now, as deep-discount retailers and category killers (huge, all-inclusive shops such as Asda) have mushroomed at the expense of these old-style malls and the 'undesirables' are actively discouraged from mall-crawling, town planners' attempts to recreate a more exclusive sense of community can be seen in the neo-colonial and traditional village designs of many of the newer suburban neighbour-hood shopping centres.

Yet if we used to brush up against each other, scrutinising each purchase and delighting in the feel of velvet against our fingers or the heady scent of a ripe quince, we can now abandon the jewel-like glow of the shop windows for the glare of LCD screens. We bat away at our keyboards with the thrilled breathlessness that comes from finding just what we want, then sit back, cocooned within our homes, and wait, like Lisa Snowdon or India Knight, for the bell to ring, our packages to arrive, 'feeling like you've got a fabulous, perfect present from someone who knows you really well. Which, in fact, you have'. Instead of the communal hunting and gath-ering in a popular and rewarding spot, we have learned to shun public spaces in favour of our private ones. Some of us even pay others to do our shopping for us, a stalwart soul who'll allow us to bypass the horror of the crowded and ill-lit changing room, and bring the loot straight to our front door – for a fee. It's an experience described with some mis-givings but chiefly with triumph by journalist Lynn Barber.

Not shopping can be a lifestyle choice in itself. If you live in New York, you can attend Reverend Billy's Church of Stop Shopping, but if New York is too far away, you can visit his blog instead at www.revbilly.com/blog for inspiration. Faith Popcorn, the American trends analyst, once predicted the end of shopping, and Judith Levine actually refused to do any for an entire year, recording both her savings and her insights in *Not Buying It*.

As an alternative, there's a special market for the unloved, once-worn, broken and now discarded in the charity or thrift shop. Whoever the beneficiary, the second-hand shop or street market can yield hip vintage gear for the shallow of pocket, and has become a common destination for shoppers from all social classes. With typical Atwoodian wry humour, *Lady Oracle* sees Joan on the Portobello Road, pawing over trinkets – 'they lurk passively, like vampire sheep, waiting for someone to buy them' – and waltzing 'to the music of the Mantovani strings, which we got at the Crippled Civilians. We got the record player there, too, for ten dollars'. Angela Carter's magic toyshop sits between 'a failed, boarded-up jeweller's and a grocer's', on the same street as a junk shop. But the penniless Polly of Mary McCarthy's *The Group* cringes when she discovers that her father has taken a job in a thrift shop.

War and revolution create special markets too. Slavenka Drakulić bemoans her addiction to the sales in Italy, just across the border from communist Yugoslavia. The anonymous Second World War diarist of *A Woman in Berlin* writes of the endless queues for anything from rancid butter to rotting potatoes, while Jung Chang remembers the thousands of prohibited books that passed through her brother's hands on the black market during the Cultural Revolution in China.

Both the thrills and the perils of capitalism were the focus of Margaret Böhme's curious 1912 novel, *The Department Store*, which fictionalises the construction of a consumers' palace, the institution of a system of credit, the addictive lure of the sales, and the installation of the in-store detective to combat the perennial problem of shoplifting. For shoplifting is a centuries-old vice, as witness the Old Bailey records of 'legerdemain ladies' tried for stealing chocolate, calico, silk, gowns and other covetables. Women have traditionally enjoyed shopping more, but a new study has shown that men are just as prone to impulse buying. Contemporary statistics suggest that men steal more, and higher value goods along predictable gender lines (for men, it's chiefly electronics). Still, men taper off in their early twenties, while women will continue to steal into their forties – though married women are less likely to do so than singles.

Shoplifters come from all classes, but the transcripts of their trials offer a rare opportunity to hear the voices of the uneducated. Bluestocking scribblers have usually ignored underprivileged shoppers, and during the Edwardian period the Fabian Society had to undertake a special study to discover the weekly expenditure of housewives on the poverty line in London's borough of Lambeth. On the other hand, the heady excitement of too much money to shop with can be dangerous and destructive, as proven by the rags-to-riches-to-rags story of the plucky pools winner, Viv Nicholson.

So what is shopping? An art, a pleasure, a chore, depending on how much time and money you have, and where you happen to find yourself. Sometimes it is simply an escape from boredom. But at its most powerful, its most seductive, shopping asks us to become complicit in our own desire, opens wide the door on our own fantasy world. It promises, usually for the length of time required to beguile us into a purchase, to transform us: to make us thinner, more beautiful, more with-it, sexy and generous, than we truly are. It whispers to us of magic, of dreams, of other selves, indeed, of escape from the self. A flight from the self that prompted the first appearance of the word 'shopping' in the eighteenth century:

> Ladies are said, to go a *Shoping*, when, in the Forenon, *sick of themselves*, they order the Coach, and driving from Shop to Shop, without the slightest Intention of purchasing any thing, they *pester* the Tradesman, by

requiring him to shew them his Goods, at a great Expence of Time and Trouble.

A Seasonable Alarm to the City of London, on the Present Important Crisis, Shewing by the Most Convincing Arguments, that the New Method of Paving the Streets, and the Pulling Down of the Signs, Must Be Pernicious to the Health and Morals of the People of England

ZACHARY ZEAL, 1764

IMPULSE AND INDULGENCE

That moment. That instant when your fingers curl round the handles of a shiny, uncreased bag – and all the gorgeous new things inside it become yours. What's it like? It's like going hungry for days, then cramming your mouth full of warm buttered toast. It's like waking up and realizing it's the weekend. It's like the better moments of sex. Everything else is blocked out of your mind. It's pure, selfish pleasure.

The Secret Dreamworld of a Shopaholic · 2000

PATRICIA HIGHSMITH

Master impressionist Tom Ripley has nothing – until he insinuates himself into the world of millionaire Dickie Greenleaf. When Dickie tires of Tom, Tom murders him and later his snidely suspicious friend Freddie Miles. With full control of Dickie's bank account, Tom makes his way to Venice.

Tom got up from the windowsill smiling, changed his shirt and tie for the evening, and went out to find a pleasant restaurant for dinner. A good restaurant, he thought. Tom Ripley could treat himself to something expensive for once. His billfold was so full of long ten- and twenty-thousand-lire notes it wouldn't bend. He had cashed a thousand dollars' worth of travellers' cheques in Dickie's name before he left Palermo.

He bought two evening newspapers, tucked them under his arm and walked on, over a little arched bridge, through a long street hardly six feet wide full of leather shops and men's shirt shops, past windows glittering with jewelled boxes that spilled out necklaces and rings like the boxes Tom had always imagined that treasure spilled out of in fairy tales . . .

11

Maybe he'd never go back to the States. It was not so much Europe itself as the evenings he had spent alone, here and in Rome, that made him feel that way. Evenings by himself simply looking at maps, or lying around on sofas thumbing through guidebooks. Evenings looking at his clothes – his clothes and Dickie's – and feeling Dickie's rings between his palms, and running his fingers over the antelope suitcase he had bought at Gucci's . . . He loved possessions, not masses of them, but a select few that he did not part with. They gave a man self-respect. Not ostentation but quality, and the love that cherished the quality. Possessions reminded him that he existed, and made him enjoy his existence. It was as simple as that. And wasn't that worth something?

The Talented Mr Ripley · 1955

Elizabeth Wurtzel

[A]ll the flights have been delayed for several hours. That's nice, I think. I'll just do some shopping. The duty-free stores in Copenhagen's airport are considered some of the best in the world. This tiny little socialist country is extremely industrious, the producer of many wonderful consumer goods – LEGO, Dansk, Royal Copenhagen, Georg Jensen, Bang & Olufsen. So much for the idea that without capitalism people are slothful, living off the dole, and wasting away. So I go on an insane, manic spree. I take my little trolley and go nuts. The stores do not have the capacity to check credit cards through to the United States, so I can spend far beyond my limit. Gucci bags, Ferragamo sandals, a Georg Jensen silver necklace, a Prada sweater, a Skagen watch for Mommy, LEGO sets for my nonexistent little cousins whom I ought to buy presents for, a Mont Blanc fountain pen for signing books. I also pick up a few bottles of Absolut Vodka, in

Citron and Kurrant and Peppar flavors, as gifts for the people in Sweden . . .

I shop until the stores close down.

More, Now, Again · 2002

SHARON ZUKIN

When terrorists struck the World Trade Center, in Lower Manhattan, on September 11, 2001, Mayor Rudolph Giuliani rapidly took command. With three hundred thousand stockbrokers, office workers, security guards, and food vendors seeking refuge in other parts of the city, emergency workers painstakingly began to clear the debris. Thousands had died, and many police officers and fire fighters also lost their lives when the towers came down. Not only the downtown financial district but most of the city – and the nation as a whole – was emotionally drained. But the mayor tried to establish a sense of normalcy. New Yorkers could find comfort, he said, if they thought of this terrible time as a day off from work. Watching the mayor on TV, I expected him to counsel us to stay at home with our families, to relax and play a game of softball, or to pray. Instead, he urged us to go shopping.

Point of Purchase · 2004

CHRISSY ILEY

It doesn't surprise me that one in four women would rather buy a pair of shoes than pay a bill. I've been there many times. It does surprise me that, according to a survey conducted by *Harpers Bazaar*, one in 10 women said she spent more than £1,000 on shoes in the past year and 8% of women own more than 100 pairs of shoes.

I think guilt, shame and a desire to be covert about their addiction means that the real figure is much higher. At my peak of shoe addiction I would be spending that in a month. I can talk about it now. I'm almost in recovery. I fell off my shoes – high suede wedges with a butterfly print. I broke two metatarsals. My foot went black, it swelled and I was not able to wear any of my 500-odd pairs of shoes for half a year.

I was resourceful though. I discovered that Louis Vuitton had an almost orthopaedic fit: very wide on the sole, low fronted with lots of toe cleavage and just about the only shoes I could bear to put on for a while. Then I realised that the mended foot was still swollen and almost a whole size bigger than it used to be. I couldn't buy shoes in the same way. Like any addiction, it defines you and for a while I didn't know who I was . . .

I remember Carrie in *Sex and the City* saying that if she hadn't spent so much money on shoes she could have bought an apartment. As the shoes of my particular delight were never cheap, always Marc Jacobs, Christian Louboutin or Louis, Emma Hope, Matthew Williamson or Michel Perry, I reckon I could have bought a small house in Camden or a farm in North Yorkshire, but instead I have a range of colour-coordinated postcards from the edge of a life I fell off . . .

My last hurrah was an encounter with bespoke shoemaker Caroline Groves. Barry Humphries had given me some poisonous toad skins in gorgeously putrid green and burnt sienna. He uses them to back books because if you rub them you hallucinate erotic thoughts, and thought I might like to turn them into shoes. Exquisite creations like small pets for my feet were made. They were the ultimate sexy beasts, one in a size larger than the other. Not too bad, I thought, at £750. The addiction mounted. I moved on to a pink suede pair lined in grey shaved mink and another in everyday stingray.

The bills I had not paid piled up. I couldn't cheer myself up with another pair of shoes. I am now in recovery and haven't bought shoes for three months. Like an ex-drinker or ex-smoker feels sick with themselves for their old weakness, so do I. When I look at shoes in magazines – I can't test myself in a shop yet – I say the mantra: you could have had a farm in Yorkshire. Don't want that? Well at least you could have had a holiday.

'Confessions of a Shoe Addict' · 2006

IMELDA MARCOS

Imelda Marcos, former First Lady of the Philippines, was famous in the 1970s for her shoe fetish. She is said to have travelled the world to buy new shoes while millions of Filipinos lived in dire poverty. President Marcos's successor, Corazon Aquino, displayed the shoes as a demonstration of Imelda's extravagance; she countered by opening her own shoe museum, protesting that instead of 3000 pairs, she owned only 1060. Whatever the figure, her pair of plastic disco sandals with three-inch high flashing battery operated heels must surely be the star of the collection.

'Win or lose, we go shopping after the election.'

*

'Funny, I never shopped. Even my jewelry – not a piece of my jewelry I bought for me . . . I was born ostentatious. They will list my name in the dictionary someday. They will use "Imeldific" to mean ostentatious extravagance . . . What's wrong with shoes? I collected them because it was like a symbol of thanksgiving and love . . . I have no weakness for shoes. I wear very simple shoes which are pump shoes. It is not one of my weaknesses.'

*

'I hate ugliness. You know I'm allergic to ugliness.'

1970s

PLUM SYKES

There's nothing Plum Sykes – once a contributing fashion editor for
American Vogue – doesn't know about shopping. Her mother was
a dress designer, and her twin sister a fashion director for Marie
Claire.

Everyone thinks it's unbelievable that a girl who is as obsessed
with Chloé jeans as I am could have studied at Princeton but
when I told one of the girls at the baby shower about school
she said, 'Oh my god! Ivy League! You're like the female
Stephen Hawking.' Listen, someone that brainy would never
do something as crazy as spend $325 on a pair of Chloé jeans,
but I just can't help it, like most New York girls . . . (I've tried
all the other jeans – Rogan, Seven, Earl, Juicy, Blue Cult – but
I always come back to the classic, Chloé. They just do something to your butt the others can't.)

Bergdorf Blondes · 2004

DOROTHEA MACKELLAR

Mackellar wrote Australia's best loved and most quoted poem,
'My Country', and her work, which was published internationally
in the Spectator, Harper's Magazine, and the Sydney Bulletin,
culminated in the award of an OBE for her contribution to
Australian literature.

14 Feb	Saw about brown evening dress . . .
23 Feb	Hardy's (lovely opal necklace) and M. got nice grey hat . . .
16 March	Saw nice three cornered hat, black with a gold quill, and wanted it very much . . .
21 March	Rain but we went for a bathe, trying in vain to buy the black hat first . . .

22 March   Got black hat.

The Diaries of Dorothea Mackellar · 1910–11

JOAN DIDION

A good center in which to spend the day if you wake up feeling low in Honolulu, Hawaii, is Ala Moana, major tenants Liberty House and Sears . . . The last time I went to the Ala Moana it was to buy *The New York Times*. Because *The New York Times* was not in, I sat on the mall for a while and ate caramel corn. In the end I bought not *The New York Times* at all but two straw hats at Liberty House, four bottles of nail enamel at Woolworths, and a toaster, on sale at Sears. In the literature of shopping centers these would be described as impulse purchases, but the impulse here was obscure. I do not wear hats, nor do I like caramel corn. I do not use nail enamel. Yet flying back across the Pacific I regretted only the toaster.

'On the Mall' · 1979

JULIET SCHOR

It appears that the more education a person has, *the less he or she saves* . . . More education also leads to more shopping, particularly for women. Women with graduate degrees spend more time shopping than individuals in any other category. (Women with college degrees are a close second.) Apparently people with more education are more status-oriented, more tuned in to identity and positional consumption, and more concerned with keeping up with the up-scale groups to which they aspire and belong . . .

Like many of the women she knows, Jennifer frequently spent her lunch hour doing recreational shopping. 'I'd be in a bad mood, I'd go shopping at lunchtime, I'd try on a dress, I'd say, "Well, I kind of like it, you know, it's only $89, I'll buy it." I buy it, I bring it home, and never wear it. I didn't really like it.' Or she'd go for one item and return with 'seven or eight other things, because I'm easily distracted and I'm not very good at making quick judgments. And so I'd stand there and waffle for a minute, and I'd say, "Ehh, do we really need another sofa pillow? Oh, all right, I'll take it. Because it was easier than walking away from it.'"

The Overspent American · 1998

JUDITH LEVINE

Judith Levine decided to forgo all but essential purchases for one year in an effort to re-evaluate her relationship with consumerism. She may have denied herself films and Q-tips, but on one foray into town couldn't resist the siren call of a skirt and some trousers.

I am in Burlington [Vermont] with Paul . . . On Battery Street, I encounter Common Threads, a clothing store. The cool, modern window display, decidedly non-Vermontesque, entices me through the door. Inside, the inventory is my aesthetic ideal: simple but not preppy, hip but not trendy, distinctive but not bizarre, with a few bright, frivolous trifles mixed in with grays and blacks like sweets after a classically prepared meal . . .

The saleswoman is about my age, maybe a little younger . . . She is wearing a skirt from the store, of gold ripstop nylon with a sewn-in flounce at the back, a joke on the bustle. I take a skirt by the same designer off the sale rack. This one is made of lavender ripstop, sewn flat around the hips with intermittently gathered seams that create billows and an uneven hem. When I put it on, the skirt delights me. It is a work of art . . . I twirl before the long oval mirror, admiring the skirt from all angles . . . [The saleswoman] says the skirt looks great on me.

We are flirting. It's a ménage à trois: salesperson, customer, product. But I'm not so smitten as to be out of my head. I reflect: where else will I wear it? Before another opportunity, the skirt will go out of fashion. At $117 on sale, it's a luxury I wouldn't indulge in even if I were buying things . . . I say no, and feel relieved – rescued from myself.

Then I see the pants: a greenish jacquard silk-polyester blend, at only $138 minus 30 percent. They are the right color . . . the right level of dressiness . . . they make me look thin . . .

I look like myself to myself, my best self. I also feel like a woman, doing what women do: preening, flirting in public. Shopping affords a woman this pleasure innocently . . .

'I'm thinking about it,' I tell the saleswoman as I dawdle around the racks, still wearing the pants.

'That's allowed,' she says, moving to the cash register counter, whose immaculate surface she busies herself tidying. She tells me again how good they look. She is smiling like a cat waiting for the bird to fly into its jaws.

I take out my credit card. Reader, I am fallen.

Not Buying It: My Year Without Shopping · 2006

SYLVIA TOWNSEND WARNER

Lolly refuses to be the perfect maiden aunt in this subversive and witty novel by one of the most original writers of the twentieth century. Warner recorded in her diary her trips to 'every counter of the domestic Woolworth, even to buying boot-polish'.

It was in Moscow Road that she began to be extravagant. But when she walked into the little shop she had no particular intention of extravagance, for Caroline's parcel hung remindingly upon her arm, and the shop itself, half florist and half greengrocer, had a simple appearance.

There were several other customers, and while she stood waiting to be served she looked about her. The aspect of the shop pleased her greatly. It was small and homely. Fruit and flowers and vegetables were crowded together in countrified disorder. On the sloping shelf in the window, among apples and rough-skinned cooking pears and trays of walnuts, chestnuts, and filberts, was a basket of eggs, smooth and brown, like some larger kind of nut. At one side of the room was a wooden staging. On this stood jars of home-made jam and bottled fruits. It was as though the remnants of summer had come into the little shop for shelter. On the floor lay a heap of earthy turnips.

Laura looked at the bottled fruits, the sliced pears in syrup, the glistening red plums, the greengages. She thought of the woman who had filled those jars and fastened the bladders. Perhaps the greengrocer's mother lived in the country . . .

She started as the man of the shop came up to her and asked her what she wished for. Her eyes blinked, she looked with surprise at the gloves upon her hands.

'I want one of those large chrysanthemums,' she said, and turned towards the window where they stood in a brown jar . . .

'Which one would you like, ma'am?' he asked, turning the bunch of chrysanthemums about that she might choose for herself. She looked at the large mop-headed blossoms. Their curled petals were deep garnet colour within and tawny yellow without. As the light fell on their sleek flesh the garnet colour glowed, the tawny yellow paled as if it were thinly washed with silver. She longed for the moment when she might stroke her hand over those mop heads.

'I think I will take them all,' she said.

Lolly Willowes · 1926

20

Barbara Pym

*Married Wilmet is well dressed and well off, and finds it a bit boring
to shop with her church friend, the self-effacing Mary. The sense of
duty leaves a bitter taste in her mouth.*

'I feel quite dashing having the afternoon off,' said Mary. 'Are
you doing anything afterwards?'

'Well, I don't know really,' I said cautiously, wondering what
she was about to suggest.

'I was just wondering if you would like to come and help me to
choose a dress,' Mary went on. 'I really do need a new one, you
know – a sort of wool dress suitable for parish evening occasions.'

'A sort of wool dress suitable for parish evening occasions' –
I turned the depressing description over in my mind. Poor
Mary, was that really all the social life she had? I supposed it
must be.

'Mother was saying that my blue is so shabby that I
must get something else.' She mentioned the name of an old-
established but fashionable shop where her mother had an
account, so we made our way there. I was surprised, knowing
the shop, that Mary did not appear better dressed.

'I usually go to the sales,' she added, explaining what I
wanted to know. 'They have some very good reductions, but I
suppose I shall have to pay more now.'

Obviously, then, it was Mary and people like her who
bought the trying electric blue or dingy olive green dress which
had been reduced because nobody could wear it. And she
probably gave the money she saved to the church or some
charitable organization. And I bought as many clothes as I
wanted in all the most becoming styles and colours, gave a
little money to the church and none at all to charitable organ-
izations. The contrast was an uncomfortable one and I did not

wish to dwell on it. It was better when we were engulfed in the perfumed air and soft carpets of the shop, and Mary, like a schoolgirl being taken out for a half holiday, was excitedly calling my attention to the various counters.

'What lovely scarves! The colours are so pretty now, aren't they? And all these beads and jewels – it's like Aladdin's cave, isn't it!' she chattered. 'But I suppose dresses will be upstairs, so we'd better not waste time down here.'

We entered the 'gown salon', which was rather empty at this time of the afternoon; acres of grey carpet seemed to stretch in front of us. A black-gowned saleswoman advanced upon us and addressed her offer of help to me.

'Well, it's really I who want to be helped,' said Mary in her open way. 'I just want an everyday wool dress in blue or green, nothing too elegant.'

'Have you ever considered black?' I asked when the saleswoman had gone away to get some dresses. 'I think it would suit you.'

'Do you?' asked Mary doubtfully. 'I've never worn it, except when Father died. Mother doesn't consider it suitable for girls. I mean,' she smiled, 'she didn't when I *was* a girl – so I've nearly always had blue or green.'

She tried a few dresses which fitted quite well but were uninteresting. Then I asked the saleswoman to bring something in black. I wondered why I was taking all this trouble over Mary Beamish, for when one came to think of it what did it matter what she wore? She might just as well buy a dress as much like her old blue as possible, for all the difference it would make to her life.

But when the black dress was brought it fitted best of all, and the plain bodice and full pleated skirt were very becoming . . .

She decided to take the black dress away with her, and I also persuaded her to buy a necklace to go with it – a double row of pearls by [sic] the faintest tinge of pink in them.

'I don't know when I shall wear them,' she laughed.

We turned into a side street where I knew of a good place to have tea, a favourite haunt of shopping women. It was already crowded but we managed to find a small table to ourselves, sitting on a narrow green banquette wedged against the silver-striped walls . . .

I looked at her dispassionately and saw almost with dislike her shining eager face, her friendship offered to me. What was I doing sitting here with somebody who was so very much not my kind of person? . . .

When we got outside I made some excuse about wanting to go into a shop before it closed and she went on the bus without me. I turned into a sweet shop that made special truffles I liked and bought half a pound, thinking rather defiantly of Mary as I did so.

A Glass of Blessings · 1958

INDIA KNIGHT

I do love the shops. Oh, God, The Shops. I can't quite remember if that almost-not-daring-to-believe, kick-in-the-stomach feeling of pure joy – 'You mean we give you a few coins and the lovely thing becomes mine?' – first happened when my paternal grandmother took me to a *pâtisserie* (Vatel in Brussels, 8 rue General Leman – they still do absolutely the best baguette in town), where I stood transfixed in front of a tiny *tartelette au citron*: pale yellow, with frilled edges and *Citron* written (just like that) in tall, thin, curly letters of darkest chocolate. I don't think I'd quite grasped that food came from shops before (sheltered childhood, and I was only six), and this *tartelette* was a revelation. The idea that you could eat delicious things all the time, if you liked, simply by taking a few steps down the street and S H O P P I N G, was just amazing to me . . .

The Shops · 2003

EDITH WHARTON

There can be no better portrait of a ruthless social climber than Wharton's Undine Spragg.

As she looked out at the thronged street, on which the summer light lay like a blush of pleasure, she felt herself naturally akin to all the bright and careless freedom of the scene. She had been away from Paris for two days, and the spectacle before her seemed more rich and suggestive after her brief absence from it. Her senses luxuriated in all its material details: the thronging motors, the brilliant shops, the novelty and daring of the women's dresses, the piled-up colours of the ambulant flower-carts, the appetizing expanse of the fruiterers' windows, even the chromatic effects of the *petits fours* behind the plate-glass of the pastry-cooks: all the surface-sparkle and variety of the inexhaustible streets of Paris.

The scene before her typified to Undine her first real taste of life. How meagre and starved the past appeared in comparison with this abundant present! The noise, the crowd, the promiscuity beneath her eyes symbolized the glare and movement of her life. Every moment of her days was packed with excitement and exhilaration. Everything amused her: the long hours of bargaining and debate with dress-makers and jewellers, the crowded lunches at fashionable restaurants, the perfunctory dash through a picture-show or the lingering visit to the last new milliner; the afternoon motor-rush to some leafy suburb, where tea and music and sunset were hastily absorbed on a crowded terrace above the Seine; the whirl home through the Bois to dress for dinner and start again on the round of evening diversion; the dinner at the Nouveau Luxe or the Café de Paris, and the little play at the Capucines or the Variétés, followed, because the night was 'too lovely', and it was a shame to waste it, by a breathless flight back to the Bois, with supper in one of its lamp-hung restaurants, or, if the weather forbade, a tumultuous progress through the midnight haunts where 'ladies' were not supposed to show themselves, and might consequently taste the thrill of being occasionally taken for their opposites.

The Custom of the Country · 1913

JANE WELSH CARLYLE

To Margaret Welsh,
  Liverpool.

Chelsea
Friday, July 15th, 1842

My dear Maggie,

It was a good thought in you to send me the little purse, and I feel very grateful to you for it. This last birthday was very sad for me, as you may easily suppose, very unlike what it was last year, and all former years; and I needed all the heartening kind souls could give me . . . Only think of my husband, too, having given me a little present! he who never attends to such nonsenses as birthdays, and who dislikes nothing in the world so much as going into a shop to buy anything, even his own trowsers and coats; so that, to the consternation of cockney tailers, I am obliged to go about them. Well, he actually risked himself in a jeweller's shop, and bought me a very nice smelling-bottle! I cannot tell you how *wae* his little gift made me, as well as glad; it was the first thing of the kind he ever gave to me in his life. In great matters he is always kind and considerate; but these little attentions, which we women attach so much importance to, he was never in the habit of rendering to anyone . . .

Ever your affectionate Cousin,
Jane Carlyle.

Letters · 1842

MICHELLE BRANDT

STANFORD, Calif. – Contrary to popular opinion, nearly as many men as women experience compulsive buying disorder, a condition marked by binge buying and subsequent financial hardship, according to new research from the Stanford University School of Medicine.

'The widespread opinion that most compulsive buyers are women may be wrong,' the researchers wrote . . .

People who have compulsive buying disorder – sometimes called compulsive shopping disorder – are often struck with an irresistible, intrusive and often senseless impulse to buy. It is common for sufferers to go on frequent shopping binges and to accumulate large quantities of unnecessary, unwanted items. Sufferers often rack up thousands of dollars in debt and lie to their loved ones about their purchases. The consequences can be bankruptcy, divorce, embezzlement and even suicide attempts . . .

Online article at EurekAlert! · 2006

JUDITH KRANTZ

Scruples is set in the eponymous Beverly Hills boutique and records the boundless appetite for luxury of customers and staff alike.

Maggie MacGregor felt both depleted and electrified by the

adrenaline of acquisition. She had just spent at least seven thousand dollars for clothes to wear on camera during the next two months and ordered an entire wardrobe for the Cannes Film Festival, which she would be covering in May. The festival wardrobe had cost an additional twelve thousand dollars for clothes that would be made by Halston and Adolfo in New York in special colours and fabrics just for her and delivered in time for her trip, or she'd have someone's head on a platter. Naturally, it was stipulated in her contract that the goniffs at the network paid. No way she'd spend her own money like that.

If anyone had ever tried to convince her, ten years ago, when she was a short, jouncingly plump teenager named Shirley Silverstein, daughter of the owner of the biggest hardware store in tiny Fort John, Rhode Island, that spending nineteen thousand dollars on clothes was hard work, she would have – laughed? No, Maggie reflected, even back then she was ambitious enough to have been able to imagine such a situation and smart enough to understand that it involved a lot of psychic strain to say nothing of what it did to her feet.

Scruples · 1978

MADELEINE ST JOHN

In this amusing short novel full of military imagery, Lisa is a schoolgirl working at Goode's department store in Sydney. The sales assistants in the Ladies' Frocks Department wear black and the names of the gowns – Rosy, Tara, Laura, Lisette – echo those at Maison Lucile, Lady Duff Gordon's couture house.

At the very end of the Ladies' Frocks Department, past Cocktail Frocks, there was something very special, something quite, quite wonderful; but it wasn't for everybody: that was the point. Because there, at the very end, there was a lovely arch, on which was written in curly letters '*Model Gowns*'. And beyond the arch was a rose-pink cave illuminated by frilly little lamps and furnished with a few elegant little sofas upholstered in oyster-grey brocade; and the walls were lined with splendid mahogany cupboards in which hung, on pink satin-covered hangers, the actual Model Gowns, whose fantastic prices were all in guineas.

To one side of the cave there was a small Louis XVI-style table and chair, where ladies could write cheques or sign sales dockets, and to each side was a great cheval glass where a lady having donned a Model Gown (did she dare) in one of the large and commodious fitting rooms might look at herself properly, walking around and turning, to get the effect of the frock in the sort of proper big space where it would ultimately be seen. A chandelier hung from the ceiling; almost the only fitment lacking to the scene was the bottle of Veuve Clicquot foaming at the mouth and the tulip-shaped glass; in all other respects the cave was a faithful reproduction of the luxurious space in which its clients were to be supposed continually to have their being: and the pythoness who guarded the cave was Magda . . .

'Well, Lisa,' said Magda, extending a graceful arm, 'here are the Model Gowns. Do you by the way know what is a Model Gown?' 'Well,' said Lisa, 'not exactly. I'm not sure—' 'Very well,' said Magda, 'I will explain to you. These frocks are all unique. There are no others like them in all this city. Oh, if you were to go to Focher perhaps you would find one or two, I don't know, that woman is capable of anything, but as far as we are concerned there can be no others of their kind in Sydney. A woman who buys one of these frocks knows that she will not meet another wearing the same frock, which is so terrible a thing to happen to a woman, even if she looks better in the frock than her rival. So to say. So we have the exclusive right to sell the frock in Sydney . . . We do not keep different sizes of the same model,' Magda continued, 'for then of course the frock would cease to be unique. Do you see?' And Lisa nodded, and gazed at the frocks, whose chiffon and taffeta edges frothed out in their luminous ranks around her . . .

Lisa had a few minutes in hand at the end of her lunch hour so she popped in to Model Gowns to say hello to Magda . . . Magda noted her involuntary tremor. 'Oh, go and look,' she said. 'See if there is anything left to tempt you.' Lisa forced herself to laugh. 'I've found the one I want already,' she said . . . Magda looked at her again. Ah, well, it was after all a case of true love: she resolved suddenly to indulge it . . . '[W]hy don't you come in here in your lunch hour tomorrow after you have changed, and try it on? It is your size I think precisely. You can have a *fantaisie* for a few moments, it is good for the soul.' . . .

Lisette was, of course, everything which could have been hoped, have been dreamed; like all the great works of the French couture, it was designed to look beautiful not simply as a thing in itself, but as the clothing of a female form. It took on then the property of vitality and movement: that is, of rhythm: it became finally incarnate. Lisa stood, overwhelmed, staring into the great cheval glass . . . The frock changed her absolutely . . .

Lisa retired to the changing room and having replaced Lisette on the hanger went to sit for the free time remaining in Hyde Park. If Lisette were to be reduced to fifty guineas she would have almost enough money in her Post Office money box to pay for it. The thought of spending this sum, which was very much more than she had ever had at her disposal before and sufficient for at least ten ordinary frocks at the usual retail prices, was utterly intoxicating.

The Women in Black · 1993

DODIE SMITH

Smith is more famous for One Hundred and One Dalmatians, *but equally charming is an earlier novel in diary form about an impoverished family, the Mortmains.*

DEAR CASSANDRA,

I am sorry not to have written before but we have been very busy. Getting a trousseau is quite hard work. I think you would be surprised at the way we do it. We hardly go to real shops at all but to large beautiful houses. There are drawing-rooms with crystal chandeliers and little gilt chairs all round and you sit there and watch the mannequins (can't spell it) walk past in the clothes. You have a card and a pencil to mark down what you like. The prices are fabulous – quite plain dresses cost around twenty-five pounds. My black suit will be thirty-five – more, really, because everything is in guineas, not pounds. At first I had a frightened sort of feeling at so much being spent but now it seems almost natural . . .

[W]hen I am married we will shop like mad for you . . .

Oh, darling, do you remember how we stood watching the woman buying a whole dozen pairs of silk stockings and you said we were like cats making longing noises for birds? I think it was that moment I decided I would do anything, anything, to stop being so horribly poor. It was that night we met the Cottons again. Do you believe one can make things happen? I do.

Love and please write often to your

ROSE

I Capture the Castle · 1949

Kate Chopin

Southerner Kate Chopin began writing when her husband died in
1882 and her novel The Awakening *is now among the top five*
most read at American universities, although it was damned as
'shocking, morbid, and vulgar', and nearly ruined her career when
first published in 1899.

Little Mrs. Sommers one day found herself the unexpected possessor of fifteen dollars. It seemed to her a very large amount of money, and the way in which it stuffed and bulged her worn old *porte-monnaie* gave her a feeling of importance such as she had not enjoyed for years.

The question of investment was one that occupied her greatly. For a day or two she walked about apparently in a dreamy state, but really absorbed in speculation and calculation. She did not wish to act hastily, to do anything she might afterward regret. But it was during the still hours of the night when she lay awake revolving plans in her mind that she seemed to see her way clearly toward a proper and judicious use of the money.

A dollar or two should be added to the price usually paid for Janie's shoes, which would insure their lasting an appreciable time longer than they usually did. She would buy so and so many yards of percale for new shirt waists for the boys and Janie and Mag. She had intended to make the old ones do by skilful patching. Mag should have another gown. She had seen some beautiful patterns, veritable bargains in the shop windows. And still there would be left enough for new stockings – two pairs apiece – and what darning that would save for a while! She would get caps for the boys and sailor-hats for the girls. The vision of her little brood looking fresh and dainty and new for once in their lives excited her and made her restless and wakeful with anticipation.

The neighbors sometimes talked of certain 'better days' that little Mrs. Sommers had known before she had ever thought of being Mrs. Sommers. She herself indulged in no such morbid retrospection. She had no time – no second of time to devote to the past. The needs of the present absorbed her every faculty. A vision of the future like some dim, gaunt monster sometimes appalled her, but luckily to-morrow never comes.

Mrs. Sommers was one who knew the value of bargains; who could stand for hours making her way inch by inch toward the desired object that was selling below cost. She could elbow her way if need be; she had learned to clutch a piece of goods and hold it and stick to it with persistence and determination till her turn came to be served, no matter when it came.

But that day she was a little faint and tired. She had swallowed a light luncheon – no! when she came to think of it, between getting the children fed and the place righted, and preparing herself for the shopping bout, she had actually forgotten to eat any luncheon at all!

She sat herself upon a revolving stool before a counter that was comparatively deserted, trying to gather strength and courage to charge through an eager multitude that was besieging breastworks of shirting and figured lawn. An all-gone limp feeling had come over her and she rested her hand aimlessly upon the counter. She wore no gloves. By degrees she grew aware that her hand had encountered something very soothing, very pleasant to touch. She looked down to see that her hand lay upon a pile of silk stockings. A placard near by announced that they had been reduced in price from two dollars and fifty cents to one dollar and ninety-eight cents; and a young girl who stood behind the counter asked her if she wished to examine their line of silk hosiery. She smiled, just as if she had been asked to inspect a tiara of diamonds with the ultimate view of purchasing it. But she went on feeling the soft, sheeny luxurious things – with both hands now, holding them up to see them glisten, and to feel them glide serpent-like through her fingers.

Two hectic blotches came suddenly into her pale cheeks. She looked up at the girl.

'Do you think there are any eights-and-a-half among these?'

There were any number of eights-and-a-half. In fact, there were more of that size than any other. Here was a light-blue pair; there were some lavender, some all black and various shades of tan and gray. Mrs. Sommers selected a black pair and looked at them very long and closely. She pretended to be examining their texture, which the clerk assured her was excellent.

'A dollar and ninety-eight cents,' she mused aloud. 'Well, I'll take this pair.' She handed the girl a five-dollar bill and waited for her change and for her parcel. What a very small parcel it was! It seemed lost in the depths of her shabby old shopping-bag. Mrs. Sommers after that did not move in the direction of the bargain counter. She took the elevator, which carried her to an upper floor into the region of the ladies' waiting-rooms. Here, in a retired corner, she exchanged her cotton stockings for the new silk ones which she had just bought. She was not going through any acute mental process or reasoning with herself, nor was she striving to explain to her satisfaction the motive of her action. She was not thinking at all. She seemed for the time to be taking a rest from that laborious and fatiguing function and to have abandoned herself to some mechanical impulse that directed her actions and freed her of responsibility.

How good was the touch of the raw silk to her flesh! She felt like lying back in the cushioned chair and reveling for a while in the luxury of it. She did for a little while. Then she replaced her shoes, rolled the cotton stockings together and thrust them into her bag. After doing this she crossed straight over to the shoe department and took her seat to be fitted.

She was fastidious. The clerk could not make her out; he could not reconcile her shoes with her stockings, and she was not too easily pleased. She held back her skirts and turned her feet one way and her head another way as she glanced down at the polished, pointed-tipped boots. Her foot and ankle looked very pretty. She could not realize that they belonged to her and were a part of herself. She wanted an excellent and stylish fit, she told the young fellow who served her, and she did not mind the difference of a dollar or two more in the price so long as she got what she desired.

It was a long time since Mrs. Sommers had been fitted with gloves. On rare occasions when she had bought a pair they were always 'bargains,' so cheap that it would have been preposterous and unreasonable to have expected them to be fitted to the hand.

Now she rested her elbow on the cushion of the glove counter, and a pretty, pleasant young creature, delicate and deft of touch, drew a long-wristed 'kid' over Mrs. Sommers's hand. She smoothed it down over the wrist and buttoned it neatly, and both lost themselves for a second or two in admiring contemplation of the little symmetrical gloved hand. But there were other places where money might be spent.

There were books and magazines piled up in the window of a stall a few paces down the street. Mrs. Sommers bought two high-priced magazines such as she had been accustomed to read in the days when she had been accustomed to other pleasant things. She carried them without wrapping. As well as she could she lifted her skirts at the crossings. Her stockings and boots and well fitting gloves had worked marvels in her bearing – had given her a feeling of assurance, a sense of belonging to the well-dressed multitude.

She was very hungry. Another time she would have stilled the cravings for food until reaching her own home, where she would have brewed herself a cup of tea and taken a snack of anything that was available. But the impulse that was guiding her would not suffer her to entertain any such thought.

There was a restaurant at the corner. She had never entered its doors; from the outside she had sometimes caught glimpses of spotless damask and shining crystal, and soft-stepping waiters serving people of fashion.

When she entered her appearance created no surprise, no consternation, as she had half feared it might. She seated herself at a small table alone, and an attentive waiter at once approached to take her order. She did not want a profusion; she craved a nice and tasty bite – a half dozen blue-points, a plump chop with cress, a something sweet – a *crème-frappée*, for instance; a glass of Rhine wine, and after all a small cup of black coffee.

While waiting to be served she removed her gloves very leisurely and laid them beside her. Then she picked up a magazine and glanced through it, cutting the pages with a blunt edge of her knife. It was all very agreeable. The damask was even more spotless than it had seemed through the window, and the crystal more sparkling. There were quiet ladies and gentlemen, who did not notice her, lunching at the small tables like her own. A soft, pleasing strain of music could be heard, and a gentle breeze was blowing through the window. She tasted a bite, and she read a word or two, and she sipped the amber wine and wiggled her toes in the silk stockings. The price of it made no difference. She counted the money out to the waiter and left an extra coin on his tray, whereupon he bowed before her as before a princess of royal blood.

There was still money in her purse, and her next temptation presented itself in the shape of a matinée poster.

It was a little later when she entered the theatre, the play had begun and the house seemed to her to be packed. But there were vacant seats here and there, and into one of them she was ushered, between brilliantly dressed women who had gone there to kill time and eat candy and display their gaudy attire. There were many others who were there solely for the play and acting. It is safe to say there was no one present who bore quite the attitude which Mrs. Sommers did to her surroundings. She gathered in the whole – stage and players and people in one wide impression, and absorbed it and enjoyed it. She laughed at the comedy and wept – she and the gaudy woman next to her wept over the tragedy. And they talked a little together over it. And the gaudy woman wiped her eyes and sniffled on a tiny square of filmy, perfumed lace and passed little Mrs. Sommers her box of candy.

The play was over, the music ceased, the crowd filed out. It was like a dream ended. People scattered in all directions. Mrs. Sommers went to the corner and waited for the cable car.

A man with keen eyes, who sat opposite to her, seemed to like the study of her small, pale face. It puzzled him to decipher what he saw there. In truth, he saw nothing – unless he were wizard enough to detect a poignant wish, a powerful longing that the cable car would never stop anywhere, but go on and on with her forever.

'A Pair of Silk Stockings' · 1897

THE COST

Desire for power and money drives Bradford's heroine, Emma Harte, a northern girl made good. Her small shop becomes the world's finest department store, so she brooks no resistance from friend and financial manager, Henry.

'Henry, where do we now stand on the liquidation of those personal assets of mine?'

'I have all the papers in front of me, Emma. I was just going over them,' he replied, clearing his throat . . . 'Everything has been sold and the prices were very good. Excellent, in fact. We realized just under nine million pounds. Not bad, eh?'

'That's marvellous, Henry! Where is the money?'

'Why, right here in the bank.' . . .

'Please transfer it today, Henry. To my current account. My *personal* current account.' . . .

'Emma, that's ridiculous! Nobody puts nearly nine million pounds in a personal current account . . .'

She laughed and could not resist teasing him a little. 'I might want to go shopping, Henry.'

'Shopping!' he exploded. 'Come now, Emma! Not even *you* can spend that amount shopping! That's the most ridiculous thing I've heard you say in all the years I've known you.' He was furious.

'I certainly can spend that amount of money shopping, Henry, depending, of course, on what exactly I'm buying,' Emma said acidly, thinking to herself that Henry's marvellous sense of humour always seemed to evaporate into thin air when he was discussing money. 'Please, Henry, no more discussion. Deduct the bank's fee for handling the sales, and the taxes to be paid, and put the rest in my personal current account.'

He sighed in exasperation. 'Very well. I suppose you know what you're doing. After all, it is your money, Emma.'

You're damn right it is, Emma thought.

A Woman of Substance · 1979

LADY MARY RHODES CARBUTT

In England one goes out shopping with money in one's pocket, and brings home one's purchases in a cart, but in the States one goes out with one's money in a cart, and returns with the purchases in one's pocket – thanks to the heavy coinage and the high prices of everything.

*Five Months Fine Weather in Canada, Western U.S.,
and Mexico* · 1889

JENNY WREN

Jenny Wren may have hidden behind a pseudonym, but her Lazy
Thoughts *are obviously a woman's take on Jerome K. Jerome's* Idle
Thoughts of an Idle Fellow.

How is it that bills mount up so quickly? You buy a little ribbon, a few pairs of gloves, some handkerchiefs – mere items in fact, and yet when quarter day comes round you are presented with a bill a yard long, which as your next instalment of money is fully mortgaged, is calculated to fill you with anything but extreme joy.

Why are the paths leading to destruction always so much easier of access than any other? It takes so much less time to run up a bill, it is so much simpler to say, 'Will you please enter it to my account?' than to pay your money down. First the bill has to be added up, and, strange as it may seem, these shop people appear to take *hours* over a simple addition sum. 'Eight and elevenpence halfpenny if you please, ma'am.' Of course you have not enough silver, and so are obliged to wait for change. Then someone has to be found to sign. Altogether it takes quite five minutes longer paying ready money; and think, how five minutes after each purchase would mount up in a day's shopping! I should say that, on an average you might call it two important hours regularly thrown away. 'And a good job, too,' perhaps our fathers, husbands, and brothers would say. But, then, you see, they are Philistines and do not understand.

But though we suffer somewhat at the hands of these shop people, I think in their turn they have to endure a great deal more from their customers. I have seen old ladies order nearly the whole shop out, turn over the articles, and having entirely exhausted the patience of their victims, say, 'Yes – all very pretty – but I don't think I will buy any to-day, thank you,' and they move off to other counters to enact the same scene over again. Selfish old things! . . .

It is well, at any rate, to consider economy in some matters in these woefully extravagant days. When the shops are decked out in their gayest colors to lure us on to destruction, why is it that 'just the very thing you want' is placed so conspicuously in the front of the window, put cunningly near a mirror too, so that you see it all the way round, and it appears doubly precious?

Lazy Thoughts of a Lazy Girl · 1891

SARAH SALWAY

Like letters he keeps her bills
on a spike by their bed,
each pierced through the heart,

43

confetti edged sums
as big as the telephone numbers
they once shyly exchanged.
The bills grow in the night,
float down to his pillow, so when he turns
they rustle, the paper tearing
so loudly it should wake her
but she just chuckles in her sleep.
He thinks of her then, prowling the shops,
licking her lips at a colour, or the cut
of a jacket, focussed ahead,
hearing nothing but the click
of her credit card until in her hands
she carries her tissue-wrapped purchase
home as carefully as any new born baby.

'Night Letters' · 2006

VIVIAN NICHOLSON AND STEPHEN SMITH

After she left school in Yorkshire, Viv Nicholson got a job making Spanish liquorice in a factory for £2 a week. Later she and her husband Keith, a miner, lived on his trainee salary of £7 – until they won £152,000 in the Pools in 1961. When Keith was killed in a car crash, Viv returned to her former lifestyle.

[W]hen I checked through my account, I found I was owing the bank four grand. But I just accepted it. I thought fate had got me into it – fate will get me out of it. No such luck though, the bank got very stroppy about it! 'Get your bungalow sold and get this paid off,' but then I was coming out of the depression. I just said to myself, 'This is it, get all you can out of life,' and as soon as I decided that I jumped in the car and headed for the shops. I found a dress I liked and decided to buy it –

'Oh, Mrs Nicholson, we have this, and Mrs Nicholson we have that.'

'I'll have it then if it fits,' I said. Everything looked so nice there. I wrote them a cheque out for £610 or something, even though the bank had told me they wouldn't cash any – and I ran all the way from Scholfields to the car, because I thought the cowing cheque would bounce before I got out of the shop. I was off like a blue-tailed fly, I couldn't get my parcels in the car fast enough. I thought, well I've got 'em, I can go to nick for them, I'm not bothered, at least they'll be there for when I come out, I'll hide them . . .

Spend, Spend, Spend · 1977

CHARLOTTE PERKINS GILMAN

Gilman, best known for her novella The Yellow Wallpaper, *was passionate about women's economic independence – and voluntary euthanasia: she took an overdose of chloroform when she learned that she had incurable breast cancer.*

Without trying to indicate any one permanent garment . . . it remains perfectly possible for man or woman to settle on some kind of costume as necessary and fitting; to allow what is necessary to provide it; and to limit their expense for dress to that amount.

Throughout the country there are women in plenty, who from economic necessity, do precisely this as far as the amount goes; but are not thereby freed from anxiety and discontent. Because of the continuous extravagance and display of those whose main business in life is to wear clothes; because of the catering of all the shops to this level of extravagance; because of the deeply rooted sentiment among men as well as women in regard to what is admirable in feminine attire; the steady influence upon all women is to spend more than is necessary, or to wish to even if they cannot.

The Dress of Women · 1915

MABEL HUBBARD BELL

10, rue Nitot   *July 24, 1895*

My dear Alec,
We went shopping this morning and have nearly bought two rugs for the Washington house and portieres. You know you told me that I could take Trust money to furnish the house and Papa cabled I might spend twenty-five hundred dollars. I won't get very far with it because I always want the handsomest and most expensive things and would rather do without them altogether than get cheap ones.

I am terribly mortified that I have had to ask for more money. I know that I have not been extravagant or rather that I have lived much more carefully than I have done for a long time, but things mount up so. I think most of my money has gone in cabs. Today for instance I spent twelve francs on cabs. That means no less than three hundred and sixty francs a month and I have spent much more, enough to buy me two of the dresses I calculated on while on the steamer.

There, all this is not interesting to you. Miss Barrington showed me her photographs today, one of them was of the Capitoline Wolf so I told her about your sheep and their nipples and Mr. McCurdy's black and white single male. She said she would always think of your sheep and their nipples when she looked at the photograph.

Do you think it would be nice for me to meet you at Rouen and stay a day at that old town. I want very much to see it. It is on the way to Paris, two hours from it. If you think well of the idea don't have your tickets taken to Paris, but check your baggage on if you can. The children are at Moret, their month is not out until the 18th August. They are very happy there and write very bright letters. They come up tomorrow for the day to do some shopping. I hope I shall see increased fluency in the use of French.

I am going to write for the club now, so goodnight my dear. I will write again to the Gilsey House, New York. You might bring Daisy a camera, she wants one very much. Be sure it is an Eastman, the one you got for Mexico is not satisfactory.

Lovingly yours,
Mabel.

Letter from Mabel Hubbard Bell to
Alexander Graham Bell · 1895

LADY MARY WORTLEY MONTAGU

Mary taught herself Latin and also spoke Italian, French and Turkish. Though her family tried to suppress them, her Turkish Embassy Letters *were an overnight sensation.*

To Jane Smith,   The Hague, 5 August
1716

. . . I dare swear you think my letter already long enough, but I must not conclude without begging your pardon for not obeying your commands in sending the lace you ordered me. Upon my word I can yet find none that is not dearer than you may buy it in London. If you want any Indian goods, here are great variety of pennyworths, and I shall follow your orders with great pleasure and exactness, being, dear madam, etc.

The Turkish Embassy Letters · 1763

JANE AUSTEN

Henrietta Street-Thursday-after dinner

1813

Thank you my dearest Cassandra for the nice long Letter I sent off this morning. – I hope you have had it by this time & that it has found you all well, & my Mother no more in need of Leeches. – . . . – I hope you will receive the Gown tomorrow & may be able with tolerable honesty to say that you like the colour; – it was bought at Grafton House, where, by going very early, we got immediate attendance & went on very comfortably. – I only forgot the one particular thing which I had always resolved to buy there – a white silk Handkf – & was therefore obliged to give six shillings for one at Crook & Besford's – which reminds me to say that the Worsteds ought also to be at Chawton tomorrow & that I shall be very happy to hear they are approved. I had not much time for deliberation. We are now all four of us young Ladies sitting round the Circular Table in the inner room writing our Letters, while the two Brothers are having a comfortable coze in the room adjoining. – It is to be a quiet evening, much to the satisfaction of 4 of the 6. – My Eyes are quite tired of Dust and Lamps. – . . . Henry is not quite well. – His stomach is rather deranged. You must keep him in Rhubarb & give him plenty of Port & Water.

. . .

– I have rejoiced more than once that I bought my Writing paper in the Country; we have not had a qr of an hour to spare. – I enclose the Eighteen pence due to my Mother. – The Rose colour was 6#s, & the other 4\s per yd. There was but 2 yd and a qr of the dark slate in the Shop, but the Man promised to match it and send it off correctly. Fanny bought her Irish at Newton's in Leicester Sqre & I took the opportunity of thinking about your Irish & seeing one piece of the Yard wide at 4#s. – and it seemed to me very good – good enough for your purpose. – It might at least be worth your while to go there, if you have no other engagements. – Fanny is very much pleased with the stockings she has bought of Remmington-Silk at 12#s.- Cotton at 4.3. – She thinks them great bargains, but I have not seen them yet – as my hair was dressing when the Man & the Stockgs came [. . .]

We then went to Wedgwoods where my Br & Fanny chose a Dinner Set. – I believe the pattern is a small-Lozenge in purple, between Lines of narrow Gold; – & it is to have the Crest.

We must have been 3 qrs of an hour at Grafton House, Edward sitting by all the time with wonderful patience. There Fanny bought the Net for Anna's gown, & a beautiful Square veil for herself. – The Edging there is very cheap, I was tempted by some, & I bought some very nice plaiting Lace at 3-4.-

Fanny desires me to tell Martha with her kind Love that Birchall assured her there was no 2d set of Hook's Lessons for Beginners – & that by my advice, she has therefore chosen her a set by another Composer. I thought she wd rather have something than not. – It costs six shillings. – With Love to You all, including Triggs, I remain

Yours very affecly J. Austen

*

Sloane St Monday 24 May

1813

My dearest Cassandra

I am very much obliged to you for writing to me. You must have hated it after a worrying morning. – Your Letter came just in time to save my going to Remnants, & fit me for Christian's, where I bought Fanny's dimity. I went the day before (Friday) to Laytons as I proposed, & got my Mother's gown 7 yds**-at 6#6 [. . .]

Friday was our worst day as to weather, we were out in a very long & very heavy storm of hail, & there had been others before, but I heard no Thunder. – Saturday was a good deal better, dry & cold. – I gave 2#6 for the Dimity; I do not boast of any Bargains, but think both the Sarsenet & Dimity good of their sort. – I have bought your Locket, but was obliged to give 18s for it – which must be rather more than you intended; it is neat & plain, set in gold [. . .]

• Henry desires Edward may know that he has just bought 3 dozen of Claret for him (Cheap) & ordered it to be sent down to Chawton. – I should not wonder if we got no farther than Reading on Thursday eveng – & so, reach Steventon only to a reasonable Dinner hour the next day; – but whatever I may write or you may imagine we know it will be something different [. . .]

J. Austen

Selected Letters · 1813

NANCY MITFORD

I remember that my mother, during one of her rare visits to England, brought me a little jacket in scarlet cloth from Schiaparelli. It seemed to me quite plain and uninteresting except for the label in its lining, and I longed to put this on the outside so that people would know where it came from. I was wearing it, instead of a cardigan, in my house when Cedric happened to call, and the first thing he said was:

'Aha! So now we dress at Schiaparelli, I see! Whatever next?'

'Cedric! How can you tell?'

'My dear; one can always tell. Things have a signature, if you use your eyes, and mine seem to be trained over a greater range of objects than yours, Schiaparelli – Reboux – Fabergé – Violet le Duc – I can tell at a glance, literally a glance. So your wicked mother the Bolter has been here since last I saw you?'

'Might I not have bought it for myself?'

'No no, my love, you are saving up to educate your twelve brilliant sons, how could you possibly afford twenty-five pounds for a little jacket?'

'Don't tell me!' I said. 'Twenty-five pounds for this?'

'Quite that, I should guess.'

'Simply silly. Why, I could have made it myself.'

'But could you? And if you had would I have come into the room and said Schiaparelli?'

Love in a Cold Climate · 1949

HELEN FIELDING

Saturday 9 December

2 p.m. Bumped into Rebecca in Graham and Greene buying a scarf for £169. (What is going on with scarves? One minute they were stocking filler-type items which cost £9.99; next minute they have to be fancy velvet and cost as much as a television. Next year it will probably happen to socks or pants and we will feel left out if we are not wearing £145 English Eccentrics knickers in textured black velvet.)

Bridget Jones's Diary · 1996

SIMONE DE BEAUVOIR

While they are doing their shopping, women exchange remarks in the shops, on the street corners, through which they affirm 'housewifely values', where each one derives a sense of her importance: they feel they are members of a community which – for a moment – is opposed to the society of men as the essential to the inessential. But above all, buying is a profound pleasure: it is a discovery, almost an invention . . . Between seller and buyer a relationship of tussling and ruses is set up: the point of the game for her is to procure herself the best buys at the lowest price; the great importance attached to the smallest of economies could not be explained merely by the concern to balance a difficult budget: the thing is to win a round. For the time she is suspiciously examining the stalls, the housewife is queen; the world is at her feet with its riches and its traps for her to grab herself some loot. She tastes a fleeting triumph when she empties the bag of provisions onto her table.

The Second Sex · 1949

MRS L. ST JOHN ECKEL

Lizzie Harper was the daughter of the famed impostor Maria Monk, who claimed in 1835 to have escaped from the Hotel Dieu convent in Montreal. When no one in that city believed her scurrilous tales of crime and adultery, she moved to New York, where the publication of her anti-Catholic 'exposé' gained her an entry into 'good' society.

Shortly after our return to the city the quarrels between my sister and myself became so frequent and so violent that our father thought it well to separate us, and placed me to board with a dressmaker. As the dressmaker was always busy, I was left to run the streets and do as I pleased. Sometimes I would pass days going from one shop to another, asking the prices of things, with, perhaps, only one cent in my pocket; and, no matter what the price of an article might be, if I wanted it, I would try to coax the shopkeeper to give it to me for the amount of money I might have. At last two shop-women took such a dislike to me, that they would lie in wait for me, and, if I attempted to pass beyond the sills, of their shops, they would seize me and give me a good shaking.

One day I had only a penny, and I wanted to buy half a yard of ribbon for my doll. I entered a fancy shop, and made a woman unroll all the narrow ribbon she had at two cents a yard. When I had made my choice, I said I would take *half* a yard, at the same time handing her the penny. She took it, threw it out on the sidewalk, and told me to go after it and never dare to come into her shop again. The very same day I saw in a shop window a little bottle of perfumery, which I coveted very much. I eagerly inquired the price. It was twelve cents; and I had only *one*. I begged the woman to give it to me for that. She sarcastically advised me to wait, till I had more to put with it. On my way home I met a ragpicker, and, as I had always been told, that all ragpickers were rich, I took it into my head that I should go at once to work, and make a fortune at ragpicking; and that then I could buy what I pleased.

Maria Monk's Daughter · 1875

AGNES DEANS CAMERON

In a store near the hotel we see a Cree boatman purchasing a farewell present for his sweetheart. As he turns over the fancy articles, we have bad form enough to observe his choice. He selects a fine-tooth comb, for which he pays fifty cents, or as he calls it, 'two skins,' and asks, as he tucks it into his jerkin, if he can change it 'if she doesn't like it.'

The New North: Being Some Account of a Woman's Journey through Canada to the Arctic · 1909

MARY E. HITCHCOCK

*In 1898, upon hearing about the discovery of gold, socialite
Hitchcock persuaded her friend Edith van Buren to accompany her
to the wilds of Alaska. It's surprising that they felt the need to do
any shopping, since they took with them a portable bowling alley,
an ice-cream maker, a Great Dane called Ivan, and a full-size
circus tent.*

Wednesday, July 6th.
A long, enjoyable tramp on shore, with an Englishman. We
finally went to the Alaska Company's Stores, which were
crowded. The men kindly offered to make way for me, on
account of my sex, but, their time being as valuable as mine, I
followed the example of other women, and sat on the counter
until my turn came. How we laughed at each new experience!
My purchases consisted of a pair of muck-a-lucks, four dollars,
which they say are worth three times that in Dawson; a small
tin of ginger wafers, fifty cents; and a bottle of lime juice, sev-
enty-five cents. Not such extravagant prices as we had been
led to expect . . .

Thursday, July 7th.
After this morning's shopping experience, will retract all written yesterday about prices.

Ordinary single blanket for Ivan, the cheapest made, seven
dollars; a very common skirt-braid, two small pieces, twenty-
five cents; writing pads, twenty-five cents each; ink,
twenty-five cents for a five-cent (retail) bottle, and the slim-
siest kind of calico, twenty-five cents a yard – all to be carried
home by the purchaser.

Two Women in the Klondike · 1899

Aphra Behn

'*All women together ought to let flowers fall upon the tomb of
Aphra Behn*', *said Virginia Woolf. Behn is said to have been the
first woman to make a living by writing. This is arguable, but she
was certainly the most prolific Restoration dramatist apart from
John Dryden. She worked as a British spy in Antwerp in 1666 but
was thrown into debtors' prison on her return to England.*

*Act Second. Scene First. Salewares Shop.
Discovers Alitia Saleware: a Prentice, the Lady Thrivewel, and a
Footman.*

Ali.

I Assure your Ladyship, there cannot be better ware in *London*,
and your Ladyship will find it such in the wearing.

La.

Have you made a Bill Mrs. *Saleware?* for I am satisfied in the
goodness of your Commodity;—a Note of the particulars I pray:
and at as low a Rate as you can afford for ready money; for I am
never in the City Books, like Heirs under age and Courtiers:

Ali.

Your Ladyships pay was ever good, and I have made the Prices
according. Here 'tis, Madam—

La.

Let me see—Boy, take you the Box, 'tis all put up.

Ali.

Yes, Madam.

La.

Give me my Purse, Boy, and go you home with the Lace. I
have only Gold, Mrs. *Saleware*, which you will weigh before
you take, I suppose.

[Ex. Boy.

Ali.
That's no great pains, Madam.
La.
How ever Ile not give you the trouble now,—pray send your man for a Glass of beer—
Ali.
Some beer for my Lady—

> *[Ex. Boy.*

La.
That I may take the opportunity to tell you, what possibly you wou'd be loth he should hear:—for 'tis more the business of the Fore-man of the Shop to keep his Mistresses secrets.
Ali.
Your Ladyship is merry.
La.
Not very merry, because I find by your Bill here that I have laid out more mony than my Husband allow'd me: here is a Hundred and Eight Pounds and Two shillings, and I am allow'd but the Hundred.

EPILOGUE:
Spoken by TOM. SALEWARE.

Dear Friends, go home and look unto your Wives,
Bid 'em keep in and mend their gadding lives;
They all have got a trick to see a Lord,
—*Yet ne'er the sooner for a hasty word.*
I mean no harm, for there are Wives that do
Keep open Shop, and trade as well as you;
Deal by retail, and are to Husbands aiding,
And oftentimes, have much the better Trading.

When time and place are fit, I'll name you some
Who keep a journy-man, or two at home.

The debauchee, or, The credulous cuckold · 1677

ELIZABETH STONOR

*This entry from the archives of the Stonor family in Oxfordshire is
selected from Elizabeth Stonor's own account book, where she notes
the cost of various foodstuffs including salt fish, salt salmon, ginger,
garlic and sugar.*

SEPT. 1478

f. I, Elysabeth Stonore . . .

f 19. It., payd the fryday the xxij day off October for salt ffysche
and salt samon, and gonger and frysche ij. s. . . . .

f. 24. Februar . . . for sourt of ffrout viij. s. iiij. d.; for a sake for
the same ffrout, xiij. d.; for viij bonches of garleke, ij. s.; to ij
porterys for the careage of the same stoffe to the barge, xij. d.
It., . . . for ij li. and di. of suger, ij. s. iij. d.; for di. li. genger, xij.
d.

The Stonor Letters and Papers · 1290–1483

ALESSANDRA STROZZI

*The letters of the widowed Alessandra Strozzi to her exiled sons,
Filippo and Lorenzo, provide invaluable information about the
expenses of a fifteenth-century patrician family in Florence.*

In the name of God.   *14 April
1470*

   In the past few days I've had several letters from you, in
which you told me how you were leaving there . . . And I've
also had the inventory for a bale of cloth and flax, and *greco*
wine, that you are sending via Pisa. They haven't turned up yet

and I don't think it's a good idea to send them to Lari because it would be too much trouble. Because it's not new there's not too much duty to pay on the cloth; we will pay for the *greco* in any case, and there's little duty on the flax. We have received what you sent with Biagio, as described on the inventory, and it's in good order. We did what you asked us to do with it . . .

About the fodder, that is the spelt, I've bought 18 bushels at 9 soldi the bushel, and one thousand two hundred sheaves of barley straw. It's dear here, worth more than 10 soldi the hundred, because the price of grain has gone up to 20 soldi the bushel. That's our luck, we're always having to buy things once they get dear. We'll have to do the same with the wine for the summer, as we'll have to buy several barrels for our own use. Because it's been so cold and still is, the grapevines aren't setting fruit and they say it's very dry for them, so they've got dearer. (These are among our other supplies.) God give us grace that things may still turn out well. If you haven't sent that powder for cleaning silver I won't be needing it . . . From your Allesandra Strozzi in Florence.

Letter from Alessandra Strozzi to her son Filippo · 1470

MAUD PEMBER REEVES

In 1913, after having recorded for several years the daily budgets of thirty working-class families, the Fabian Women's Group published what became a classic study of poverty in Lambeth, an inner borough of London.

Without a doubt, the chief article of diet in a 20s. budget is bread. A long way after bread come potatoes, meat, and fish. Bread is bought from one of the abundance of bakers in the neighbourhood, and is not as a rule very different in price and quality from bread in other parts of London. Meat is generally bargained for on street stalls on Saturday night or even Sunday morning. It may be cheaper than meat purchased in the West End, but is as certainly worse in original quality as well as less fresh and less clean in condition. Potatoes are generally 2 lbs. for 1d., unless they are 'new' potatoes. Then they are dearer. When, at certain seasons in the year, they are 'old' potatoes, they are cheaper; but then they do not 'cut up' well, owing to the sprouting eyes. They are usually bought from an itinerant barrow. Bread in Lambeth is bought in the shop, because the baker is bound, when selling over the counter, to give legal weight. In other words, when he is paid for a quartern he must sell a quartern . . .

The usual plan for a Lambeth house-keeper is to make her great purchase on Saturday evening when she gets her allowance. She probably buys the soap, wood, oil, tea, sugar, margarine, tinned milk, and perhaps jam, for the week. To these she adds the Sunday dinner, which means a joint or part of a joint, greens, and potatoes. The bread she gets daily, also the rasher, fish, or other relish, for her husband's special use. Further purchases of meat are made, if they are made, about Wednesday, while potatoes and pot herbs, as well as fish, often come round on barrows, and are usually bought as required . . .

The regular shopping is monotonous. The order at the grocer's shop is nearly always the same, as is also that at the oilman's. The Sunday dinner requires thought, but tends to repeat itself with the more methodical housewife, who has perhaps a leaning towards neck of mutton as the most interesting of the cheaper joints, or towards a half-shoulder as cutting to better advantage. It is often the same dinner week after week – one course of meat with greens and potatoes. Some women indulge in flights of fancy, and treat the family to a few pounds of fat bacon at 6d. per pound, a quality which is not to be recommended, or even to the extravagance of a rabbit and onions for a change. These women would be likely to vary the vegetables too; and in their accounts tomatoes, when tomatoes are cheap, may appear. It is only in the budgets of the very small family, however, that such extravagant luxuries would creep in . . .

Another reason for buying all necessaries daily is that many men, though in a perfectly regular job (such as some kinds of carting), are paid daily, as though they were casuals. The amounts vary, moreover. One day they bring home 4s. 6d., another 3s. The housewife is never sure what she will have to spend, and as the family needs are, so must she supply necessaries out of the irregular daily sum handed to her.

The daily purchases of the wife of a dustsorter are given below.

Tuesday, 3s.:

2 ozs. tea, 2d.; ½lb. sugar, 1½d.; 4 ozs. butter, 3½d.; bread, 3d.	0	10
One tin of milk, 3½d.; relish for husband's tea, 2d.	0	5½
Potatoes, 2d.; greens and pot herbs, 3½d.; meat, 7d.	1	0½
Gas	0	2
	2	6
In hand	2	1½

Friday, 3s.:

2 ozs. tea, 2d.; ½lb. sugar, 1½d.; 4 ozs. butter, 3½d.; bread, 3d.	0	10
Suet, 2d.; flour, 2½d.; treacle, 1½d.	0	6

Gas	0	2
Five days' pay for neighbour's girl to take out the baby	0	6
	2	0
In hand	3	6½

Saturday, 3s + 3s. 6½d. = 6s. 6½d.:

2 ozs. tea, 2d.; ½lb. sugar, 1½d.; 4 ozs. butter, 3½d.; bread, 6d.	1	1
One tin of milk, 3½d.; bacon, 6d.; eggs, 2d.; potatoes, 2d.; greens, 2d.	1	3½
Gas	0	1
Sunday's joint	2	0
Bakehouse	0	2
Blacklead, hearthstone, matches, soda	0	4
Husband's shirt	1	0
Baby's birth certificate	0	3
Girl to mind baby	0	2
	6	6½

Round About a Pound a Week · 1913

AGNES DEANS CAMERON

Cameron was one of British Columbia's first female journalists and, with her niece, the first white woman to reach the Arctic overland in 1908. She returned determined to promote the equality of the Inuit. It was the Hudson's Bay Company which supplied her for her trip.

When you obtain credit from a Hudson's Bay store, you 'get debt.' A Factor's unwillingness to advance you goods on credit would be expressed thus, 'The Company will give me no debt this winter.' From here northward the terms 'dollars' and 'cents' are unheard. An article is valued at 'three skins' or 'eight skins' or 'five skins,' harking back to the time when a beaver-skin was the unit of money. The rate of exchange to-day is from four skins to two skins for a dollar. Trapping animals is 'making fur.' 'I made no fur last winter and The Company would give me no debt,' is a painful picture of hard times.

The New North: Being Some Account of a Woman's Journey through Canada to the Arctic · 1909

SARA JEANNETTE DUNCAN

Duncan made a journey round the world with her friend 'Orthodocia' – and met her husband in India, where this extract is set, and where she remained for the next three decades.

I almost forget what we saw, which is the penalty attached to craning one's neck round the whole of the world at once; but there remains with me the picture of a great fair city lying under a dusky yellow glory where the sun sloped to the west – lying low and level under it, piercing it with masts that seemed to rise round half her boundary, cleaving it with a shaft in the midst of a green *maidan*, reflecting it in a wide water-space darkling in her heart, breaking it softly with the broad, heavy clusters of the gold-mohur tree . . .

We found ourselves among the shops, and then even to my untutored perception from over seas, it became absolutely clear that we were in British territory. For, from the saddler to the draper, from the confectioner to the great diamond-merchant who has set his seal on three-quarters of the engagements in India, they were all blazoned high 'Under the distinguished patronage' of somebody or other – the Viceroy if they could get him, and failing His Excellency, the next luminary in line . . .

Temptation stalked on every counter in the shape of delicately embroidered 'Indian' fabrics made in Manchester, but purchaseable only here, they told us; and we discovered, in paying one bill, the temptation made easy.

'Will you pay for it now,' said the shopman, 'or sign a chit?'

We asked to have the alternative explained, and were informed that 'the more popular way' in Indian shopping was to sign for the amount of the bill a *chit*, which means a note, a memorandum, anything – and to have the chits added up and sent in at the end of one month or six in the shape of a bill. A certain discount was allowed for cash, but it was the same, quite the same – politely – to them whether we paid or signed. And would we look at their new assortment of parasols?

A Social Departure · 1890

LADY JEUNE

Here, Lady Jeune contrasts shopping in the 1890s with shopping as she remembered it in the 1870s. The shop with 'young men for dancing' was William Whiteley's.

We are not able to stand against the overwhelming temptations which besiege us at every turn . . . We go to purchase something we want; but when we get to our shop there are so many more things that we never thought of till they presented their obtrusive fascinations on every side. We look for a ribbon, a flower, a chiffon of some sort or other, and we find ourselves in a Paradise of ribbons, flowers, and chiffons, without which our life becomes impossible and our gown unwearable. There are many shops in London into which one cannot safely trust oneself. There are the drawbacks of noise, heat, and overcrowding, but they are more than counterbalanced by the brightness of the electric light and the brilliancy of the colours, and the endless variety on either side. There are two very important changes which have contributed to the temptation of spending money nowadays. One is the gathering together under one roof of all kinds of goods – clothing, millinery, groceries, furniture, in fact of all the necessities of life . . . nearly all the great shops in London are becoming vast stores, one of which, more enterprising than the others, is said to supply young men for dancing and coffins to bury them in.

Many more people than formerly come to London, and to the large centres, to do their shopping; they prefer to make their purchases where they can concentrate their forces and diminish fatigue. The shops which still cling to the old-fashioned way of carrying on business are being pressed out by the keen competition which increases so rapidly. What an amount of trouble and expense is avoided where one can order one's New Zealand mutton downstairs, buy one's carpet on the ground floor, and deck oneself out in all the glory of Worth or La Ferrier, on the top floor, to all of which one is borne on the wings of a lift, swift and silent.

The other reason for the increased temptation to spend money is the large numbers of women which are now employed . . . women are so much quicker than men, and they understand so much more readily what other women want; they can enter into the little troubles of their customers; they can fathom the agony of despair as to the arrangement of colours, the alternative trimmings, the duration of a fashion, the depths of a woman's purse, and, more important than all, the question of the becomingness of a dress, or a combination of material, to the wearer.

'The Ethics of Shopping' · 1895

KARYN BOSNAK

In 2002, Karyn Bosnak found herself in New York – and over $20,000 in debt. Her brassy solution was to set up a low-budget website and ask 20,000 people to donate just $1 to rescue her from her own poor choices. Incredibly, people from all over the world responded to her chutzpah and her sense of humour, and she became an overnight news sensation. To view the original website, click on:
www.savekaryn-originalsite.com.

After all the distractions [in cosmetics], I finally made it up to the floor where the lingerie department was. I started looking around and saw some bras and panties by the designer La Perla. I frequently saw La Perla ads in magazines, so I decided to check them out. After finding a bra that I liked, I was horrified to see that the price was almost $200! . . . Who in their right mind would spend $200 on a bra? Not me.

I quickly moved on and soon found the nightgown section, because that was what I was there to buy . . . As my hands were getting full, a saleslady came up to me and asked me if I needed a fitting room.

'Oh, yes, please,' I said while handing her all my nighties. She led me to a fitting room that she said no one knew about.

'It's huge, and it's hidden away from the others, so it's always empty. You'll love it,' she said.

Once we arrived, I was delighted to see that she was indeed correct. It was enormous, and almost as big as my apartment. Yes, it's a sad day when a fitting room at a department store is as big as your apartment, but I tried not to let it get me down.

As I undressed and started to put on the nightgowns, I imagined myself sashaying around in my fabulous but small New York apartment, looking like Krystle Grant Jennings

Carrington or Alexis Morrell Carrington Colby Dexter Rowan. I used to watch a lot of *Dynasty* when I was younger, and always dreamed of looking like those women. Maybe someday someone would even name a perfume after me . . .

As thoughts of a perfect life filled my head, I slipped an Oscar de la Renta silk nightgown off the hanger and over my head. I adjusted the straps and turned around to look in the mirror and . . . ugh! It looked just horrible! I did not look like Alexis or Krystle. I was too short and my breasts were too small to pull a long nightgown off.

. . . [T]he saleslady . . . suggested I try younger more hip styles from designers like Only Hearts and Eberjey. With her help, I picked out a cute tie-dyed sheer camisole and brief set, and an orange-and-yellow short nightgown. I also selected some short D&G spaghetti-strap nightgowns.

After a short while, I went back to my favorite hidden fitting room and tried them on. And bingo! She was right . . . I never knew lingerie could be so much fun!

After three more trips to the fitting room, I ended up also giving the saleslady a D&G nightgown, two more short nightgowns and a great camisole/pant set by Josie Natori, and a great bra and panty set from a designer called Princess Tam-Tam. I wasn't there to get bras and panties, but once I saw this set, I just couldn't pass it up! It was periwinkle and had the most beautiful lace stitching I ever saw! And every girl should have at least one nice bra and panty set.

On my way up to the counter to pay, I grabbed a few more black lace boy-cut undies that I knew would look so flattering on my big booty. As the saleslady rang it all up, I tried to add it all up in my head. It couldn't be that much. A few seconds later she was done.

'Okay, the total is $778,' she said.

'How much?' I asked, shocked that it was so expensive.

'$778,' she repeated. 'You had two Only Hearts camisole sets for $72 each, one Eberjey nightgown for $80, one D&G nightgown for $123, one Natori camisole/pant set that was $100, two Natori nightgowns for $50 each, one Princess Tam-Tam bra for $72, one pair of Princess Tam-Tam panties for $42, and three pairs of Wacoal black lace panties for $20 each. That comes to $721. And with tax the total is $778.'

I stood there in awe not knowing what to do. It was expensive, but I had to be honest with myself. I was twenty-seven years old and wasn't going to be a spring chicken much longer. So I needed these nighties to look as sexy as I could because I needed to land a man. So they were kind of like an investment. An investment in my sex life and an investment in my future. Just like my favorite makeup products, they served two purposes. And if they didn't work with Brad, then hopefully they'd work with the next guy.

And how 'out of style' can lingerie really go? Sexy is sexy. Lace panties have been in style forever and weren't going anywhere. These weren't like a trendy top or something. They were pajamas. Lingerie. I'd be able to wear them for seasons. So I needed to chill out and not fret over my $778 lingerie purchase. It was going to be okay. With that, I gladly handed over my Amex card, and a few moments later I was out the door . . .

When I got home, I opened my pajama drawer. There comes a time in your life when you have to say goodbye to old T-shirts and college sweatshirts that have been masquerading as pajamas for years and make room for more adult stuff. And for me, now was that time . . .

Over the next two weeks, Brad slept over almost every night. Things were going pretty well between us. And my financial life seemed to be picking up as well. American

Express upgraded me to a Gold card. And if they were confident that I could pay it off every month, then so was I! Life was good!

Save Karyn · 2003

EDITH WHARTON

As the day of departure approached, Undine's absorption in her dresses almost precluded the thought of amusement. Early and late she was closeted with fitters and packers – even the competent Céleste not being trusted to handle the treasures now pouring in – and Ralph cursed his weakness in not restraining her, and then fled for solace to museums and galleries.

He could not rouse in her any scruple about incurring fresh debts, yet he knew she was no longer unaware of the value of money. She had learned to bargain, pare down prices, evade fees, brow-beat the small tradespeople and wheedle concessions from the great – not, as Ralph perceived, from any effort to restrain her expenses, but only to prolong and intensify the pleasure of spending. Pained by the trait, he tried to laugh her out of it. He told her once that she had a miserly hand – showing her, in proof, that, for all their softness, the fingers would not bend back, or the pink palm open. But she retorted a little sharply that it was no wonder, since she'd heard nothing talked of since their marriage but economy; and this left him without any answer. So the purveyors continued to mount to their apartment, and Ralph, in the course of his frequent flights from it, found himself always dodging the corners of black glazed boxes and swaying pyramids of pasteboard; always lifting his hat to sidling milliners' girls, or effacing himself before slender *vendeuses* floating by in a mist of opopanax. He felt incompetent to pronounce on the needs to which these visitors ministered; but the reappearance among them of the blond-bearded jeweller gave him ground for fresh fears. Undine had assured him that she had given up the idea of having her ornaments reset, and there had been ample time for their return; but on his questioning her she explained that there had been delays and 'bothers' and put him in the wrong by asking ironically if he supposed she was buying things 'for pleasure' when she knew as well as he that there wasn't any money to pay for them.

The Custom of the Country · 1913

BARGAINS AND SALES

Alkalay-Gut begins her poem with a quote from Aristotle's lectures on rhetoric.

> We must consider, as a red cloak suits a young man, what suits
>   an old one; for the same garment is not suitable for both.

Aristotle and I go shopping at Bloomingdales.
It is one of those sales when everything
is seventy per cent off and if you don't grab the stuff first
and decide later if it suits you, you'll lose the opportunity.

So we come home, totally blown,
with a dozen robes between us,
a bottle-green pantsuit, some tight dresses,
a pale cashmere sweater, and a red cloak.

Aristotle wants to try it all on at once –
he's such a dandy – and begins dreaming,
immediately, of where he will wear each treasure.
The cloak is perfect for tonight's lecture,
he declares. It gives me energy,
imagination.

Listen, Dear,
I try to remind him of his own philosophies,
there is the matter of proportion.
Your size, your age, your dignity –
Stay out of this sister, he explodes.
If I want your friendly advice, I'll ask for it.

'Consider the Red Cloak' · 1999

CHICSHOPPINGPARIS.BLOGSPOT.COM

Tuesday, June 13, 2006

6 Tips for Doing the Sales from a Chic Shopper:
1. Hold a stake out: Visit the store before the sale starts, see how many of your beloved item is still in stock, and try to get some information from the *vendeuse* about its sale price.
2. Avoid the first day: The stores are packed with people and while marathon shopping can be a great sport, shopping the sales on the first day is bound to leave you frustrated.
3. Shop with a friend: She'll talk you out of that pair of neon green cowboy boots, even if they are 75% off.
4. Get out of bed: Go first thing in the morning to avoid lines or look for special opening hours during the evenings or on weekends.
5. Dress for success: If shopping for clothing, wear layers and clothing that is simple to remove to facilitate trying on.
6. Shop well-armed: Bring multiple forms of payment – credit cards and cash – just in case.

posted by chicshopper @ 8:42 PM, June 13, 2006

PLUM SYKES

Even in my most imaginative nightmares I never dreamed a day could start with an invitation to the Chanel sample sale and end with a New York nervous breakdown.

'Don't tell her I said this or she'll think I'm a two-faced liar,' whispered Julie conspiratorially one beautiful May morning over café au lait at Tartine, 'but K.K.'s New York City Opera benefit, which is universally considered to be *the* benefit of benefits, is not even five percent as thrilling as the Chanel sample sale. Show me a Manhattan girl who'd rather watch *Don Giovanni* than shop Chanel at Target prices, and I'll renew my membership at Equinox Gym on Sixty-third Street and actually start going on a semi-regular basis.'

According to Julie, the Chanel sample sale is *the* event of New York events: absolutely no one gets invited except 'very few, very exclusive girls. But you're in,' Julie said, handing me a white envelope. 'I got you on the list.'

Inside was a stiff white card from Chanel. I was beyond excited, which was *très* alarming actually. I adore Julie but her shopping habits are not exactly healthy. I didn't want to turn into a girl like her, whose hormone system is ruled by retail opportunities. But apparently everyone's estrogen sky-rockets the first time they get this particular invitation, so there's no need to be freaked by it. It read,

CHANEL SAMPLE SALE
TUESDAY, MAY 7, 7:15 A.M.
PARK LANE HOTEL
58TH STREET, BTW. 6TH AND 7TH
BRING PHOTO ID
NO ADMITTANCE WITHOUT THIS CARD.
THIS IS YOUR SECURITY PASS.

. . . The annoying thing was, I couldn't go to the sample sale because of work. Careers are very unreliable things and you have to be attentive to them or they just disappear. NY girls who go to too many parties and sample sales tend to have disappearing-type careers and I didn't want to be one of them. I was booked to fly down to Palm Beach to do an interview with a society girl. She'd just inherited an Art Deco beach mansion. She lived there all alone like a millenial Doris Duke. It was sad, really, but very glamorous.

'*Fool*,' said Julie when I told her I wasn't coming. 'You cannot miss this.'

I knew I should do the interview, but I just couldn't resist the idea of shopping Chanel like it was the Gap. Occasionally my value system inexplicably abandons me, and I find myself doing things I never usually would. Feeling unbelievably guilty, I called the office and said that the Palm Beach heiress had cancelled due to 'fatigue'.

Bergdorf Blondes · 2004

ANONYMOUS

A careful buyer can really spend profitably at the sales without suffering from sale mania. For, on the other hand, there are many women for whom sales are a positive vice. They exercise so little control when they see a bargain. They stop at each counter and find the wares spread thereon irresistible. Whereas the systematic bargain-seeker has her mind fairly well made up concerning her purchases. She will never leave the remnant baskets out; she will always expect the best models in the 'ready-to-wear' sections.

Ladies' Sphere · 1922

SLAVENKA DRAKULIĆ

When a friend from abroad visited me in the mid-seventies, he noticed that women in Zagreb were dressed very elegantly and wondered how it was possible on the little income they had. But at that time the cost of living was still low and spending the little surplus money was the only fun we had. The result was that we all looked and behaved as if we were rich. We developed an easy-come, easy-go attitude to money.

But even spending what we did demanded a strategy. Travelling abroad, I could afford to buy clothes only in sales. I am not bothering to discuss shopping in my own country, because there was not much to buy there in the first place. Sale goods there were real rubbish. The things in sales in Graz or Trieste were rubbish, too, but there was a difference between our rubbish and the rubbish produced abroad. It was all cheaply made, it's true, but sometimes, if you searched hard enough and were lucky, you could find cheap things that looked expensive.

God only knows if these sales, or *sconti*, in Trieste were genuine sales. I always suspected that they were not, and I felt cheated. I thought then, as I do today, that shop owners had discovered the magic attraction the word 'sale' held for us poor Balkan suckers. Piles of underwear, T-shirts, shoes, dresses – anything labelled 'sale', drew us like flies. There was also a ritual in the way you shopped: you went in the morning, early enough to be able to check all the usual places (Giovanni, Standa, Ponte Rosso) early, because, you told yourself, you would be able to snap up the 'bargains' before anyone else. You would not even look at the 'better' – that is, normal, shops. What would be the point? The *magazini* we regularly visited were stuffed with the same cheap crap, but prices were lower and saving a few thousand lire meant you could afford to buy yet another pair of jeans or sneakers, which is what it was all about.

Years and years of such habits have moulded my attitude towards shopping and indeed to money in general. Not my taste – taste is something you develop independently of your resources. Taste, when you have no money, is about what you do with cheap things you buy, how you wear and combine them. But to this day, as soon as I see the magic word 'sale' and spot something reduced to £9.99 in England or $19 in America – or 99 German marks, 199 Swedish crowns, 199 Austrian schillings – any small sum in any currency, in fact, I have to investigate, if only to see for myself what they are selling – kitchenware, sheets, towels, detergent – even if I'm actually shopping for shoes. It is a compulsive act for me, I have to look to avoid the feeling that perhaps I'm missing a good opportunity. Of course, I end up buying ten T-shirts (they will always come in handy), three pairs of espadrilles (I need them), and a dozen pairs of panties I can't resist, just because they are cheap. All at the cost, as I explain to myself as soon as I am back at home, of 'no money at all'. What is more important is that buying so much for so little gives me a sense of satisfaction.

This is an art, I think, proud of myself for a moment. But no, it is not, and deep down I know it. I am aware that the T-shirts will fall apart after two washes and the espadrilles after I have worn them for a week; the elastic in the panties was already going when I bought them. Buying junk is not an art, it is only a sad necessity. Or, in my case, a bad habit that you can't get rid of, like smoking.

Café Europa · 1996

SOPHIE KINSELLA

'Bex, open it up!' Suze is begging. 'Let me see!' She's grabbing inside the bag with eager long fingers, and I pull it away quickly before she rips it. This bag is going on the back of my door along with my other prestige carrier bags, to be used in a casual manner when I need to impress. (Thank God they didn't print special 'Sale' bags. I *hate* shops which do that. What's the point of having a posh bag with 'Sale' splashed all over it? You might as well splash 'Cheapskate'.)

Very slowly, I take the dark green box out of the bag, remove the lid and unfold the tissue paper. Then, almost reverentially, I lift up the scarf. It's beautiful. It's even more beautiful here than it was in the shop.

The Secret Dreamworld of a Shopaholic · 2000

MARY WOLLSTONECRAFT

Caroline and Mary are staying in the country when their father writes to ask their guardian, Mrs Mason, to take them to town. There, the girls are given a lesson in compassion and unselfishness as they meet many less fortunate people.

The wished for morning arrived, and they set off in a tumult of spirits; sorry to leave the country, yet delighted with the prospect of visiting the metropolis . . .

For some time after their arrival, every thing they saw excited wonder and admiration; and not till they were a little familiarized with the new objects, did they ask reasonable questions.

Several presents recruited their purses; and they requested Mrs Mason to allow them to buy some trifles they were in want of. The request was modest, and she complied.

As they walked in search of a shop, they both determined to purchase pocket-books . . .

They stopped at a small shop, Mrs Mason always sought out such; for, said she, I may help those who perhaps want assistance; bargains I never seek, for I wish every one to receive the just value for their goods.

In the shop which they chanced to enter, they did not find the kind of pocket-book that they had previously fixed on, and therefore wished precipitately to leave it; but were detained by their more considerate friend. While they had been turning over the trinkets, the countenance of the woman, who served them, caught her eye, and she observed her eager manner of recommending the books. You have given much unnecessary trouble, said she, to the mistress of the shop; the books are better, and more expensive than you intended to purchase, but I will make up the deficiency.

Original Stories from Real Life · 1791

MARGARETE BÖHME

Covering several generations of shopkeepers and the evolution of their premises, Böhme's melodramatic novel fictionalises the institution of credit, the building of consumer paradises such as Selfridges 1909 department store, and in-store detection.

The ground floor was the El Dorado for bargains. On long tables the staple commodities were heaped: cheap glass and china, linen goods, bundles of remnants, embroideries, gloves.

Friedrich felt, as ever, unhappy at the sight of these countless pennyworths. Everywhere reigned the principle of cheapness as opposed to good value; and it was that principle which chiefly attracted people to the big shops. 'Some day,' thought he, 'it must all be changed.' . . .

[T]raffic in the shop had increased, for it was the last quarter of an hour before closing. Like a swift seething wave of dark human bodies, the stream poured between the counters; the strange, indefinable, immanent noise in the air now sounded like the distant, menacing growl of hungry beasts of prey . . .

The Department Store · 1912

TAMMY FAYE BAKKER

Jimmy Bakker and his wife Tammy Faye held sway over a vast televangelising empire, the Praise the Lord Club, until scandal

involving love affairs, attacks on their opulent lifestyle, and
financial misdeeds ended their reign.

'There's times when I just have to quit thinking . . . and the
only way I can quit thinking is by shopping.'

*

'I take Him shopping with me. I say, "Okay, Jesus, help me
find a bargain."'

*

'I always say shopping is cheaper than a psychiatrist.'

1980s

RAHILA GUPTA

Coleen McLoughlin is the star of Asda's £80m campaign to
promote its Must Have fashion range, modelling the clothes in
a series of TV adverts. The press release that accompanied last
week's launch declared breathlessly: 'Must Haves come with
Must Buy price tags, with items starting from as little as £3.'

Now, far be it from me to spoil the party, but somebody has
to ask about the true cost of cheap clothes. When the media
starts dribbling over Primark's business model, it is time to
look at the bigger picture. Primark sources materials from the
cheapest possible supplier, moving quickly on to a cheaper
and faster option where possible, meaning its relationships
with suppliers are short-lived.

Trendspotters gleefully talk of the end of the designer label,
a tyranny from which we would all happily be released.
Celebrities are now seen gracing the aisles of cut-price clothing chains. 'Bag a better bargain than your buddy' is apparently
the competitive mantra for today's teenagers getting their fix
at the shopping centre.

Before the love of cheap chic was being hyped up by the

fashionistas, we might have understood that poverty drives people to buy cheap. The morality of the poor exploiting the poor (if you ignore the profiteers in the middle) is certainly more palatable than those with disposable cash buying cheap because it's fashionable.

Even Radio 4's *Woman's Hour* carried an uncritical piece on this trend recently, debating whether cheap really was the new chic. Surely it should have been debating the question posed by the title of a revealing report, Who Pays for Cheap Clothes?, published in July by a campaigning group called Labour Behind the Label.

Where does this downward pressure on prices lead us? In some cases to places such as Bangladesh, where the cost of clothing production is half that of China's; and to textile factories where women earning just £7 a month and often working 80-hour weeks make up more than 90% of the workforce.

According to this report, women's clothing prices have fallen by a third in 10 years. The cheap end of the market has doubled in size in just five years to notch up £6bn of sales in 2005. We now buy 40% of our clothes at stores such as Primark and its competitors with just 17% of our clothing budget.

If we are prepared to spend more on organic food and goods produced by companies with a green halo, surely we should be prepared to boycott those companies whose buying policies seem to leave no room for a living wage. Maybe, as with messages on cigarette packets, we should pass legislation to ensure that every item produced in inhumane conditions comes with a warning. This is exactly what Jonah Peretti, an American student, tried to do in 2001. He responded to Nike's offer of a personalised ID in every pair of shoes with a tongue-in-cheek request to have the word 'sweatshop' stitched into his. The company refused. One of the reasons cited was: 'Your personal ID contains profanity or inappropriate slang.' I hope the multinationals remember this notion of sweatshop being an obscenity the next time they squeeze suppliers in the developing world.

At the very least, we should demand that fair-trade certification be extended to garments, and not just agricultural commodities. Of course, at these prices who needs a certificate to know that fair trade is impossible? Surely our list of Must Haves should include basic human rights for those producing our hot-off-the-catwalk clothes.

'Sweatshop Till You Drop' · 2006

MADELEINE ST JOHN

The great doors were opened and the phalanx of grim-faced viragos cantered through the breach and down the marble steps: it took a good five minutes for the whole formation to pass him . . . Well done, ladies, he said to himself: off to as fine a flying start as I have seen these dozen years.

This he knew was merely the advance guard: supplementary troops would continue to arrive in large numbers for the next hour, in slightly lesser numbers up until lunchtime, and in still-considerable force throughout the afternoon. The élite regiment of the first day would be replaced by the only slightly less determined battalions of the second and subsequent days, but look at it as one would, the scene at Goode's for the next ten days would be, not to put too fine a point on it, a battlefield; honours would be won, and indeed merited; trophies would be displayed; lives might not be lost but wounds of one kind or another would most certainly be sustained: the sale was now in progress.

Each floor of the great building revealed substantially the

same sight: of hundreds of women, all caution, all dignity abandoned, fighting for their rights to possession of frocks, skirts, jerseys, shoes, blouses and hats at greatly reduced prices. Who could blame them, who so much as criticise? They were driven not by any impulse so mere as greed or vanity, but by a biological law which impelled them to make themselves fine: and now they hoped to fulfil its diktat without at the same time making themselves broke.

The Women in Black · 1993

LADY JEUNE

The complaints which have lately appeared in many papers about the rudeness, the insolence, and discourtesy of customers to shop-women are not really exaggerated. One very rarely hears 'please' or 'thank-you' and no expression of gratitude for trouble taken is vouchsafed by many an over-dressed and mon-eyed boor. Many people complain that the shop assistants bore them by their persistent appeals to buy things they do not require . . . but many women go to shops for no reason beyond the desire to look round. The ingenious entrepreneur of today, has, however, hit on the scheme which offers the greatest seductions to the shopping women, in the sales which take place twice every year. At these times women can walk about unmolested, turning over laces and ribbons and finery of all sorts without being pressed to purchase, though they are possibly tempted and succumb before leaving.

'The Ethics of Shopping' · 1895

MARY WOLLSTONECRAFT

The conversation of French women, who are not so rigidly nailed to their chairs to twist lappets, and knot ribands, is frequently superficial; but, I contend, that it is not half so insipid as that of those English women whose time is spent in making caps, bonnets, and the whole mischief of trimmings, not to mention shopping, bargain-hunting, &c. &c.: and it is the decent, prudent women, who are most degraded by these practices; for their motive is simply vanity.

A Vindication of the Rights of Woman · 1792

DOLLY PARTON

Country singer Dolly Parton was one of twelve children growing up in a one-room cabin in the Smoky Mountains, Tennessee.

My life is like unto a bargain store
And I may have just what you're lookin' for
If you don't mind the fact that all the merchandise is used
But with a little mending it could be as good as new

Why you take for instance this old broken heart
If you will just replace the missing parts
You would be surprised to find how good it really is
Take it and you never will be sorry that you did

The bargain store is open come inside
You can easily afford the price
Love is all you need to purchase all the merchandise
And I will guarantee you'll be completely satisfied

'The Bargain Store' · 1975

SHARON ZUKIN

[I]f you shop at Kmart on a weekday morning, you could get lonely cruising the wide, empty aisles of the upper floor, with its random assortment of suitcases, picture frames, Martha Stewart sheets and towels, and a few racks of children's clothing.

It's sad up there. Although you can sit on plastic chairs in the Kmart café and gaze through a large, plate-glass window onto the bustling street below, you can't escape the feeling of emptiness . . .

Everyone comes to Kmart. Even my neighbor, who paid a million dollars for his apartment several years ago, smiles when he sees my Kmart plastic shopping bag and I tell him about the paper towels. 'Sure,' he says, 'and they're even cheaper at Costco.'

Point of Purchase · 2004

JANE AUSTEN

Tuesday 11 June 1799

My dear Cassandra,

Though you have given me unlimited powers concerning Your Sprig, I cannot determine what to do about it, & shall therefore in this & in every future letter continue to ask you for further directions.—We have been to the cheap Shop, & very cheap we found it, but there are only flowers made there, no fruit—& as I could get 4 or 5 very pretty sprigs of the former for the same money which would procure only one Orleans plumb, in short could get more for three or four Shillings than I could have means of bringing home, I cannot decide on the fruit till I hear from you again.—Besides, I cannot help thinking that it is more natural to have flowers grow out of the head than fruit.—What do you think on that subject? . . . Now I will give you the history of Mary's veil, in the purchase of which I have so considerably involved you that it is my duty to economise for you in the flowers.—I had no difficulty in getting a muslin veil for half a guinea, & not much more in discovering afterwards that the Muslin was thick, dirty & ragged, & would therefore by no means do for a united Gift.—I changed it consequently as soon as I could, & considering what a state my imprudence had reduced me to, I thought myself lucky in getting a black Lace one for 16 shillings—. I hope the half of that sum will not greatly exceed what You had intended to offer up on the altar of Sister-in-law affection.—Yours affe:

Jane

Selected Letters · 1799

ANNE TYLER

She had been taught to buy only top-quality underwear, however else she might economize, but this was an emergency. She crossed the street and entered the dime-store smells of caramel and cheap cosmetics and old wooden floors. Apparently the notion of consolidated checkout lanes had not caught on here. At each and every counter, a clerk stood by a cash register. A floss-haired girl rang up a coloring book for a child; an elderly woman bagged a younger woman's cookie sheets. The lingerie department was staffed by a man, oddly enough; so Delia made her selections in haste and handed them over without quite raising her eyes. A plain white nylon bra, white cotton underpants. The underpants came three to a pack. Other styles could be purchased singly, but it was the pack of three that her fingers alighted on. *Just in case I'm away for more than one night*, she caught herself thinking. Then, as she counted out her money, she thought, *But I can always use them at home, of course, too. This doesn't mean a thing . . .*

At four-fifteen she returned to the dime store and bought one cotton nightgown, white, and two pairs of nylon panty hose. At four twenty-five she crossed the square to Bassett Bros. Shoe Store and bought a large black leather handbag. The bag cost fifty-seven dollars. When she first saw the price she considered settling for vinyl, but then she decided that only genuine leather would pass muster with Miss Grinstead.

Ladder of Years · 1995

SARA JEANNETTE DUNCAN

Lady Torquilin and I were going shopping. I had been longing to shop in London ever since I arrived, but, as Lady Torquilin remarked, my trunks seemed to make it almost unreasonable. So up to this time I had been obliged to content myself with looking at things in the windows, until Lady Torquilin said she really couldn't spend so much time in front of shop-windows – we had better go inside. Besides, she argued, of course there was this to be said – if you bought a good thing, there it was – always a good thing! 'And it isn't as if you were obliged to pinch, my dear. I would be the last one to counsel extravagance,' said Lady Torquilin. 'Therefore we'll go to the cheapest place first' – and we got an omnibus . . .

We went in with a throng that divided and hurried hither and thither through long 'departments', upstairs and down, past counters heaped with cheapnesses, and under billowing clouds and streaming banners of various colours, marked 1s. 1½d. and 1¾d. on very black letters on a very white ground. The whole place spoke of its cheapness, invited you to approach and have your every want supplied at the lowest possible scale of profit – for cash. Even the clerks – as we say in America, incorrectly, I believe – the people behind the counter suggested the sweet reasonableness of the tariff; not that I mean anything invidious, but they seemed to be drawn from an unpretending, inexpensive class of humanity. The tickets claimed your attention everywhere, and held it, the prices on them were so remarkably low, and it was to me at first a matter of regret that they were all attached to articles I could not want under any circumstances. For, the moment I went in, I succumbed to the cheapest place; I desired to avail myself of it to any extent – to get the benefit of those fascinating figures personally and immediately. I followed Lady Torquilin with eagerness, exclaiming: but nothing would induce her to stop anywhere; she went straight for the trifles she wanted, and I perforce after her. 'There are some things, my dear' she said, when we reached the right counter, 'that one *must* come here for, but beyond those few odds and ends – well, I leave you to judge for yourself.'

This was calculated to dash a person's enthusiasm, and mine was dashed at once. There is nothing, in shopping, like a friend's firm and outspoken opinion, to change your views. I began to think unfavourably of the cheapest place immediately, and during the twenty-five minutes of valuable time which Lady Torquilin spent, in addition to some small silver, upon a box of pink paper trimmings for pudding-dishes, I arrived at a state of objection to the cheapest place, which intensified as we climbed more stairs, shared more air with the British Public of the cheapest place, and were jostled at more counters. 'For,' Lady Torquilin said, 'now that we *are* here, though I loathe coming, except that it's something you ought to do, we really might as well see what there is!' – and she found that there were quite a number of little things at about a shilling and a ha'penny that she absolutely needed, and would have to pay 'just double for, my dear, anywhere else.' By that time my objection became active, and embraced the cheapest place and everything connected with it, quite unreasonably . . . It was the deadly monotony of goodishness and cheapishness in everything and everybody that oppressed you. There were no heights of excellence and no contrasting depths – all one level of quality wherever you looked – so that the things they sold at the cheapest place – sold with mechanical respect, and as fast as they could tie them up – seemed to lack all individuality, and to have no reason for being, except to become parcels. There was none of the exultation of bargain-getting; the bargains were on a regular system of fixed laws – the poetic delight of an unexpected 'reduction' was wholly absent. The cheapest place resolved itself into a vast, well-organised Opportunity, and inside you saw the British Public and Opportunity together . . .

'Now, what do you think of the cheapest place,' asked Lady Torquilin as we walked together in the Edgware Road. I told her as I have told you. 'H'mph!' said she. 'It's not a shop I like myself, but that's what I call being *too* picksome! You get what you want, and if you don't want it you leave it, and why should you care! Now, by way of variety, we'll go to the dearest place;' and the omnibus we got into rattled off in the direction of Bond Street.

An American Girl in London · 1891

EMILY FITZGERALD

There are some people at the Agency who, in some way or other, come across advertisements in New York, the cheap things they get just astonish me . . . Can you do any better than that? . . . I see in the Altman's Catalogue calico wrappers trimmed with a dark band, pockets and all fixings—for one dollar. *What is the use of sewing any more?*

Letters · 1876

SARA HUTCHINSON

Sara Hutchinson was Wordsworth's sister-in-law, and the beloved of Samuel Taylor Coleridge, with whom she edited the literary and political magazine The Friend. *Her letters are full of references to shopping.*

Miss J. Hutchinson, Radnor
Kendal, Novr 24th 1815

I hope dearest Mary that you will take care of yourself & not
suckle too long for notwithstanding the fine tales you tell me
of your strength it is evident by the falling-off of your hair,
& weakness in your eyes it takes great hold of you – this
latter being often the effect of it disagreeing with the
constitution. I shall send you a pattn Night Cap when I send
off the Bed &c & if you want aught else from this country
you need but mention it & it shall be done – You often
disbelieved me about the cheapness of articles here – for
instance we can get handsome cut glass wine glasses at
15/per doz the common 12/. Tumblers common at 8d & I/ a
piece the best 16d & 19d cut &c – & Scotch carpetting
handsome at . . . & mahogany furniture is dog cheap by
comparison . . . at Young-husbands till I longed to buy a side
board which was sold for 3 £ made by Gillow of the very
kind which would have suited you but the Carriage is so
promiscuous that I feared it might be spoilt or broken . . . I
have a long list of commissions from Betsy about silk Gowns
& Silver spoons – which last articles I believe are at
Hindwell or Radnor . . . Farewell ever yours S.H.

Letters · 1815

BARBARA COMYNS

*The impoverished heroine of Comyns's second novel was based on
Comyns herself during her first marriage to a painter, when she
supported her family by dealing in antiques and classic cars.*

The next free afternoon we had, we went to the address in
Haverstock Hill she had given us. A woman with very fuzzy
black hair came to the door . . . She showed us the flat, which

consisted of a large basement room with an old-fashioned dresser, and a small kitchen and use of bath and lav. When we had seen it she said we had better meet her sister 'GER-G E R', so we went upstairs and met the sister, who had even more fuzzy hair, but it was fair, and her eyes were round and blue and her face like a melting strawberry ice cream, rather a cheap one, and I expect her body was like that, too, only it was mostly covered in mauve velvet. She spoke to us a little and said we were little love-birds looking for a nest. She made us feel all awful inside. Then she suddenly went into a trance. We thought she was dying, but her sister explained she was a medium and governed by a Chinese spirit called Mr Hi Wu. Then Mr Hi Wu spoke to us in very broken English and told us we were so lucky to be offered such a beautiful flat for only twenty-five shillings a week; it was worth at least thirty-five . . .

After this we had a frantic time shopping; we did most of it in Chalk Farm Road, N.W. We bought a massive oval table for seven-and-six, and chairs for one-and-six . . . We found the rugs rather expensive; we had to have two and they were a pound each. The sheets and blankets were a great worry, too. We had to get the divan on hire purchase and for months after were having trouble over it; we nearly lost it several times, but after two years it really belonged to us, and they sent us a large and legal paper to say it did . . .

We had white walls in the kitchen, and Charles painted a chef by the gas cooker. The thing we were most pleased about was the dresser; there were drawers for our clothes and shelves for the china. We had a proper tea-set from Waring and Gillow, and a lot of blue plates from Woolworths; our cooking things came from there, too. I had hoped they would give us a set of real silver teaspoons when we bought the wedding-ring, but the jeweller we went to wouldn't, so our spoons came from Woolworths, too.

Our Spoons Came from Woolworths · 1950

FIVE-FINGER DISCOUNTS

ENGLISH BALLAD

Oh, don't we live in curious times.
You scarce could be believing,
When Frenchmen fight and Emperors die
And ladies go a-thieving.
A beauty to the West End went,
Around a shop she lingers,
And there upon some handkerchiefs
She clapped her pretty fingers.
Into the shop she gently popped;
The world is quite deceiving
When ladies have a notion got
To ramble out a-thieving.

'Ladies, Don't Go Thieving' · *c.* 1867

SMARTJUSTICE.ORG

More women are sentenced to prison for shoplifting than any
other crime, according to official figures released today. The
Home Office figures reveal one third of all women sentenced
to custody in 2002 had been convicted of stealing from shops.

And locking up women shoplifters does little to increase
public safety – as official figures show that eight out of ten
commit more crimes within two years of leaving jail.

'Female Jails Bursting With Shoplifters' · 2004

ELIZABETH WURTZEL

I walk into Saks Fifth Avenue in the Galleria one afternoon
and wander around. I am looking for something, I am always
looking for something. Makeup, jewelry, bubble bath, a pair of

spiky red heels that I will never wear, certainly not here in Fort Lauderdale.

But truly, I am looking for something to steal, for no reason other than that I feel like stealing something . . .

It started out with small items, lipstick and mascara at drugstore chains. Then one day I was at Macy's trying to buy a silver bracelet with the seven deadly sins engraved into it. I was standing in my winter coat for at least a half hour, waiting for a clerk to let me buy this way overpriced item, and I was getting hot and nauseated and yawning in that way that you do when you are overbundled indoors. I had already loosened my scarf and pulled off my hat, I felt faint and shaky, and finally I just said fuck it, stuffed the thing into one of my capacious pockets, and walked out the door. Since then it's been Gucci sunglasses from Bloomingdale's, a silver butterfly anklet from Burdines, any number of tester lipsticks from any number of Estée Lauder counters – mostly because I feel like it, but partly because in the crowds of department stores, it's easier to steal things than buy them. I will never take anything from a privately owned store – I have scruples, really I do. But these messes of emporia owned by Federated and other huge conglomerates that don't care enough about their employees to pay them decently and don't regard their customers highly enough to make sure there is an adequate sales staff to serve them – as far as I'm concerned, they are asking for me to become a thief . . .

More, Now, Again · 2002

ANONYMOUS

AMERICA. Dec. 5. – Two Gothamite authoresses recently tried their hands at shoplifting, in order to get punch into their literary work. Now the unliterary laws of New York will give them further realistic experience in the workhouse.

The Stars and Stripes · 1918–19

ELIZA SMITH

I was born in the County of Galway of very respectable parents, but my father was rather extravagant, and made no provision for his children, and at his death left four, of whom I was the youngest . . .

On the 29th of September [1835], I became acquainted with a woman whose line of life was that of shop-lifting, and with her I went into many shops to deprive my fellow-creatures of their property. Many times I have trembled with my ill-got prize, lest the Lord should strike me dead, and cast me into hell. So strong did my conscience accuse me, that I often came out without taking what my sinful companions would offer me, and have borne their ill-treatment sooner than the guilt of my conscience; of all people I was the most miserable. In October, I was taken and sent to Newgate for trial, and was sentenced to six month's [sic] imprisonment in Grange Gorman Prison. I felt thankful I was any place, and not obliged to rob; but I still continued in my sins, and at the end of that time I came out determined to return to my old trade. I often thought to gather a few shillings and give up my robbing, but so strong was my love of spirits that I still went on. It made me forget my misery for a while, but in my sober hours my mind was a perfect hell to me . . .

During my stay in the prison, I have been treated with the greatest kindness by the ladies I had the honour to be placed under; may every blessing attend them. And now I am placed on board ship, which is to carry me to a distant land . . .

neither husband or children know any thing of me: may the Lord bless them, and keep his watchful care over them— Amen.

On Board ship February 9th
Memoir of Eliza Smith, Who Was Transported for Shoplifting,
Written by Herself · 1839

WILLA CATHER

Fred strolled over to the sofa, lifted a scarf from one of the trays and stood abstractedly drawing it through his fingers. 'You've been so kind these last few days, Thea, that I began to hope you might soften a little; that you might ask me to come over and see you this summer.'

'If you thought that, you were mistaken,' she said slowly. 'I've hardened, if anything. But I shan't carry any grudge away with me, if you mean that.'

He dropped the scarf. 'And there's nothing – nothing at all you'll let me do?'

'Yes, there is one thing, and it's a good deal to ask. If I get knocked out, or never get on, I'd like you to see that Dr. Archie gets his money back. I'm taking three thousand dollars of his.'

'Why, of course I shall. You may dismiss that from your mind. How fussy you are about money, Thea. You make such a point of it.' He turned sharply and walked to the windows.

Thea sat down in the chair he had quitted. 'It's only poor people who feel that way about money, and who are really honest,' she said gravely. 'Sometimes I think that to be really honest, you must have been so poor that you've been tempted to steal.'

'To what?'

'To steal. I used to be, when I first went to Chicago and saw all the things in the big stores there. Never anything big, but little things, the kind I'd never seen before and could never afford. I did take something once, before I knew it.'

Fred came toward her. For the first time she had his whole attention, in the degree to which she was accustomed to having it. 'Did you? What was it?' he asked with interest.

'A sachet. A little blue silk bag of orris-root powder. There was a whole counterful of them, marked down to fifty cents. I'd never seen any before, and they seemed irresistible. I took one up and wandered about the store with it. Nobody seemed to notice, so I carried it off.'

Fred laughed. 'Crazy child! Why, your things always smell of orris; is it a penance?'

The Song of the Lark · 1915

ELAINE ABELSON

Abelson's study of Victorian women shoplifters looks at middle-class women who could not resist the lure of the new department stores. Unlike their working-class sisters in crime, middle-class shoplifters were allowed to plead 'incapacitating illness', or kleptomania, a new term coined by psychiatrists to excuse them and prevent scandal.

Mrs. Dora Landberg, a wealthy widow and a frequent customer in the store that finally had her arrested, claimed to be 'suffering from Kleptomania'. A twenty-seven-year-old woman, Sarah Dengler, told court authorities that she was a kleptomaniac and 'vainly sought to resist the temptation to steal'. She added that 'she had pains in her head at times during which she was subject to the disease'. The report ended with the notation, 'The police were inclined to believe Miss Dengler's story'. Fannie Lendrum, forty-five and from 'respectable family' in Brooklyn, was defended in court by her husband, who said that 'her mental aberration lately had been due to her physical condition. She had no reason to steal and never before had developed any dishonest characteristics'. The attorney for another suspect, arrested in a Sixth Avenue department store in 1904, described her as 'a very studious girl. She has studied art and is somewhat literary. She has long suffered from a nervous trouble. Her father is heartbroken and has done everything to cure her. She spent the summer in a sanitorium, and has been to Bermuda . . .'

When accused nineteenth-century shoplifters had described the physical inability to resist the temptation that assailed them in the dry-goods bazaars, their excuses were generally understood in terms of female hysteria and mental degeneration. Women seem to have accepted this interpretation, as well as the popular medical dogma that viewed the female body as the basis of social behavior.

When Ladies Go A-Thieving · 1989

CRIMEPREVENTION.RUTGERS.EDU/CRIME/
SHOPLIFTING/TECHNIQUES.HTM

'Crotch-walking' is a technique used by women wearing full skirts and dresses. They simply place the merchandise between their thighs and walk away. Thieves who are good at this have been known to steal hams, typewriters, and other large objects . . .

The baby carriage or stroller is a great tool for shoplifters. There are always blankets, toys, and other things in strollers (including the baby) that merchandise can be hidden under.

Some thieves have even built false bottoms in baby carriages.

'Favorite Shoplifter Clothing and Devices' · 2006

CHRISSY ILEY

Lady Isabel Barnett is memorialised in David Bowie's song, 'God Knows I'm Good'. During her funeral service, thieves broke into her house and stole nearly £6000 worth of silver.

Shoplifting is profoundly middle class. People who are hungry or deprived rob, burgle or beg. People who are bored or sad, or who need to airlift themselves out of the comfort zone, shoplift. It's the emotional equivalent of having a relationship with a bad boy, except you are your own bad boy.

Millions of bikinis, batteries, chocolates and lipsticks get nicked every year. One boutique owner reported that he considered teenage girls who stole an important marketing tool, because then he really knew what the hot trends were, how much to invest and in what. While Winona Ryder might have encouraged the leader pages which suggested that having it all was not good enough for her, she clearly never thought she did anyway. The likelihood is that if you hit the shops with a pair of scissors, you know what you're doing and you've done it before.

I read that she'd recently given about $50,000 worth of clothes to a children's charity. How's that for gorging and purging? Shoplifting and bulimia have so much in common. They usually hit the teenage psyche or the hormonally deranged. They create in the brain a misguided belief that eating or not eating, stealing and getting caught, means you are in control of one aspect of your life – and of course that is the very aspect that controls you.

Shoplifters, like bulimics, are compulsive. And after they

have filled up the hole with clothes, trinkets or food, they are left with a pudding of guilt inside them which they must rid themselves of by being sick or, in Winona's case, either giving it to charity or getting caught.

Tracy Shaw, the Coronation Street actress, was a shoplifter. She stole strawberries and confessed that she had a compulsion to steal that was connected to her anorexia. Lena Zavaroni was charged with stealing jelly the year she died from a slimming disease; her thinking was, bizarrely: 'If I steal the food it doesn't count as eating it.'

Shoplifting is just a vehicle, a big old juggernaut, in fact, in which to put bucketloads of celebrity guilt; it is an exorcism. Tennis star Jennifer Capriati was arrested when she was 17 for stealing a cheap silver ring from a shopping mall. Years later she spoke of how she had wanted to kill herself at that time because she felt so ugly and fat. It was as if she didn't deserve success, so she subconsciously tried to ruin her career.

It might be fairer to say that, at 32, she came to shoplifting a little late because she missed out on that part of her life when she was a teenager, as she was working so hard and being so successful.

The 76-year-old Hedy Lamarr's career as a purring glamourpuss was well over in 1991 when she was charged with stealing laxatives and eyedrops. She had faced shoplifting charges before, probably because she needed to replace the adrenaline rush she used to get from all the attention . . .

This year, former Olympic gymnast Olga Korbut stole food from the humdrum aisles of an Atlanta mall. She also had a strange relationship with food, having been forced into gruelling regimes of diet and 20-hour training days as a teenager. So much repression then, rebellion now.

Tracy Shaw said, 'It's not that you go out to shoplift, it's just something that happens,' apparently agreeing with the assertions of psychologists that shoplifters are suffering from nothing more exotic than an addictive compulsive disorder . . .

A quarter of shoplifters are teenagers and a lot of the rest are middle-class women suffering from a manipulating consumer culture that has seduced them, mainly because they have not been seduced by any other passion recently.

Victorian middle-class ladies used to stuff their corsets with swag, and hide their booty under their bustles when department stores first came into being. The Victorians called their disorder kleptomania and doctors said it originated in the uterus.

I don't think that's such nonsense because I believe it is hormonally driven. You do get male shoplifters, however, which is all the more shocking because it strips them of their machismo . . . some people are addicted to the guilt as much as to the excitement and the act of possessing.

The feeling is, it's there, it's yours. You feel empowered, elated, slick, cool and cunning . . .

There isn't always a happy ending, though. In 1980, Lady Isabel Barnett, who had been a radio and TV panellist in the 1950s and 1960s on programmes like *What's My Line?* and *Twenty Questions*, committed suicide after being fined for stealing a can of tuna and a carton of cream from her village shop. The court refused to believe that the poacher's pocket sewn into the lining of her coat was intended to carry her purse in case she got mugged.

Two days before her death she admitted she was a compulsive thief. She got into a bath with pills, alcohol and an electric heater, her terrible feelings of remorse bringing about her final drama.

'Celebrity Shoplifting' · 2002

THE PROCEEDINGS OF THE OLD BAILEY

Legerdemain Ladies, theft: shoplifting, 13th December, 1676
Two Legerdemain Ladies of profound experience in the mysteries of Shoplifting; one of them having been whipt at the Carts tail but the very last Sessions, were convicted for stealing two pieces of Callicoe, under pretence of buying o kerum. The Goods were taken before they got out of sight in one of their aprons, who alleadged a very civil excuse, assuring the Court that she was drunk with Brandy, and knew not what she did; but that Plea was overrul'd, and both of them found guilty.

*

30th June, 1714
Margaret Stevenson, of the Parish of St. Paul Covent Garden, was indicted for privately stealing a Piece of Persian Silk, Value 3l. out of the Shop of John Johnson, on the 25th of May last. The Prosecutor's Servant swore, That the Prisoner came pretending to buy, and the Shop being pretty full, she found an opportunity to take the Goods, and go away; but he having some Suspicion, pursu'd, and brought her back to the Shop, where she dropt the Silk. She had nothing to say in her Defence, nor any to her reputation, so was found Guilty of Shoplifting.

*

Frances Jacobs, theft: shoplifting, 30th May, 1718
Frances Jacobs, of the Parish of Christ Church, was indicted for feloniously stealing 26 Ounces of Gum Elamy, value 10s. in the Shop of John Antrim, the 20th of May last. The Prosecutor's Servant deposed, That the Prisoner came into his Master's Shop under pretence of buying some Coco-Nuts, and took the Opportunity to steal the Gum Elamy. Another Evidence deposed, that the Prisoner brought it to his Shop to

sell, and he suspecting she had stollen it, remembring he had seen such Gum lie in his Neighbour a Druggist's Window, and sending to enquire, the Prosecutor's Servant came and owned it. The Prisoner deny'd the Fact, pleading she used to deal in such things; and that finding it in her Handkerchief among some Chocolate, she did not know but that she had brought it from home. This did not avail but that the Jury found her Guilty to the Value of 4 s. 10 d. Transportation for 7 Years.

*

Rachel Palmer, theft: simple grand larceny, 13th January, 1744
Rachel Palmer, was indicted for stealing one pound of chocolate, value 18 d. the goods of John Barton, Dec. 17th.

Charles Gataker. I am apprentice to Mr. Barton, the Prisoner came into my master's shop to buy a pound of sugar, about 9 o'clock at night, she brought a guinea to change, I gave her 20s. but had not given her a groat, which was her due; there was some chocolate lay upon the counter, I looked to see if it was right, and I missed a pound, she was going away, and our young man brought her into the shop, and she dropped it down behind her.

Q. How do you know this to be your master's chocolate?

Gataker. It was marked with our mark; I believe she was a little in liquor when she did it; she lived a servant upon Ludgate-Hill. Guilty.

1676–1744

HOW TO SHOP

As I stepped into Market Square, leaving Papists' Corner behind, I breathed in deeply. I had not realised that I had been holding myself in tight all the time I was with the family.

I . . . passed along the stalls to Pieter's. He seemed surprised to see me. 'Here already, are you? Couldn't wait to get here for more of that tongue?'

'I'd like a joint of mutton today, please.'

'Now tell me, Griet, was that not the best tongue you have had?'

I refused to give him the compliment he craved. 'The master and mistress ate it. They did not remark on it.'

Behind Pieter a young man turned round – he had been cutting a side of beef at a table behind the stall. He must have been the son, for though he was taller than his father, he had the same bright blue eyes. His blond hair was long and thick with curls, framing a face that made me think of apricots. Only his bloody apron was displeasing to the eye.

His eyes came to rest on me like a butterfly on a flower and I could not keep from blushing. I repeated my request for mutton, keeping my eyes on his father. Pieter rummaged through his meat and pulled out a joint for me, laying it on the counter. Two sets of eyes watched me.

The joint was grey at the edges. I sniffed the meat. 'This is not fresh,' I said bluntly. 'Mistress will be none too pleased that you expect her family to eat meat such as this.' My tone was haughtier than I had intended. Perhaps it needed to be.

Father and son stared at me. I held the gaze of the father, trying to ignore the son.

At last Pieter turned to his son. 'Pieter, get me that joint set aside on the cart.'

'But that's meant for—' Pieter the son stopped. He disappeared, returning with another joint, which I could immediately see was superior. I nodded. 'That's better.'

The Girl with a Pearl Earring · 1999

ELIZA SMITH

Although she wrote it in her native England, Smith's Compleat Housewife *was the first cookbook to be printed in the United States.*

To Chuse Butter and Eggs.

When you buy butter taste it yourself at a venture, and do not trust to the taste they give you, least you be deceived by a well tasted and scented piece artfully placed in the lump. Salt butter is better scented than tasted, by putting a knife into it, and putting it immediately to your nose; but if it be a cask it may be purposely packed, therefore trust not to the top alone, but unhoop it to the middle, thrusting your knife between the staves of the cask, and then you cannot be deceived.

When you buy eggs put the great end to your tongue; if it feels warm, it is new; but if cold it is stale; and according to the heat or coldness of it, the egg is newer or staler. Or take the egg, hold it up against the sun or a candle, if the white appears clear and fair, and the yolk round, it is good; but if muddy or cloudy, and the yolk broken, it is nought. Or take the egg and put it into a pan of cold water; the fresher it is the sooner it will sink to the bottom but if it be rotten, or addled, it will swim on the surface of the water. The best way to keep them is in bran or meal; though some place their small ends downwards in fine wood-ashes.

The Compleat Housewife · 1742

FANNY FERN

*Fanny Fern was one of the first American women journalists and
her weekly column, for which she was paid the then enormous sum
of $100, had half a million readers.*

When the spirit moves you to amuse yourself with 'shopping',
be sure to ask the clerk for a thousand-and-one articles you
have no intention of buying. Never mind about the trouble
you make him; that's part of the trade. Pull the fingers of the
gloves you are examining quite out of shape; inquire for some
nondescript color, or some scarce number, and, when it is
found, 'think you won't take any this morning'; then, keep
him an hour hunting for your sun-shade, which you, at length,
recollect you 'left at home'; and depart without having
invested a solitary cent.

'Advice to Ladies' · 1853

MAUD C. COOKE

*Among other social necessities, Cooke's book advises on how to eat
grapes (by gently squeezing the pulp into your mouth and leaving
the skin on your plate) and the delights of a 'Chocolataire', or party
at which all food and drink contains chocolate.*

In visiting a store for the purpose of examining the goods or
making purchases, conduct yourself with courtesy and amia-
bility.

Speak to the clerks and employés [sic] of the store with
courtesy and kindness. Do not order them to show you anything. Request them to do so in a polite and ladylike or
gentlemanly manner. Give them no more trouble than is
necessary, and express your thanks for the attentions they
may show you. In leaving their counter, say pleasantly

'Good-morning,' or 'Good-day'. By treating the employés of a store with courtesy, you will render your presence there, welcome, and will receive all the attention such conduct merits.

Should you find another person examining a piece of goods, do not take hold of it. Wait until it is laid down, and then make your examination.

To attempt to 'beat down' the price of an article is rude. In the best conducted stores the price of the articles is 'fixed', and the salesmen are not allowed to change it. If the price does not suit you, you are not obliged to buy, but can go elsewhere.

Pushing or crowding at a counter, or the indulgence in personal remarks, handling the goods in a careless manner, or so roughly as to injure them, lounging upon the counter, or talking in a loud voice, are marks of bad breeding.

Never express your opinion about an article another is buying, unless asked to do so. To say to a customer about to make a purchase that the article can be bought cheaper at another store, is to offer a gratuitous insult to the clerk making the sale.

You should never ask or expect a clerk engaged in waiting upon another customer to leave that person and attend to you. Wait patiently for your turn.

It is rude to make unfavorable comparisons between the goods you are examining and those of another store.

Have your parcels sent, and so avoid the fatigue of carrying them.

It is best to buy for cash. You can always buy cheaper in this way. If you make bills, however, pay them promptly. Make no bill you are not sure of paying at the time promised by you. Avoid debt as the greatest curse of life.

Social Etiquette · 1896

ETHEL TURNER

From Yorkshire, Ethel Turner and her mother moved to Sydney,
Australia. Her first novel, Seven Little Australians, *was*
published internationally and a $15,000 literary prize was named
for her.

Just how ill-dressed she was Nicola saw vividly in one of the
full-length mirrors of the shop; gazing at the models in the
window had swiftly educated her eyes and she stared at herself
with a critical intentness.

The ground floor of the shop was strewn with things that
did not matter – lovely and desirable things, no doubt, like
bead-necklaces and coloured sunshades, and glittering trimmings and toilet powders and handkerchiefs and silver
puff-boxes, but still things that did not in the least matter –
yet.

'I want clothes,' said Nicola at last in an intense voice to
the shop-walker, – 'just like those in the window.'

She was put gravely into a great lift, drawn up to a great
height and discharged into an immense place of green velvet
carpets and long mirrors and beautifully gowned and haughty-
seeming shopwomen.

She looked at these last in a despairing fashion; she felt she
would never dare to tell to such her needs, never dare to
protest if they told her she had better choose a green gown
even though she was ardently longing for a pink one.

And then her eager, troubled gaze fell on a slender, fair-
haired girl who was adjusting a pale pink frock flowered with
roses upon a model in a show-case. A pale-faced girl she was,
with shoulders a little drooping beneath the black silk elegant frock she wore; but she was clearly intent upon her
work, was clearly bringing all her artistic powers to bear upon

it. She tried a black lace hat on the model's head, – stood back, examined it with her own head a little on one side, took it off and tried a Leghorn trimmed with long streamers of blue satin ribbon – rejected this in favour of a large white straw.

'Oh,' said a voice at her elbow, positively shaking with emotion, 'could you do that with me, – try things on me – help me to choose properly.'

Nicola Silver · 1924

LOUISA LAWSON

Poet, publisher and women's rights advocate, Lawson worked on the Australian journals The Republican *and* The Dawn, *from which this piece is taken.*

It ought to be recognised as a part of a girl's education to shop wisely and well – to know that bargain counters are to be avoided if they do not present something that one really wants.

Music, art, languages are looked upon as desirable for a thorough general education for women but parents do not seem to consider that it is necessary to train a girl in the line of shopping, that she will look upon a thrifty management of her purse as an accomplishment and not a bore.

There are very few women to whom it is unnecessary to count the cost of what they buy.

'Teach Girls How to Shop' · 1893

JENNIFER CROSS

[The supermarket is a] bewildering, enticing, craftily packaged trap that awaits every housewife during her weekly shopping expeditions, which all too often leave her numb, fatigued, and slightly poorer than she anticipated. The contest is not an equal one, largely because most people are unaware that the trap exists, and of the competitive conditions within the food industry that sprung it, the marketing techniques that bait it so cunningly, or the waste that is one by-product of all this effort . . .

Keep a small notebook with each week's shopping list in the front and a permanent alphabetical reference section at the back . . . Prices should be entered in pencil, and a pencil with an eraser top should accompany all major shopping trips for piecemeal revisions.

The Supermarket Trap · 1970

MARY VIVIAN HUGHES

Bessie . . . had advised me to get everything at Whiteley's. 'You've only got to walk into the shop, order what you want in the different departments, and you find everything delivered at your door'. She was right, but I soon found that this easy way of buying had to be paid for by too high prices, so I determined to explore the neighbourhood, buy what I wanted and bring it home myself.

One fortunate morning I found, quite a short distance away, another of London's oddities. It was a complete contrast to our row of respectable shops – no outward attractions and yet enjoying the liveliest trade. In an old narrow winding lane, once no doubt a medieval thoroughfare, I found shops and stalls catering for those who have no money to waste and mean to get the utmost value for their outlay. They were not to be put off with stale vegetables or doubtful fish – such as I had experienced in 'better-class' shops.

One shop, a greengrocer's, was the most satisfactory place of business I have ever been in, for there seemed to be no waste at all . . . The premises were allowed to remain ramshackle, no books were kept, no credit given, and the whole energy of the staff was devoted to getting the best they could every morning from Covent Garden and selling it quickly at a small profit. By the 'best' I don't mean exotic fruits, but great piles of what was 'in' – such as fresh strawberries, raspberries, currants – served out to the first comers (often little children) with good humour, homely manners, and very little wrapping up. Once I had already filled my shopping basket when I spied some sprouts and begged for a paper bag to put them in. 'Not for greens, my dear' was the inexorable reply.

A London Home in the Nineties · 1937

JENNY DISKI

Anyone troubled by thoughts of the afterlife, and their likelihood, or otherwise, of having one, could do worse than make regular visits to the supermarket. They are, of course, very useful for shopping, but their function as spiritual gymnasiums shouldn't be overlooked. I can think of few situations which offer as many opportunities for practising virtue, all under the same roof.

Abstinence, for example: go to Waitrose and only buy necessities. Ignore the Cappuccino Chocolate Cake and Häagen-Dazs. Don't buy onion bhajis or, if you do, don't eat half of them by the time you get to the checkout.

Work on laziness: no ready-washed bags of three different kinds of exotic lettuce, or pre-julienned carrots. Buy organic cos and fat leeks with earth in every crevice. Avoid trimmed sugar snap peas and miniature cauliflower in a microwave tray. Only buy loose fruit and vegetables, so you have to queue to get them weighed.

Love your neighbour: shop on Saturday afternoon and take

every opportunity (even if you're still there on Sunday) to back your trolley up the aisle you've just struggled down, so that your fellow shoppers can make easy progress. And smile as they pass. Pretend you feel nothing when the children behind ram you. Gaze indulgently at the high spirits of the younger generation and indicate to their mother your admiration for the tremendous job she's doing bringing them up.

By the time you've reached the checkout, you should be feeling pretty other-worldly, but don't relax yet. Choose the longest queue and watch those in front of you unload their goods without making a single judgment about what they've bought. Finally, as your turn comes, turn to the man behind and suggest that, since he's only got a basketful of shopping, he should go in front. When the woman behind him looks at you, then at her watch, don't hesitate. Insist you're in no hurry, of course she can go first. And smile, smile, smile.

'Supermarket Sweep' · 2003

HELEN FIELDING

Tuesday 19 December
9st 7 (but still nearly one week to lose half-stone before Christmas),
alcohol units 9 (poor), cigarettes 30, calories 4240, Instants 1
(excellent), cards sent 0, cards received 11, but include 2 from
paper boy, 1 from dustman, 1 from Peugeot garage and 1 from
hotel spent night in for work four years ago. Am unpopular, or
maybe everyone sending cards later this year.

9 a.m . . . Ugh. Would that Christmas could just *be*, without presents. It is just so stupid, everyone exhausting themselves, miserably haemorrhaging money on pointless items nobody wants: no longer tokens of love but angst-ridden solutions to problems.

. . . What is the point of entire nation rushing round for six weeks in a bad mood preparing for utterly pointless Taste-of-Others exam which entire nation then fails and gets stuck with hideous unwanted merchandise as fallout? If gifts and cards were completely eradicated, then Christmas as pagan-style twinkly festival to distract from lengthy winter gloom would be lovely. But if government, religious bodies, parents, tradition, etc. insist on Christmas Gift Tax to ruin everything why not make it that everyone must go out and spend £500 on themselves then distribute the items among their relatives and friends to wrap up and give to them instead of this psychic-failure torment?

Bridget Jones's Diary · 1996

JAN STRUTHER

One of the minor arts of life, thought Mrs. Miniver at the end of a long day's Christmas shopping, was the conservation of energy in the matter of swing doors. With patience and skilful timing it was very seldom necessary to use your strength on them. You could nearly always follow close behind some masterful person who had already done the pushing; and if you were too late for that and the door had begun to swing towards you, then it was well worth pausing for a second until it swung away again and needed only a gentle encouragement. This seemed obvious enough; but there was an astounding number of people who seemed to glory in taking the line of most resistance, hurling themselves against an approaching door and reversing its direction by brute force, as though there were virtue in the act. They must lead, she reflected, very uncomfortable lives.

Placing herself neatly in the wake of a bull-necked woman in tweeds, she slipped out of the shop. There was a raw wind;

sleety rain was beginning to fall, blurring the lamplight; the pavements were seal-sleek; it was settling down into one of those nasty wet evenings which the exiled Londoner longs for with a quite unbearable nostalgia . . .

Getting home was evidently going to be a long job. The usual six o'clock home-going stream was in spate with Christmas crowds, and Oxford Street was a solid jam. It was her own fault, she had to admit, as she sat back and waited for the lights to change. Every year the same thing happened. At the beginning of November she made up her mind that this time, for once, she would get her Christmas shopping done early. She went as far as writing out a list – and there, for several weeks, the matter rested. At intervals she tried to pretend that Christmas Day fell on the 5th of December, or, alternatively, that all her friends and relations lived in South Africa and that she had to catch an early mail; but it was no use. The feeling of temporal urgency cannot be artificially produced, any more than the feeling of financial distress. The rich young man who determines to work his way round the world may gain many things, but the experience of poverty is not one of them. He knows that in the ultimate emergency he can always cable home for funds; and Mrs. Miniver knew perfectly well that Christmas was not until the 25th of December, and that all the people on her list lived in England . . .

Besides, successful present-choosing depends very largely upon the right atmosphere, upon the contagious zest of crowds, upon sudden inspirations and perceptions, heightened rather than otherwise by a certain sense of pressure in space and time. To do it cold-bloodedly, in a half-empty shop, without any difficulty or competition, is as joyless as a *mariage de convenance*. So perhaps it was just as well, she told herself consolingly, that she had, as usual, left it till the middle of December.

Mrs Miniver · 1939

RATIONING OF CLOTHING, CLOTH, FOOTWEAR FROM JUNE 1, 1941
Rationing has been introduced, not to deprive you of your real needs, but to make more certain that you get your share of the country's goods – to get fair shares with everybody else.

When the shops re-open you will be able to buy cloth, clothes, footwear and knitting wool *only if you bring your Food Ration Book with you*. The shopkeeper will detach the required number of coupons from the unused margarine page. Each margarine coupon counts as one coupon towards the purchase of clothing or footwear. You will have a total of 66 coupons to last you for a year; so go sparingly. You can buy *where* you like and *when* you like without registering.

THESE GOODS MAY BE BOUGHT *WITHOUT* COUPONS
Children's clothing of sizes generally suitable for infants less than 4 years old. Boiler suits and workmen's bib and brace overalls. Hats and caps. Sewing thread. Mending wool and mending silk. Boot and shoe laces. Tapes, braids, ribbons and other fabrics of 3 inches or less in width. Elastic. Lace and lace net. Sanitary towels. Braces, suspenders and garters. Hard haberdashery. Clogs. Black-out cloth dyed black. All second-hand articles.

The Board of Trade · 1941

KATE PHIPPS

During the Second World War, Kate Phipps served as a nurse in various posts. When she wrote the extracts below, she was working at the Emergency Medical Service Hospital in Ashridge,

*Hertfordshire and at University College Hospital, but she also acted
as the warden of a Women's Land Army Hostel near Baldock,
Hertfordshire.*

Sat 12th Oct 1940
Went to London today to do Xmas shopping, because after all
one never knows how long ones favorite shops will be standing. John Lewis is a blackened skeleton and so many smaller
places burnt out. Decided also to get some canned goods for
Lizzie to pack in a parcel for Oswald, via the Red Cross. Found
to my delight some really nice scented soap which will make
nice presents together with tins of tinned fruit (getting very
scarce) for my hostesses around Beechwood. People are so very
kind in having me over on my days off. But I was truly loaded
up when I arrived home!

Oct 4th 1942
Shopping takes a long time. One has to get to know the various tradespeople, and a gossip over the counter often brings
treasures out from under it!
    The Second World War Diary of Kate Phipps · 1939–45

ELISABETH RUSSELL TAYLOR

*The novelist Elisabeth Russell Taylor remembers shopping with her
grandmother during rationing.*

Two conventions formed themselves around shopping during
World War II: the trial and the conspiracy. Every man,
woman and child was issued with a ration book and registered
with a grocer and a butcher, probably merchants with whom
they had dealt in peacetime. One was entitled to shop for
the exiguous rations only where one was registered, but it was
not uncommon for those shops to run out of supplies and for

shoppers to have to return, day after day, just for an egg or two and a twist of tea. At the sight of a queue forming housewives rushed to join, not knowing what the queue was for; anything would be a bonus and the queue itself a social occasion where one might offload legitimate discontents, for it really was miserable having to forgo the pleasures of the table at the same time as being bombed to blazes.

Then there was the conspiratorial side to shopping, an agreement forged to the advantage of supplier and recipient that was private, beyond the grasp of the state, not illegal but somewhat reprehensible. It was to this exchange that my grandmother lent her not inconsiderable charm, and financial wherewithal.

In the years before the war my grandmother had the use of her own chauffeur-driven car. She kept Mr Hudson modestly liveried and the car unostentatious and I believe her feet rarely, if ever, came in contact with London tarmac. Whether she suffered a painful bunion or was protecting dainty footwear I do not know, but looking back on those times I do not remember her ever setting out on foot. When World War II deprived her first of Mr Hudson (called up) and then of petrol, expropriated for more essential use, the car was evacuated to the country and placed on bricks and my grandmother took to the Black Cab. She negotiated this transfer enthusiastically, keeping the telephone numbers of local ranks on her bedside table, by the telephone in the hall, in her diary and no doubt secreted in other places unknown to me.

I joined her sometimes on her errands. I was aware that her appearance excited attention: she was beautiful and she dressed with a confidence quite out of keeping with the national mood. She favoured colour for the coats she wore – parma violet, jade, topaz and amethyst – turbans of oriental silks, cobweb-light veils that fell from sprays of flowers to frame her face. She was like none other and this only added to my love and admiration of her. However, children can be hide-bound and I was a product of undemocratic schooling and my grandmother's behaviour surprised me: was it not over familiar, I wondered? For having ordered a taxi from home or hailed one at the front gate, before climbing in she would always make certain she recognised the driver so as to address him by name, and were he unknown to her she would insist upon learning his name before bestowing her salutation and direc-tions. Once settled in her seat she would lean forward, push back the glass separating her from the cabbie, and call out, 'Not too fast, if you please; I am not in a hurry!' And on alight-ing, not only thank the driver for his consideration but exchange with him all sorts of views: on the efficacy of the gas mask, the shortages of soap and other necessities and, of course, the genius of Mr Churchill, before tipping generously and wishing him and his family godspeed. My grandmother became so well known to London's cabbies that with many she had only to ask to be taken to her daughter's, her hairdresser's or to the doctor without having to mention the address.

Stringent food rationing was introduced three months into the war but it was not before my grandmother had struggled for a year with its exigencies that she introduced the subject into her exchange of confidences. Finally, she was to admit – for she was not one normally to complain, and adhered strictly to the government's exhortation to 'keep cheerful' – that she was finding it impossible to manage; indeed it was all driving her to distraction. This pathetic and dramatic admission received an immediate response from a cabbie named Mr Bates. He ordered my grandmother to 'climb back in, my dear' and drove her post-haste into the city to a fashionable fish, poultry and game merchant, to be introduced to his friend, Albert Corringer, 'who will look after you', a promise Mr Corringer was to keep throughout the war and well into lean peace.

Fish, poultry and game were classed 'off ration' for the duration but it was often the case that the men left to run this type of shop had not only their own allotments, on which they kept a few chickens for eggs, but relatives who had been farming for generations and made butter, cheese and cream. Although these products were not allowed to be sold off ration, they did find their way to the tables of special friends. My grandmother became such a special friend to Mr Corringer.

Once Mr Bates had effected the introduction, my grandmother made and received many more telephone calls than usual behind closed doors and took sudden journeys across London on the tacit understanding that no questions were to be asked. Celebration lunches and dinners took place throughout the war, at which Leah, the cook, produced succulent pheasant with all the trimmings, halibut in egg and lemon sauce, stuffed roast chickens, jugged hare and fruit-filled sponge concoctions, accompanied by a jug of cream. No wrong was done, precisely, rules bent a little, perhaps, but not broken, and no doubt each life involved improved somewhat. Bartering of coupons would have taken place, so that Mr Corringer's daughter's sweet tooth might be catered to, and his wife's need for stockings met and, I believe, some whisky and brandy found for Mr Corringer himself.

The Mr Corringers of war-torn Britain needed customers like my grandmother as much as weary, anxious housewives, like my grandmother, needed a Mr Corringer. But as in all social exchange, such relationships depend on more than mere commercial reciprocation and my grandmother, like Mr Corringer, understood the full implications attached to 'looking

after': time-consuming courtesies, imaginative thoughtful-
nesses, above all an absence of servility on the one hand and
condescension on the other. Indeed, a perfect entente.

'A Perfect Entente' · 2006

MISS J.C. STRANGE

One of four children of a Worthing draper, Joan Colebrook Strange
trained as a physiotherapist and, with her own car, tended patients
in the Worthing/Brighton district.

Paper is very scarce – we have to take bags wherever we go
shopping. Many people go out with baskets on wheels & a
handle. There are few advertisements on boardings & these
are mostly advising us to 'Save more & lend it to the
Government.' 'Less shopping means more shipping for vital
war supplies'.

The Second World War Diaries of Miss J.C.
Strange · 1939–1945

PAMELA KLAFFKE

Klaffke, a pop-culture journalist from Canada, illustrates eBay
madness.

In November 2002, a man from Orange County, California
auctioned off his services in an ad titled 'I Will Go Shopping
for Jeans With You'. George, of item #983171300, was pictured
sitting on a sofa, clad in boxer shorts and posing like the mus-
cled he-man he wasn't. Bidding began at one cent, with
interested parties undoubtedly sucked in by the tempting
description of the merchandise:

> This auction is for a 100% pure Man. He lives in Orange County
> and wants to go shopping with you. High bidder agrees to pick him

up in Newport Beach so he can go shopping with them. He will carry bags and give expertise [*sic*] fashion advice. He can also go out to eat if you would like him to, his treat. This item measures 5′9″ and is stocky build. The item you are bidding on likes designer jeans, candle light dinners, and long walks on the beach. Please, serious bidders only. I prefer PayPal but will also accept money orders, checks, and food stamps.

After seven days and seven bids, George's services were sold. He went for 55 cents, proving that shoppers really can find it all on eBay.

Spree · 2003

LADY JEUNE

The writer recalls shopping as a girl in the 1870s.

There was little or no display in the windows. Each shop had its own speciality, and the more expensive and costly its goods, the more unremittingly conservative was the way of carrying on its business. Jones sold the best silks, Smith the best gloves, Brown the best bonnets, Madame X was far and away the only good milliner and dressmaker . . . We bought our goods at these various shops, and dutifully followed in the steps of our forefathers, paying for the things at the end of the year, for no well-thought-of firm ever demanded or expected more than a yearly payment of debts. If residence in the country made a visit to London to choose what was wanted an impossibility, Jones, Brown or Smith knew the need of their particular customer, and the orders sent were expedited and despatched with unfailing accuracy.

With what interest and excitement the arrival of the case containing the garments was awaited, and the new mode canvassed! How quietly but certainly the appearance of the new garments at church heralded a reproduction of the same in the persons of the parson's wife and the smaller ladies of the community, who considered the big lady a faithful apostle of the gospel of dress! Even the dwellers in big cities carried on their shopping in a dignified and easy way, and the time devoted to shopping was laid aside as a concession which every woman felt bound to devote to the mysteries of her clothes. An afternoon's shopping was a solemn and dreary affair, when one was received at the door of the shop by a solemn gentleman in black, who in due time delivered one to another solemn gentleman, and perhaps again to a third, who found one a chair, and in a sepulchral tone of voice uttered some magic word such as 'Silk, Mr Smith' or 'Velvet, Mr A'. and then departed to seek another victim. One bought what was wanted and nothing more, and having secured the goods left the shop as seriously as one arrived. The whole performance left an impression of responsibility and sadness on one's mind and whether desiring wedding or funeral garments, the same solemnity characterized it, and with as great sense of relief the large doors closed behind one.

'The Ethics of Shopping' · 1895

LYNN BARBER

Almost every woman I meet now claims to have a personal shopper, whose name and number she insists on giving me – I always take it badly because it seems tantamount to saying I need someone else to buy my clothes.

Of course, maybe I *do* need someone else to buy my clothes? I floated this idea past my good friend . . . whose opinion I trust on most subjects, and she said tactfully that, well, *she* had certainly found having a personal shopper very helpful . . . [S]he explained that most people who say they have personal shoppers actually mean they have shop shoppers, ie they go to Selfridges or Liberty and sit in a changing-room while the in-house shopper whizzes round the store finding them clothes to try on. Which is fine up to a point, but what these in-house shoppers won't tell you is that, actually, there's a little boutique in Notting Hill that has just what you want. Whereas . . . [my friend] has a *real* personal shopper, who goes round *all* the shops on her behalf and is truly independent. She takes no commission but only charges for her time. Ooh, give me her name, I cried . . .

The list of fees . . . is fairly jaw-dropping – £100 an hour for consultation and £50 an hour for shopping time – but it seems almost worth it if I won't have to spend those tragic Saturdays trudging round the West End, sobbing quietly in changing rooms.

'What sane and sensible woman would pay
£1,000 for a makeover? Er, me' · 2006

MRS HENRY WARD BEECHER

Mrs Henry Ward Beecher was the sister-in-law of Harriet Beecher Stowe, who wrote Uncle Tom's Cabin.

Now we cannot understand what pleasure there can be in the fatiguing business of shopping, only so far as it is gratifying to accomplish any necessary labour successfully. To hang about a counter, examining things one has no intention of buying – jostled, crowded and made uncomfortable by the ever-surging throng, is fatiguing in the extreme, and exceedingly bewildering unless a list of what is needed has been carefully prepared before entering the store. According to our mode of looking at the work, this should always be done, even in home shopping, but is much more desirable when abroad. Decide what you must have; and fix, as near as possible, the quality and price. This settled, begin your researches – no need of buying in haste and repenting at leisure. If the purchase to be made is of any great importance, never decide at first sight. Take a pattern of the goods with you, after having spent all necessary time in the examination.

When you return to your hotel, compare the sample with something similar which you have brought from home – and the price also – and in the quiet of your room you will decide far more wisely than will be possible in the confusion of tongues which distracts you in all stores; especially when partially tongue-tied yourself by inability to speak the language. By this mode of procedure you will have a better opportunity to complete your purchase the next time you enter the stores, having clearly arranged in your own mind just what you intend to buy, and the price you are willing to pay.

Notwithstanding the term 'fixed price', often seen in large letters in many stores, it is true that the merchant does often make many changes in the sum demanded – perhaps compelled to do so by the determination on the part of his customers to 'beat him down', and never satisfied until that consummation, so devoutly wished for, has been achieved . . .

But, although fully aware that it may not be always safe to accept the first price named, it must be acknowledged that higgling and chaffering in making a bargain is not in good taste. It would greatly lower our self-respect, and we will never stoop to it. To say, in a quiet, lady-like manner, 'The price is higher than I am prepared to give,' is usually quite sufficient.

All Around the House · 1881

ELAINE SHOWALTER

'Shopping for pleasure': is the title tautological or oxymoronic? On one side, the joys of shopping seem almost axiomatic, especially now that every newspaper and magazine offers tips on how to do it, and Zagat is about to bring out a series of retail-tourist guidebooks. In a recent poll taken in London, more than a quarter of respondents said that shopping was what they liked best about the city. In her fashion guidebook, Mimi Spencer exhorts her readers to 'shop for England . . . just for the sheer entertainment value of it all'. Suzy Gershman, the American author of *Born to Shop: Great Britain*, is 'so enamoured' of the January sales that she recommends flying in from Cleveland or Omaha for a long weekend. On the other hand, there are – there actually are – women living in Zone 1 who hate to shop, and many feminists who regard shopping as selfishness, frivolity or political deviance. When I wrote an essay for American *Vogue* a few years ago on my own fondness for department stores, catalogues and shopping malls, I was attacked by academic radicals as the Marie Antoinette of the MLA, whose answer to the sweated and unemployed must be 'Let them wear Prada.' . . .

So-called 'luxury' shopping can be the most uncomfortable of all, at least in the pricey boutiques where status is the chief pleasure for sale. Despite my notoriety as the Prada Queen, my only Prada had been a counterfeit handbag (with triangular logo) bought from a street vendor outside Bloomingdale's for $30. It has given me much more pleasure than the Prada shop on New Bond Street, which is about as much fun as an hour in a bank, and is even decorated in the subtle beige and green shades of money. You could spend a weekend in New York for the price of a Prada item. The security guard is the most attentive employee, and the buying is hyper-discreet. The best thing is the packaging: a chic black box, a creamy white bag with Prada insignia, tied on both sides with bows of Prada-Milano ribbon. Last summer I saw one of those ribbons used as a pullcord for a naked light-bulb in the loo of a coffee-shop on Brick Lane – the height of reverse chic and Post-Modern marketing style.

If shopping is going to continue to be a pleasure in the age of the Web, it's going to have to offer both men and women a lot more in the way of real comfort and psychological intangibles. It will have to be hooked up to a status and aesthetic aspiration in a way that pleases even those who disapprove of mere consumerism and detest marketing. In London, it seems to me, designer paint is the class signifier of the millennium. Of course, paint has been aspirational before. Mr Pooter got the enamel craze in the 1890s. 'In consequence of Brickwell telling me his wife was working wonders with the new Pinkford's enamel paint, I determined to try it. I bought two tins of red on my way home . . . went out into the garden and painted some flowerpots . . . Went upstairs into the servant's bedroom and painted her washstand, towel-horse and chest of drawers.' Not only middle-class suburbanites like the Pooters but even an impeccable left-winger like Eleanor Marx discovered the joys of enamel paint in 1895 and did up everything in the house: 'If the climate only permitted,' she wrote to a friend, 'I should enamel myself.'

American shoppers have no status codes for paint. Thus I was embarrassed to discover in London last summer that my enthusiasm for Dulux was considered as tacky as a taste for Madame Tussaud's. The only aesthetically satisfying and socially acceptable wall colour, I was informed, comes from Fired Earth. Connoisseurs, moreover, have a paint merchant, just as they have a wine merchant. At one end of the spectrum, J.W. Bollom on the Old Brompton Road caters to the masculine museum and exhibition trade. There are no concessions to frivolity – nothing in the windows, no little samples, no reason to browse. At the other extreme, Jocasta Innes's Paint Magic shops are totally *femme*; shopping for paint there is like buying make-up, with lots to touch and try, and glamorous ranges of suede paints, colourwash, impasto, marmorino, limewash, distemper, tinters, craquelure and sparkle dust. With colours like Hummous and Guacamole, you know you're in Islington. John Oliver in Notting Hill is the epitome of Posh Paint, elegant, with shelves of leather-bound sample books, like an aristocratic library in a gentleman's or ladies' club. Here the paints are called Shrinking Violet, Purple Heart, British Navy, Betty Blue, Grays Inn, Golders Green, Cotswold Cream, Fromage and Not Quite White.

The future of shopping, I think, will belong to the places that provide a social service as well as a product. The new Waterstone's bookshop in Piccadilly, for example, in the former Simpson's, looks like it is selling books and magazines, but it's also a perfect place to spend an evening and to meet potential companions. It stays open late, has food and drink, live entertainment, comfortable seating, state-of-the-art loos and great people-watching in a central location. For the books alone, why bother to leave home? For women in the 21st century, shopping is going to be about belonging to a club.

'Prada Queen' · 2000

WINDOW-SHOPPING

VIRGINIA WOOLF

They were driving along a bright crowded street; here stained ruby with the light from picture palaces; here yellow from shop windows gay with summer dresses, for the shops, though shut, were still lit up, and people were still looking at dresses, at flights of hats on little rods, at jewels.

The Years · 1937

MARGARETE BÖHME

The great electric lamps shone like moons in the pale violet twilight of the spring evening. From the baskets of the flower sellers floated the sweet breath of blossoms. And all was enjoyment, beauty, refinement, with their many accompaniments. Behind the immense panes of a flower shop there shone a charming arrangement of orchids and La France roses – a symphony in mauve and rose colour. Waves of fragrance from the exotic butterfly-blooms and the pale roses seemed to penetrate the crystal, whose soft, enhancing clearness gave to the flowers almost the illusion of life. Agnes sighed with enchantment . . . Slowly she went on, to stop again before the display of a great jeweller. Over the black velvet cushioning there flowed a stream of petrified rainbows. Electric reflectors drew chords of colour from the bewildering glory of the gems. Between the sparkling dewdrops of the diamonds shone the deep radiant green of emeralds, the fresh dark crimson of rubies, the grave tranquil blue of sapphires. Dead-white pearl necklaces seemed, with their soft glimmer, like dreams amid that arrogant, insistent life. Agnes held her breath, a hot glow throbbed to her temples, her heart pounded . . . And a couple of doors farther on, a charming boudoir 'interior' was arranged behind the glass: a gilded toilet-table in rococo-style, and lying on it a great, flung-down bunch of Parma violets, and an old Venetian fan. Elsewhere there stood a bronze vase with a bouquet of giant poppies, against a background of tapestry in splendid, faded colours. And a glass case held all sorts of costly trifles – porcelain, miniatures, chains of coloured beads, gems, clasps. Right in front, cast as if negligently on a gilded chair, was a dress – a dress? No! but a fairy-tale, a poem, of a strange opalescent silk and silver-glittering lace, fragile as a breath, fragrant as a meadow mist in moonlight. On the old-rose coloured screen hung a hat in white chiffon with cloudy, uncurled feathers . . .

'My God, my God!' said Agnes softly to herself. Her lips quivered, she tottered rather than walked, as she looked from the brilliant façades towards the dim promenade. But after about fifty steps she literally threw herself against the dazzling window of a *lingerie* shop. Almost deliriously her eyes fastened on the sea of lace that flowed in foamy billows over a bright gold velvet background. She pressed her face close against the pane that she might see it all the better, as if drunk with the colour and beauty that she had fed on for the last half-hour. Her hat, with its 'crow-quills', had fallen back on her neck; she cared not, she had but one burning, irresistible desire – to fling herself headlong into this rippling mass, and revel in it, feeling the cobweb-like loveliness against her skin, burying her face in the rapturous whirl of cambric and lace.

The Department Store · 1912

WILLA CATHER

Thea Kronberg is the opera-star heroine of Cather's third novel, a woman who typically defies the conventions of her time and gender.

Thea never went into shops unless she had to, and she felt no interest in them. Indeed, she shunned them, as places where one was sure to be parted from one's money in some way. She was nervous about counting her change, and she could not accustom herself to having her purchases sent to her address. She felt much safer with her bundles under her arm.

During this first winter Thea got no city consciousness. Chicago was simply a wilderness through which one had to find one's way. She felt no interest in the general briskness and zest of the crowds. The crash and scramble of that big, rich, appetent Western city she did not take in at all, except to notice that the noise of the drays and street-cars tired her. The brilliant window displays, the splendid furs and stuffs, the gorgeous flower-shops, the gay candy-shops, she scarcely noticed. At Christmas-time she did feel some curiosity about the toy-stores, and she wished she held Thor's little mittened fist in her hand as she stood before the windows. The jewelers' windows, too, had a strong attraction for her – she had always liked bright stones. When she went into the city she used to brave the biting lake winds and stand gazing in at the displays of diamonds and pearls and emeralds; the tiaras and neck-laces and earrings, on white velvet. These seemed very well worth while to her, things worth coveting.

The Song of the Lark · 1915

SOPHIE VON LA ROCHE

Sophie von la Roche praised the shops on 'lovely Oxford Street' when she wrote to her home in Germany. Goethe admired her History of Lady Sophia Sternheim, *which was the first epistolary novel in Germany and the first to be published by a German woman writer.*

Behind the great glass windows absolutely everything one can think of is neatly, attractively displayed, in such abundance of choice as almost to make one greedy. Now large slipper and shoe-shops for anything from adults down to dolls, can be seen; now the confectioner's goodies, the pewterer's wares, fans, etc . . . There is a cunning devise for showing women's materials. They hang down in folds behind the fine, high windows so that the effect of this or that material, as it would be in a woman's dress, can be studied . . .

We also passed shops where animals were for sale, which goods were both novel to us and comical. Peacocks were placed on pretty perches, bright cages with songsters hanging in between; there were cases of monkeys, large bird-cages containing turtle-doves, others with fine domestic fowls; lap-dogs of every type followed in nicely padded kennels; pointers lay at the bottom on leads, and by their side baskets of all kinds of game – all grouped so artistically that the whole made a charming picture . . .

We strolled up and down lovely Oxford Street this evening, for some goods look more attractive by artificial light. Just imagine . . . a street taking half an hour to cover from end to end, with double rows of brightly shining lamps . . . and the pavement, inlaid with flag-stones, can stand six people deep and allows one to gaze at the splendidly lit shop fronts in comfort. First one passes a watchmaker's, then a silk or fan store, now a silversmith's, a china or glass shop. The spirit booths are particularly tempting for the English are in any case fond of strong drink. Here crystal flasks of every shape and form are exhibited; each one has a light behind which makes all the different coloured spirits sparkle. Just as alluring are the confectioners and fruiterers, where, behind the handsome glass windows pyramids of pineapples, figs, grapes, oranges and all manner of fruits are on show. We enquired the price of a fine pineapple and did not think it too dear at 6s. Most of all we admired a stall with Argand lamps, situated in a corner house and forming a really dazzling spectacle.

Sophie in London · 1786

MRS GASKELL

It is a pretty sight to walk through a street with lighted shops; the gas is so brilliant, the display of goods so much more vividly shown than by day, and of all shops a druggist's looks the most like the tales of our childhood, from Aladdin's garden of enchanted fruits to the charming Rosamond with her purple jar.

Mary Barton · 1903

VIRGINIA WOOLF

Bond Street fascinated her; Bond Street early in the morning in the season; its flags flying; its shops; no splash; no glitter; one roll of tweed in the shop where her father had bought his suits for fifty years; a few pearls; salmon on an iceblock.

'That is all,' she said, looking at the fishmonger's. 'That is all,' she repeated, pausing for a moment at the window of a glove shop where, before the War, you could buy almost perfect gloves. And her old Uncle William used to say a lady is known by her shoes and her gloves . . . Gloves and shoes; she had a passion for gloves; but her own daughter, her Elizabeth, cared not a straw for either of them.

Not a straw, she thought, going on up Bond Street to a shop where they kept flowers for her when she gave a party . . . pushing through the swing doors of Mulberry's the florists.

She advanced, light, tall, very upright, to be greeted at once by button-faced Miss Pym, whose hands were always bright red, as if they had been stood in cold water with the flowers.

There were flowers: delphiniums, sweet peas, bunches of lilac; and carnations, masses of carnations. There were roses; there were irises. Ah yes – so she breathed in the earthy garden sweet smell as she stood talking to Miss Pym who owed her help, and thought her kind, for kind she had been years ago; very kind, but she looked older, this year, turning her head from side to side among the irises and roses and nodding tufts of lilac with her eyes half closed, snuffing in, after the street uproar, the delicious scent, the exquisite coolness. And then, opening her eyes, how fresh like frilled linen clean from a laundry laid in wicker trays the roses looked; and dark and prim the red carnations, holding their heads up; and all the sweet peas spreading in their bowls, tinged violet, snow white, pale – as if it were the evening and girls in muslin frocks came out to pick sweet peas and roses after the superb summer's day, with its almost blue-black sky, its delphiniums, its carnations, its arum lilies was over; and it was the moment between six and seven when every flower – roses, carnations, irises, lilac – glows; white, violet, red, deep orange; every flower seems to burn by itself, softly, purely in the misty beds; and how she loved the grey-white moths spinning in and out, over the cherry pie, over the evening primroses!

Mrs Dalloway · 1925

EDITH WHARTON

The ramshackle wooden hotels about the square were all hung with flags and paper lanterns, and as Harney and Charity turned into the main street, with its brick and granite business blocks crowding out the old low-storied shops, and its towering poles strung with innumerable wires that seemed to tremble and buzz in the heat, they saw the double line of flags and lanterns tapering away gaily to the park at the other end of the perspective. The noise and colour of this holiday vision seemed to transform Nettleton into a metropolis. Charity could not believe that Springfield or even Boston had anything grander to show, and she wondered if, at this very moment, Annabel Balch, on the arm of as brilliant a young man, were threading her way through scenes as resplendent.

'Where shall we go first?' Harney asked; but as she turned her happy eyes on him he guessed the answer and said: 'We'll take a look round, shall we?'

The street swarmed with their fellow-travellers, with other excursionists arriving from other directions, with Nettleton's own population, and with the mill-hands trooping in from the factories on the Creston. The shops were closed, but one would scarcely have noticed it, so numerous were the glass doors swinging open on saloons, on restaurants, on drug-stores gushing from every soda-water tap, on fruit and confectionery shops stacked with strawberry-cake, cocoanut drops, trays of glistening molasses candy, boxes of caramels and chewing-gum, baskets of sodden strawberries, and dangling branches of bananas. Outside of some of the doors were trestles with banked-up oranges and apples, spotted pears and dusty raspberries; and the air reeked with the smell of fruit and stale coffee, beer and sarsaparilla and fried potatoes.

Even the shops that were closed offered, through wide expanses of plate-glass, hints of hidden riches. In some, waves of silk and ribbon broke over shores of imitation moss from which ravishing hats rose like tropical orchids. In others, the pink throats of gramophones opened their giant convolutions in a soundless chorus; or bicycles shining in neat ranks seemed to await the signal of an invisible starter; or tiers of fancy-goods in leatherette and paste and celluloid dangled their insidious graces; and, in one vast bay that seemed to project them into exciting contact with the public, wax ladies in daring dresses chatted elegantly, or, with gestures intimate yet blameless, pointed to their pink corsets and transparent hosiery.

Summer · 1917

LADY VIOLET GREVILLE

How rich England must be to have a demand for the number-less lace trifles, gaudy ribbons, satins, delicate frills and confections and head-dresses, and whatever all the names may be of the various articles that sparkle and dangle and shine and attract in the plate-glass squares that make the delight of ladies' eyes! Gold embroidery, the products of Indian looms, Syrian dyes, American furs, the finest of Belgian lace, the thickest of French silks, the warmest of Scotch wool tissues . . . 'Come in and be dressed' the shops seem to chant in a kind of deep chorale; 'come and put off your own individuality and put on the livery of your master, the despot of civilisation – Fashion.' So the women come, like ducks in the old nursery rhyme, come and are fleeced and made happy. Vanity Fair, indeed! Its presence is stronger, louder, more blatant than ever . . .

A greengrocer's shop is not without charm: piles of scarlet tomatoes repose cheerfully near a mass of Brussels sprouts – pretty little vegetables that might almost pass for flowers, they are so dainty; oranges from Seville set us thinking of blue skies and serenades, and love-making in the moonlight, and the fairy arches of the Alhambra. Poor fruits, the companions of the gutter, how sweet they are, and what a contrast must the London streets be to their sunny home! Then there are the rows of cabbages, under whose weight line upon line of market-carts toil every night to Covent Garden. Who eats all those thousand mawkish-tasting vegetables, that leave such a very disagreeable odour behind them when they are being cooked? To be sure bacon and cabbage is a very good dish, but then it is not 'genteel,' so the rich don't often get a chance of tasting it . . .

A saddler's shop . . . Those bright-coloured horse-cloths those glittering bits, how they take us back to our first gallop over grass . . . and to the first steeple-chase we ever won! There is a racing saddle, a whip – can it be that we are grey and weigh fourteen stone? . . .

And now we come to a fashionable fishmonger's. What a wealth of beauty is here! No wonder the Dutch painters covered reams and reams of canvas with the presentment of fish in every attitude and of all colours. The loveliness of hue, the infinite gradations of tone, are unrivalled; only a master like Turner showed himself in his famous picture of mackerel, can reproduce the silveriness of the salmon, the true grey of the mackerel, and the indefinite variety of shades in the finny tribe . . .

A continuation of our stroll lands us before a bookseller's shop . . . Alas! bookstalls will soon be obsolete delights. When you can buy Gibbon's 'Decline and Fall' for 4s., and 3s. 6d. is the price of the Elizabethan dramatists, where can one go for a delightful old-fashioned, well-thumbed dirty bargain of a book? Everything is cheap nowadays . . .

'Shop Windows' · 1880

MARGERY SHARP

Mr Joyce suddenly stopped before a lighted window. It was another of his street-arab habits – staring into shops. Except at certain jewellers, he had the money to buy almost anything

145

that caught his fancy; he remained content with staring. It irritated Miranda that he now stopped to examine a straight-grain briar pipe with every appearance of attention. There was an irritating *insouciance* even in the way he stood: his hat on the back of his head, his loud check overcoat flapping open – this indeed because it was really too close to wear it – and his new regimental scarf sticking up round the collar . . .

'Dadda!' said Miranda sharply. 'This is an important conversation! Will you please think about Harry and me?'

'Harry I am thinking about this moment,' returned Mr Joyce benevolently. 'I am going to buy that boy a pipe.'

The Eye of Love · 1957

SHOPPING HELL

GEORGE ELIOT

To Mrs Elma Stuart   *June 27, 1878*

I have a fine genius for knowing that I have bought or ordered
the wrong thing as soon as it is brought home, and hence my
house comes to represent with some accuracy what I least
prefer – a sort of scum thrown up by my poor mind in the
boiling agitation of shopping.

Letters · 1878

RACHEL BOWLBY

Cultural historian Bowlby's studies of shopping include Carried
Away, Shopping with Freud *and* Just Looking.

Saturday, 21 September 1996; IKEA, Purley Way, South London
It is late in the afternoon and the lines of wide carts loaded up
with flatpacks of future furniture stretch back from the row of
checkouts. Back and back, right into the warehouse section,
they bump up against the people still trying to pick out their
own cardboard packages and happily oblivious, as yet, to the
fate in store for them.

But gradually the news is getting through. The computers are
down, all the purchase transactions are having to be done man-
ually. The prospect of a handwritten receipt from IKEA seems
quaintly unreal. Nobody, nothing moves, forwards or backwards.
Nobody protests. Nobody seems to be talking to anyone else,
passing the time in complaint or chat. We all stand sullenly by
our carts keeping our places, half-heartedly trying to decode the
announcements. And nobody walks out, back through the stores
or out past the checkouts, leaving their cart behind.

We just can't leave now. These carts bear the tangible results of an afternoon's hard work. It may have been fun at the time, but now the prospect of going home empty-booted obliterates that from view. If we let go of the goods, we would have nothing to show for all this time and effort. And we are attached to these things already. This big brown box contains what a joyous, newly verbal two-year-old, still trailing clouds of consumerly innocence, is already proudly calling 'my IKEA bed'. Here we are voluntarily trapped inside a store that we are unable to leave. Why did we come here in the first place? What is keeping us here? Is our behaviour perverse, a stubborn refusal to give up? Or is it calmly rational, suffering the short-term frustrations and making the best of a bad situation? In this IKEA world, there isn't much to choose between the two, or much to choose at all.

Carried Away · 2000

ANNE FRIEDBERG

As if in distant reverberation of the darker consequences of . . . [women's] newfound consumer power, Dutch filmmaker Marleen Gorris's 1982 film, A *Question of Silence*, has its women shoppers bludgeoning a male store manager to death with hangers and a shopping cart. A woman caught shoplifting in a shopping mall boutique is joined by two other women in an improvised collective lynching of the imperious store man-ager. In the subsequent trial, all of the other female customers remain silent, an act of subversive solidarity. In the courtroom, they begin to laugh, as if the pleasurable extension of such empowerment – the true 'Ladies' Paradise' – is the laughter of revolt against scopic regulation of their consumer autonomy.

Window Shopping: Cinema and the Postmodern · 1993

ELIZABETH PUREFOY

*The inscription on the tombstone of Elizabeth Purefoy (which she
wrote herself) calls her 'prudent and frugal', qualities evidenced in
the letters she wrote and kept from 1735 to 1753. For ninety years,
she lived in the village of Shalstone, Buckinghamshire. After
Thomas Robotham married Elizabeth Purefoy's former maid, she
addressed many of her letters and personal requests to him.*

for Mr. Robotham at
   the King's Head at
   Islington near London

May the 29th 1737

I was in hope by this time Mr. Fisher could have sent me some
mackerell accordingly to my order, but since none are come.
The weather is now so exceeding hot that what fish you sent
last week stank and could not be eat so I desire you would not
send any more fish until further orders, let me have a letter
what they come to and will order you payment, and Am

Your humble servant
Elizabeth Purefoy

for Mr. James Fisher
   a fishmonger in
   Newgate Market, London

March the 4th 1739

This is to let Mr. Price know that I shall send Mr. Moulson his
money for the sack next week. Therefore desire that you will
send the money for yours between this and next Saturday.

Your daughter, Mrs. Betty, might have saved yourself and me
this trouble but she never mentioned neither the price of the
wine, nor to pay for it.

The price is as usual eight shillings a gallon, the vessell of

sack was 13 gallons, I should have been glad if Mrs. Betty Price
came soon enough to see it drawn of. I had no more than 6
gallons and 1 quart. She had 6 gallons and 1 quart all but a
glasse or two in bottles, and 1 quart bottle of yours besides these
was broke as soon as it was filled it being crackt first; so there
wanted a quart of 13 gallons wch. I suppose I must bear the losse
of. Mrs. Betty Price wrangled a little about it but this is the very
Truth of the matter. So the money you are to pay comes to
£2.10s. and I shall have no more at that price Mr. Moulson sent
me word. We would have waited on you ourselves but are very
busie on sowing Beans and with our service and respect to you
and all am

Your humble servt.
Elizabeth Purefoy

The Purefoy Letters · 1737

ISABELLA L. BIRD

*Plagued by ill health, Bird was ordered by her doctor to take to her
bed. Instead, she took to the road, and a series of remarkable
journeys.*

The streets of Yamagata are broad and clean, and it has good
shops, among which are long rows selling nothing but ornamental iron kettles and ornamental brasswork. So far in the
interior I was annoyed to find several shops almost exclusively
for the sale of villainous forgeries of European eatables and
drinkables, specially the latter. The Japanese, from the Mikado
downwards, have acquired a love of foreign intoxicants, which
would be hurtful enough to them if the intoxicants were genuine, but is far worse when they are compounds of vitriol, fusel
oil, bad vinegar, and I know not what. I saw two shops in
Yamagata which sold champagne of the best brands, Martel's

cognac, Bass' ale, Medoc, St. Julian, and Scotch whisky, at about one-fifth of their cost price – all poisonous compounds, the sale of which ought to be interdicted.

Unbeaten Tracks in Japan · 1911

DOROTHY DAVIS

Far more sinister . . . than all the complaints about frowsy meat and dirty fruit which the customer could at least see and judge for himself, was the opportunity . . . offered to the small trader to make money by deliberate adulteration and fraud. It was in this century of plentiful food [18th c] that the first mutterings against poisonous contamination were first heard; against beer that was 'pernitiated' with vitriol, and wine with copperas, and that boiled sweets sometimes contained a species of rat's bane to give them 'a fine but excessively dangerous sparkle'. Cupidity, ignorance and irresponsibility combined to tempt shopkeepers and stallholders not only to mingle harmless dust with the tea but brickdust with the cocoa; not only sand with the sugar but lime with the flour; not only to cheat on their own account but also to buy cheap food without question from rogues with more specialized cunning like the manufacturers of imitation vinegar from diluted sulphuric acid coloured with oak chips or the makers of bright green pickles who poisoned them with verdigris . . . But the only case of adulteration that really aroused widespread public alarm was the state of London's bread . . . [There were] allegations, for example that the alum used was often dissolved in human urine; that often one part in six of a loaf was either lime or chalk or whiting and ground bones from the graveyard; that purgatives were sometimes added to offset the constipating effect of the alum . . . Not for another hundred years, until 1860, did the first Food and Drugs Act begin the slow process of relieving the consumer of the hazard of impure food.

A History of Shopping · 1966

JANE WELSH CARLYLE

This letter was written on notepaper printed with a picture of Ramsgate Harbour.

T. Carlyle, Esq., 5 Cheyne Row.

Wellington Crescent, Ramsgate:
Tuesday, August 6,1861.

Very charming doesn't that look, with the sea in front as far as eye can reach? And that seen (the East Cliff), you needn't wish to ever see more of Ramsgate. It is made up of narrow, steep, confused streets like the worst parts of Brighton. The shops look nasty, the people nasty, the smells are nasty! (spoiled shrimps complicated with cesspool!) Only the East Cliff is clean, and genteel, and airy; and would be perfect as sea-quarters if it weren't for the noise! which is so extraordinary as to be almost laughable.

Along that still-looking road or street between the houses and gardens are passing and repassing, from early morning to late night, cries of prawns, shrimps, lollipops – things one never wanted, and will never want, of the most miscellaneous sort; and if that were all!

Letters · 1861

FAY INCHFAWN

Fay Inchfawn was the pseudonym of Elizabeth Rebecca Ward.

The shopping had been tedious, and
   the rain

Came pelting down as she turned home
   again.

The motor-bus swirled past with rush and
   whirr,
Nought but its fumes of petrol left for
   her.

The bloaters in her basket, and the cheese
Malodorously mixed themselves with
   these.

And all seemed wrong. The world was
   drab and grey
As the slow minutes wept themselves
   away.

And then, athwart the noises of the street,
A violin flung out an Irish air.

'I'll take you home again, Kathleen.'
Ah, sweet,
How tender-sweet those lilting phrases
   were!

They soothed away the weariness, and
   brought
Such peace to one worn woman, overwrought,

That she forgot the things which vexed
   her so:
The too outrageous price of calico,

The shop-girl's look of pitying insolence
Because she paused to count the dwindling
    pence.

The player stopped. But the rapt vision
    stayed.
That woman faced life's worries unafraid.

The sugar shortage now had ceased to be
An insurmountable calamity.

Her kingdom was not bacon, no, nor
    butter,
But things more costly still, too rare to
    utter.

And, over chimney-pots, so bare and tall,
The sun set gloriously, after all.

'The Street Player' · 1920

KATHERINE MANSFIELD

Mansfield wrote from Paris to her former schoolmate and devoted friend about a shopping trip in Bon Marché, the world's first department store.

To Ida Baker   *April 1922*
[sic]
[W]e went off to the Bon Marché to buy a very simple light hat. Have you been there? Its [sic] one of the wonders of the world. Having fought to the lift we got out on to an open gallery with about 5,000 hats on it 10,000 dressing gowns, and so on. But the gallery looked over the entire ground

floor and the whole of the ground floor was taken up with
untrimmed 'shapes' and litera[ll]y, hundreds and hundreds of
women – nearly all in black wandered from table to table
turning and turning over these shapes. They were like some
terrible insect swarm – not ants more like blow flies. Free
balloons were given away that day and fat elderly women
with little eyes and savage faces carried them. It was exactly
like being in hell. The hats were loathsome. Jack as usual on
such occasions would not speak to me and became furious. If
I said 'Do you like that?' he replied 'No. Horribly vulgar!' If I
timidly stretched out a hand he hissed 'Good God!' in my
ear. We got out of the place at last. Then while waiting for a
taxi a woman tried to commit suicide by flinging herself at
his umbrella with which he was prodding the pavement. *She*
was violently angry. I ran away to where a man was selling
easter chickens that cheeped when you blew a whistle. The
taxi came and Jack had by this time lost me. Finally both of
us raging we got in, drove to the hotel, got out, got in again,
and drove to another hat shop. 'Get this damned thing
over!' was Jack's excuse. There [was] a quiet shop we both
knew. We found only about 25 people and hats flying
through the air. One woman put on another woman's old
dead hat with the pins in it and walked off to pay the
cashier. The owner dashed after her, with a face of fury and
snatched it off her astonished head. My one stipulation was I
didn't mind what kind of hat I bought but it must have no
feathers. And I finally decided on a little fir cone with 2
whole birds on it!

Letters and Journals · 1922

LOUISA MAY ALCOTT

Louisa's letters to her sister make frequent mention of shopping.

To Anna Alcott Pratt   *c. August?*
1860?

My Lass,—This must be a frivolous and dressy letter, because
you always want to know about our clothes, and we have been
at it lately. May's bonnet is a sight for gods and men. Black and
white outside, with a great cockade boiling over the front to
meet a red ditto surging from the interior, where a red rainbow
darts across the brow, and a surf of white lace foams up on each
side. I expect to hear that you and John fell flat in the dust with
horror on beholding it.

My bonnet has nearly been the death of me; for, thinking
some angel might make it possible for me to go to the
mountains, I felt a wish for a tidy hat, after wearing an old one
till it fell in tatters from my brow . . . I was in woe for a spell,
having one dollar in the world, and scorning debt even for that
prop of life, a 'bonnet.' Then I roused myself, flew to Dodge,
demanded her cheapest bonnet, found one for a dollar, took it,
and went home wondering if the sky would open and drop me a
trimming. I am simple in my tastes, but a naked straw bonnet is
a little too severely chaste even for me.

Selected Letters · 1889

GERTRUDE BRAAT VANDERGON

*The family of Gertrude Vandergon left Holland for Minnesota in
1867. There they experienced long winters and bug infestations
curiously unmentioned in the glowing descriptions of the territory
by land agents.*

Clothes for the growing children was a real problem. Mother

seldom went to Monticello and father had to purchase our shoes also dress material as well as the general shopping. Mother made our coats, dresses, and the suits for the men. I remember so well the time father purchased a pair of shoes for me. They were the real lumber jack type. The store keeper told father that was what all the children in America were wearing, besides it was all he had to show him. When Mother and I looked at them, we both seemed to think the same thing. We were heart sick and were certain he was getting rid of some old stock. The shoes could not be exchanged for it would be many weeks before father would go for supplies. My shoes from Holland were made of soft leather. They however were too small for me, especially when I had to wear the red woolen hose. It hurt my pride to wear these lumber jack shoes, so I chose to wear the shoes from Holland, even though they pinched my feet and I froze two toes the first cold winter we were in Minnesota.

Our Pioneer Days in Minnesota · 1949

CAROLYN KEENE

The Nancy Drew detective series for girls was begun in the 1930s with an admirably independent and self-confident heroine. During the following decades, particularly the 1950s, Nancy became much more submissive and reliant on those around her. This episode in the series dates from the 1970s. It is interesting to note the service afforded customers in shops long before the invention of the in-store personal shopper.

'What are your plans for this morning, Nancy?' her father asked at the breakfast table.

'I thought I'd do a little shopping,' she replied. Her eyes twinkled. 'There's a dance coming up at the country club and I'd like to get a new dress.'

'Then will you phone me about lunch? Or better still, how about eating with me, whether Mr Rolsted comes or not?'

'I'll be there!' Nancy declared gaily . . .

After her father had left, Nancy finished her breakfast, then went to the kitchen to help Hannah Gruen, who had already left the table.

'Any errands for me?' Nancy asked.

'Yes, dear. Here's a list,' the housekeeper replied. 'And good luck with your detective work.'

Hannah Gruen gazed at the girl affectionately and several thoughts raced through her mind. In school Nancy had been very popular and had made many friends. But through no fault of her own, she had made two enemies, Ada and Isabel Topham.

This worried Hannah. The sisters, intensely jealous of Nancy, had tried to discredit her in positions she had held in school. But loyal friends had always sprung to Nancy's defence. As a result, Ada and Isabel had become more unpleasant than ever to Nancy . . .

Becomingly dressed in a tan cotton suit, Nancy set off in her convertible for the shopping district. She drove down the boulevard, and upon reaching the more congested streets, made her way skilfully through heavy traffic, then pulled into a parking lot.

'I think I'll try Taylor's Department Store first for a dress,' she decided.

Taylor's was one of River Heights' finest stores. Nancy purchased several items for Hannah on the main floor, then went directly to the evening dresses section on the second floor.

Usually Nancy had no trouble finding a sales-clerk. But this particular morning seemed to be an especially busy one in the department, and an extra rush of customers had temporarily overwhelmed the sales force.

Nancy sat down in a convenient chair to await her turn . . . She was suddenly brought out of her reverie by loud-voiced complaints.

'We've been standing here nearly ten minutes!' a shrill voice declared. 'Send a saleswoman to us immediately!'

Nancy turned to see Ada and Isabel Topham speaking to the floor manager.

'I'm afraid I can't,' the man replied regretfully. 'There are a number of others ahead of you. All our salespeople are—'

'Perhaps you don't know who we are!' Ada interrupted rudely.

'Indeed I do,' the floor manager told her wearily. 'I will have a saleswoman here in a few moments. If you will only wait—'

'We are not accustomed to waiting,' Isabel Topham told him icily.

'Such service!' Ada chimed in. 'Do you realize that my father owns considerable stock in Taylor's? If we report your conduct to him, he could have you discharged.'

'I'm sorry,' the harassed man apologized. 'But it is a rule of the store. You must await your turn.' . . .

Suddenly Ada and Isabel saw Nancy, who nodded a greeting. Isabel coldly returned the nod, but Ada gave no indication that she had even noticed Nancy.

At that moment a saleswoman hurried toward the Topham sisters. At once they began to shower abuse upon the young woman for her failure to wait on them sooner.

'What is it you wish to look at, Miss Topham?' the clerk said, flushing.

'Evening dresses.'

The saleswoman brought out several dresses. Nancy

watched curiously as the Tophams, in an unpleasant frame of mind, tossed aside beautiful models with scarcely a second glance. They found fault with every garment.

'This is a very chic gown,' the saleswoman told them hopefully, as she displayed a particularly attractive dress of lace and chiffon. 'It arrived only this morning.'

Ada picked it up, gave the dress one careless glance, then tossed it into a chair, as the distracted clerk went off to bring other frocks.

The fluffy gown slipped to the floor in a crumpled mass. To Nancy's horror Ada stepped on it as she turned to examine another dress. In disgust, Nancy went to pick it up.

'Leave that alone!' Ada cried out, her eyes blazing. 'Nobody asked for your help.'

'Are you buying this?' Nancy asked evenly.

'It's none of your business!'

As Nancy continued to hold the dress, Ada in a rage snatched it from her hands, causing a long tear in the chiffon skirt.

'Oh!' Isabel cried out. 'Now you've done it! We'd better get out of here, Ada!'

'And why?' her haughty sister shrilled. 'It was Nancy Drew's fault! She's always making trouble.'

'It was *not* my fault,' Nancy said.

'Come on Ada,' Isabel urged, 'before that clerk gets back.'

Reluctantly Ada followed Isabel out of the department. As they rushed toward a waiting elevator, Nancy gazed after them. At this moment the saleswoman reappeared with an armful of lovely frocks. She stared in bewilderment at the torn dress.

'Where did my customers go?' she asked Nancy worriedly.

Nancy pointed to the elevator, but made no comment.

Instead she said, 'I'm looking for an evening dress myself. This torn one is very pretty. Do you think it could be mended?'

'Oh, I don't know,' the woebegone clerk wailed. 'I'll probably be held responsible and I can't afford to pay for the dress.'

'I'm sure Taylor's wouldn't ask you to do that,' Nancy said kindly. 'If there's any trouble, I'll speak to the manager myself. What usually happens is that such a dress is greatly reduced.'

'Thank you,' the clerk replied. 'I'll call Miss Reed, the fitter, and see what can be done.'

'First, let me try on the dress,' Nancy said, smiling.

They found a vacant fitting room and Nancy took off her suit and blouse. Then she slipped the lovely pale-blue dance creation over her head and the saleswoman zipped it up.

'It's darling on you,' she said enthusiastically.

Nancy grinned. 'I kind of like myself in it,' she said. 'Please call the fitter now.'

Presently Miss Reed, a grey-haired woman, appeared. Within seconds she had made a change in an overlap of the chiffon skirt. The tear was no longer visible and the style of the dress was actually improved.

'I told our manager what happened,' said the saleswoman. 'If you want the dress, he will reduce the price fifty percent.'

'How wonderful!' Nancy exclaimed. Laughing, she said, 'That price will fit into my budget nicely. I'll take the dress. Please send it.' She gave her name and address. To herself she added, 'Ada Topham did me a favour. But if she ever finds out what happened, she'll certainly be burned up!' Nancy suppressed a giggle.

'It's been a real pleasure waiting on you, Miss Drew,' the saleswoman said after Miss Reed left and Nancy was putting on her suit. 'But how I dread to see those Topham sisters come in here! They're so unreasonable. And they'll be even worse when they get Josiah Crowley's money.' . . .

Nancy was too discreet to engage in gossip with the saleswoman.

The Secret of the Old Clock · 1972

ISABELLA D'ESTE

With an appetite for luxury and the money to satisfy it, Isabella d'Este patronised the finest craftsmen of her time and her studio at the Ducal Palace in Mantua was renowned for the costly decoration she devised for it. At the time she wrote this letter, she had already refused an earlier shipment from Prospero.

To Bernardino Prospero
We gave ten ducats to Sanzio to buy as many gloves of d'Ocagna for our use when he went to Spain, and being in Ferrara we spoke to him that he should serve us well. It has now been many days since his return, and since then he has sent us twelve dozen of the saddest gloves that had he searched all of Spain in order to find such poor quality I don't believe he could have found as many. In Rome, Genoa and Florence there are better ones without comparison and using some diligence in Ferrara itself he could have found some that were as good and perhaps even better. Therefore we have decided to return them so that you do not think that we have such little judgement in gloves that we would think that these were good enough to give to our ladies-in-waiting and to some of our friends. We would be ashamed to give them to people whom we love and they would never wear them. Can you please send them back and tell him how badly we have been served?

Letters of Isabella d'Este · late 1400s – early 1500s

FRANCES KEMBLE

The English actress Fanny Kemble toured the United States in
1832 and later married a plantation owner in Georgia. Her
Journal of a Residence on a Georgia Plantation *was written in*
letter form and is said to have influenced British opinion during the
Civil War. Horrified to discover that her husband's income was
reliant on slave labour, Kemble divorced him in 1848. She is buried
in Kensal Green Cemetery.

As for my shopping, the goods or rather 'bads,' at which I
used to grumble, in your village emporium at Lenox, are what
may be termed 'first rate,' both in excellence and elegance,
compared with the vile products of every sort which we
wretched southerners are expected to accept as the conveniences of life in exchange for current coin of the realm. I
regret to say, moreover, that all these infamous articles are
Yankee made – expressly for this market, where every species
of *thing* (to use the most general term I can think of), from list
shoes to pianofortes, is procured from the North – almost
always New England, utterly worthless of its kind, and dearer
than the most perfect specimens of the same articles would be
anywhere else. The incredible variety and ludicrous combi-
nations of goods to be met with in one of these southern
shops beats the stock of your village omnium-gatherum
hollow to be sure, one class of articles, and that probably the
most in demand here, is not sold over any counter in
Massachussetts – cow-hides, and man-traps, of which a large
assortment enters necessarily into the furniture of every
southern shop.

Letter from Frances Kemble to Elizabeth Dwight
Sedgwick Rackemann · 1839

MELESINA CHENEVIX ST GEORGE

To Mary Shackleton Leadbeater   *June 14, 1816*
Bursledon Lodge

You do me too much honour in supposing me well dressed. I am rather negligently than carefully; I mean negligent, as opposed to fashionable and studied, but not to neat or fresh; and as I think there cannot be too little seen of my present changed appearance, I always wear a veil and shawl when I can, partly, perhaps, from pride, but partly from modesty, having observed how much pains are thrown away by my cotemporaries to make their *exposures tolerable*, 'et pour réparer des années les outrages irréparables.'

I am, besides, of an indolent disposition on many subjects, and dress is one. I hate shopping, dislike conferences with milliners and dressmakers, fidget while anything is trying on, and give no credit to the pert Miss who always assures me the most expensive of her caps is exactly the one which becomes me the best.

1816

ANONYMOUS

Next to mental improvement, shopping is now the business of life, and a most bewildering and exhausting business it is . . . Strong is the character demanded for wise shopping! Exalted are the Christian virtues needed to make that peculiarly feminine labor anything but anguish, mortification and a sad waste of money!

Woman's Journal · 1873

CHARLOTTE BRONTË

When the governess Jane Eyre accepts the hand of her employer,
Mr Rochester, she is urged by him to spend, for her forthcoming
wedding, according to her new station.

The hour spent at Millcote was a somewhat harassing one to me. Mr Rochester obliged me to go to a certain silk warehouse: there I was ordered to choose half a dozen dresses. I hated the business, I begged leave to defer it: no – it should be gone through with now. By dint of entreaties expressed in energetic whispers, I reduced the half-dozen to two: these, however, he vowed he would select himself. With anxiety I watched his eye rove over the gay stores: he fixed on a rich silk of the most brilliant amethyst dye, and a superb pink satin. I told him in a new series of whispers, that he might as well buy me a gold gown and a silver bonnet at once: I should certainly never venture to wear his choice. With infinite difficulty, for he was stubborn as a stone, I persuaded him to make an exchange in favour of a sober black satin and pearl-gray silk. 'It might pass for the present,' he said; 'but he would yet see me glittering like a parterre.'

Glad was I to get him out of the silk warehouse, and then out of a jeweller's shop: the more he bought me, the more my cheek burned with a sense of annoyance and degradation . . . He smiled; and I thought his smile was such as a sultan might, in a blissful and fond moment, bestow on a slave his gold and gems had enriched: I crushed his hand, which was ever hunting mine, vigorously, and thrust it back to him red with the passionate pressure.

'You need not look in that way,' I said; 'if you do, I'll wear nothing but my old Lowood frocks to the end of the chapter. I'll be married in this lilac gingham: you may make a dressing-gown for yourself out of the pearl-gray silk, and an infinite series of waistcoats out of the black satin.'

He chuckled; he rubbed his hands, 'Oh, it is rich to see and hear her!' he exclaimed. 'Is she original? Is she piquant? I would not exchange this one little English girl for the Grand Turk's whole seraglio – gazelle-eyes, houri forms, and all!'

The Eastern allusion bit me again. 'I'll not stand you an inch in the stead of a seraglio,' I said; 'so don't consider me an equivalent for one. If you have a fancy for anything in that line, away with you, sir, to the bazaars of Stamboul, without delay, and lay out in extensive slave-purchases some of that spare cash you seem at a loss to spend satisfactorily here.'

'And what will you do, Janet, while I am bargaining for so many tons of flesh and such an assortment of black eyes?'

'I'll be preparing myelf to go out as a missionary to preach liberty to them that are enslaved – your harem inmates amongst the rest.'

Jane Eyre · 1847

ELIZA BENTLEY

I went out one day to do a little shopping for myself with my fingers in my gloves . . . It was a memorable day to me. The Good Shepherd was watching over His own.

I was standing by the counter of a store looking at some ribbons and choosing for my spring bonnet when I heard the Voice divine say distinctly, 'The lust of the eye.' It was a kind warning and meant 'Don't be fancy led.' The lesson was never forgotten but has followed me through life . . .

Also, in a dream . . . I saw the houses near the market all in flames inside, and the meat in the market stalls turning putrid . . .

About this time, having shopping to do, I took my little

three-year-old girl and went up town, dressed as lightly as possible, the heat was so intense. The sun glared fiercely down. There had been no rain for some time. As we walked along I was praying and lifting my face heavenward. I said, 'O Lord, we are all as dead sheep, except Thou send us rain.' I could say nothing else but repeat these words, and while looking up, I felt, I thought, a single drop of moisture on my face, and some little birds went twittering over my head, and these words were spoken to my heart with great assurance:

'Lo! the promise of a shower
  Drops already from above,
But the Lord will shortly pour
  All the fulness of His love.'

And I felt it would be love indeed to send us rain, but there was not the least sign of it. By the time my shopping was done and we were about halfway home, we had to take to our heels and run as fast as possible, there came such a sudden downpour.

Precious Stones for Zion's Walls · 1897

GRACE NICHOLS

Born in Guyana, Grace Nichols is a Commonwealth Prize-winning poet. Her collection, Lazy Thoughts of a Lazy Woman, *echoes the title of Jenny Wren's* Lazy Thoughts of a Lazy Girl.

Shopping in London winter

is a real drag for the fat black woman
going from store to store
in search of accommodating clothes
and de weather so cold

Look at the frozen thin mannequins
fixing her with grin
and de pretty face salesgals
exchanging slimming glances
thinking she don't notice

Lord is aggravating

Nothing soft and bright and billowing
to flow like breezy sunlight
when she walking

The fat black woman curses in Swahili/Yoruba
and nation language under her breathing
all this journeying and journeying

The fat black woman could only conclude
that when it come to fashion
the choice is lean

Nothing much beyond size 14

'The Fat Black Woman Goes Shopping' · 1984

SECOND-HAND

Richard Papin succeeds in wheedling an advance on his work-study cheque in Donna Tartt's first novel about class and corruption at a New England boarding school.

I walked down the hall with spirits soaring, and two hundred dollars in my pocket, and the first thing I did was to go downstairs to the pay phone and call a cab to take me into Hampden town. If there's one thing I'm good at, it's lying on my feet. It's sort of a gift I have.

And what did I do in Hampden town? Frankly, I was too staggered by my good fortune to do much of anything. It was a glorious day; I was sick of being poor, so, before I thought better of it, I went into an expensive men's shop on the square and bought a couple of shirts. Then I went down to the Salvation Army and poked around in bins for a while and found a Harris tweed overcoat and a pair of brown wingtips that fit me, also some cufflinks and a funny old tie that had pictures of men hunting deer on it. When I came out of the store I was happy to find that I still had nearly a hundred dollars. Should I go to the bookstore? To the movies? Buy a bottle of Scotch? In the end, I was so swarmed by the flock of possibilities that drifted up murmuring and smiling to crowd about me on the bright autumn sidewalk that – like a farm boy flustered by a bevy of prostitutes – I brushed right through them, to the pay phone on the corner, to call a cab to take me to school.

Once in my room, I spread the clothes on my bed. The cufflinks were beaten up and had someone else's initials on them, but they looked like real gold, glinting in the drowsy autumn sun which poured through the window and soaked in yellow pools on the oak floor – voluptuous, rich, intoxicating.

The Secret History · 1992

ANGELA CARTER

Early on in her career Angela Carter was a fashion critic for
New Society.

The taxi climbed through gaunt, grey streets with, here and there, ragged October trees dropping sad leaves into a deepening, sheep-white and shaggy mist. Melancholy, down-on-its-luck South London . . .

They reached a wedge-shaped open space on a high hill with, in the centre, a focus, a whimsical public lavatory ornately trimmed with rococo Victorian wrought ironwork and, drooping over it, a weary sycamore tree with white patches on its trunk, like a skin disease. There were a number of shops, all brightly lighted now. A fruitshop, with artificial grass banked greenly in the windows and mounds of glowing oranges, trapped little winter suns; groping, mottled hands of bananas; giant crinkly green roses which turned out to be savoy cabbages when you looked more closely; buds of blackcurrant cordial which were red cabbages, to be cooked in spices and vinegar. A butcher's shop, where a blue-aproned, grizzle-headed man in a bloodstained straw boater reached between two swinging carcasses of lamb for sausages from a marble slab. A sweetshop with crackers and sweets done in reindeer and holly Christmas packs and a crêpe paper Santa Claus in the window, already, jostling the Roman candles, fairy fountains and whizz-bangs for November 5.

More shops. A junk-shop, where a withered, pale woman

sat and knitted by a paraffin stove among broken old things – pitchers, candlesticks, a few books, a sagging chair, a limping table, a chipped enamel bread-bin full of cracked saucers. A new furniture shop with a three-piece suite in uncut moquette in the window next to a cocktail cabinet shiny as toffee. All the shops were in the lower parts of tall, old houses and had curly, old-fashioned lettering on them, but for the furniture shop, which winked in faulty neon:

'Everything for the 'ome.' . . .

'But where is Uncle's house?' asked Melanie.

'His shop. We live over the shop. Over there.'

Between a failed, boarded-up jeweller's and a grocer's displaying a windowful of sunshine cornflakes was a dark cavern of a shop, so dimly lit one did not at first notice it as it bowed its head under the tenement above. In the cave could be seen the vague outlines of a rocking horse and the sharper scarlet of its flaring nostrils, and stiff-limbed puppets, dressed in rich, sombre colours, dangling from their strings; but the brown varnish of the horse and the plums and purples of the puppets made such a murk together that very little could be seen.

Over the doorway was a sign, 'TOYS PHILIP FLOWER NOVELTIES', in dark red on a chocolate ground. Stuck in the door, under a card on which was written 'Open' in an italic hand, was a smaller visiting card reading: 'Francis K. Jowle. Fiddle Reels and jigs, etc. A breath of Auld Ireland. Generally available. Moderate fees.' And a shamrock and the pencilled message, 'Enquire within.'

The Magic Toyshop · 1967

JUSTINE PICARDIE

Picardie has written about fashion for British Vogue, Marie
Claire, *the* Daily Telegraph *and other major British newspapers.*

Do clothes have ghosts, or do ghosts have clothes? There's no
evidence one way or the other, as you might expect: but there
are stories, some of which survive long after their telling. I
was talking about this, quite recently, to a friend of mine,
Harriet Quick, the fashion features editor at *Vogue* (whose
name, incidentally, has always seemed to me most fitting for
her work, as a translator of rapidly shifting trends). We were
having lunch together, and I asked her if she'd ever felt
haunted by a piece of clothing, and she told me the following
tale.

'There's a second-hand shop, around the corner from the
football ground in Fulham Road, and I used to go there quite
often, on Saturdays, to hunt for stuff. And one day, I found a
jet-beaded top that fell from the shoulders in butterfly sleeves,
and fastened with minute black buttons from the waist to a
gentle décolletage.

'The label in the top said "Biba", and I remembered my
mother telling me about the Biba shop in the Sixties, and how
she used to sit me under the Victorian hat-stands that displayed the stock. Apparently I sat there and chewed shirttails,
while she tried on the clothes. So when I slipped into the
changing cubicle in the second-hand shop, and put on the
black top, I had already opened a small peephole of memory. It
took me a little while to fasten all those tiny buttons, and
then I looked at myself in the mirror: but the face that stared
back at me wasn't mine.'

Harriet paused at this point in her monologue, and looked
over at me, to check that I wasn't laughing at her. And I

wasn't, because she was so serious; in fact, I felt the hairs standing up on the back of my neck; had that creeping sensation over my skin, that Freud called 'the Uncanny'. 'Go on,' I said to Harriet. 'What happened next?'

'Well, it sounds impossible, but in the mirror, instead of my reflection, there was a girl with flame-red hair and porcelain-pale skin. She had green eyes – I could see her eyes, but I don't think she could see me – and she was thin, terribly thin. And as I looked at her, she seemed to be falling, and I nearly fell, too, and beyond the mirror, I felt that she was swaying in a room in a white stuccoed London town house, filled with people jostling and screeching at each other.'

As Harriet described the girl, I could not help but imagine my slender redheaded mother, who wore Biba clothes and whose green eyes shone out of porcelain skin; but I knew that was another reflection in a different looking glass, that my mother's past should have no place in Harriet's story. 'So what did you do?' I said to Harriet, who was now paler than usual, herself.

'I took the top off, straight away, but it was hard, because I was fumbling with all the buttons, but I wanted it off – I couldn't bear being inside it – because it felt funereal, like a shroud.'

'As if someone had died in it?' I asked.

'Yes,' said Harriet, 'I felt sure that the girl in the mirror had been wearing it on the night she died. So I put the top back where I'd found it, and left the shop, feeling very shaken. And I tried not to think about it again – I didn't tell anyone, because it seemed so irrational – but I was just reading the diaries of [the fashion designer] Ossie Clark, and I came across an entry which describes an infamous party-girl with flame-red hair, who lived near the King's Road, and who died of an overdose.'

'And you think it was her Biba top that you tried on?'
'Yes,' said Harriet. 'I think so.'

My Mother's Wedding Dress · 2005

MARGARET ATWOOD

It was over the Portobello Road that we came to the parting of the ways. [Paul] himself introduced me to it, and it quickly became an obsession with me. I would pore for hours over the stalls of worn necklaces, sets of gilt spoons, sugar tongs in the shape of hen's feet or midget hands, clocks that didn't work, flowered china, spotty mirrors and ponderous furniture, the flotsam left by those receding centuries in which, more and more, I was living. I had never seen things like this before; here there was age, waves of it, and I pawed through it, swam in it, memorized it – a jade snuffbox, an enameled perfume bottle, piece after piece exact and elaborate – to fix and make plausible the nebulous emotions of my costumed heroines, like diamonds on a sea of dough.

What amazed me was the sheer volume of objects, remnants of lives, and the way they circulated. The people died but their possessions did not, they went around and around as in a slow eddy. All of the things I saw and coveted had been seen and coveted previously, they had passed through several lives and were destined to pass through several more, becoming more worn but also more valuable, harder and more brilliant, as if they had absorbed their owner's sufferings and fed on them. How difficult these objects are to dispose of, I thought; they lurk passively, like vampire sheep, waiting for someone to buy them.

*

Finally I had someone who would waltz with me, and we waltzed all over the ballroom floor of his warehouse, he in his top hat and nothing else, I in a lace tablecloth, to the music of the Mantovani strings, which we got at the Crippled Civilians. We got the record player there, too, for ten dollars. When we weren't waltzing or making love, we frequented junk shops, combing them for vests, eight-button gloves, black satin Merry Widows and formal gowns of the fifties. He wanted a sword cane, but we never did find one. We did find a store in Chinatown which had button boots for sale, left over from 1905. They hadn't sold because they were odd sizes, and I had to sit down on the curb and let the Royal Porcupine try to cram my feet into each pair, beautiful half-tones, white glacé kid, pearl gray. I felt like Cinderella's ugly sister. The only pair I could get on were black lace-ups with steel toes, washer-woman boots, but even these were desirable. We bought them, and later a pair of black net stockings to go with them.

Lady Oracle · 1982

MARY MCCARTHY

McCarthy's satirical novel features eight Vassar graduates of the 1930s. Here Polly, the penniless Cinderella of The Group, returns home newly engaged from a date with Jim to find her father waiting up for her.

'He's going to get married,' she exclaimed to herself. But no; he had got a job. In a thrift shop on Lexington Avenue, where he was going to be assistant to the manageress, who ran it for a charity. The pay was not much, but he had only to sit in the shop afternoons and talk to customers; he would have his mornings to himself.

'Why, that's wonderful, Father!' said Polly. 'How did you ever get it?' 'Julia arranged it,' he said. 'Julia's on the board. The position's usually kept for "reduced gentlewomen", but she lobbied me through. I believe I'm being exchanged for a club membership' ... 'That's wonderful,' Polly repeated. 'When do you start?' 'Tomorrow. This afternoon the manageress explained my duties to me and itemized the stock. A preponderance of white elephants. The stuff is all donated. "The Antimacassar", it's called. I advised them to change the name to "The Dust Catcher".' 'Is it all bric-à-brac?' said Polly. 'By no means. We have second-hand furs, children's clothes, old dinner jackets, maids' and butlers' uniforms. A great many of those, thanks to the late unpleasantness.' This was his name for the depression. Polly frowned; she did not like the thought of her father selling old clothes. 'They come from the best houses,' he said. 'And there are amusing French dolls and music boxes. Armoirs, *étagères*, jardinieres. Whatnots, umbrella stands, marble-topped commodes. Gilt chairs for musicales. Gold-headed canes, fawn gloves, opera hats, fans, Spanish combs, mantillas, a harp. Horsehair sofas. An instructive inventory of the passé.'

The Group · 1963

SARA HUTCHINSON

Penrith Sep: eleven 1830
Edward Quillinan Esq, 12 Bryanston Sqe, London
W. Marsham

My dear Friend,
Amongst the luxuries of this House *good* pens are not of the number. I have tried 3 & can scarcely make a stroke – tho' they are all new & tempting looking Pens as you would wish to see – I hope this will find you in Town for we have an important commission for you to execute (if you will be so kind as undertake it) & there is no one else in Town upon whose *taste* we can rely – We have 70 or 75 £ to spend in

Plate for John & it has been suggested that second hand Plate may be had in London as good as new and at the difference of 7/- old & 10/6 new – Therefore if you just take the trouble of going to Rundles where you are sure to find *good old* if it is to be had – & purchase a Tea & Coffee Pot, Sugar & Cream Jug *to match* – what is called a set – as observe they are not however cheap & handsome to be *odds & ends* – & we should prefer what is called the melon pattern – which is without any chasing or frosting – Also a Toast Rack – A Soup Ladle – Sugar Tongs & Spoon & 4 *old fashioned* salt cellars round ones with little feet which are very common & plentiful in all shops – Dora ought to have made a sketch of this article – for if you do not hit upon the right Pattern She will be quite unhappy as our little Salt sellars are her *pets* & she wishes these to be the same – If you meet with the Tea set second hand to suit – & the Salts the proper kind second hand also – the smaller articles you will buy new – as they are not likely to be found good – But if second-hand is not to be had I think we can please ourselves with *new* here – & beg you may not trouble yourself any further than going to Rundles – I feared I had made too many words but I have read my production to Dora who lazy thing is yet in bed, & she says it is quite clear & intelligible – but I greatly fear you will not be in Town & we are in wedding haste – Mr W. has given you such a *Newsy* Letter that I have nothing left to say – only love to the dears – & believe me truly yours S.H.

Letters · 1830

SUZANNE HORNE AND AVRIL MADDRELL

Consumers have varied motives when they approach the charity shop as a consumption space. The thrifty . . . are looking, out of necessity or desire, for a bargain. The elderly or those with limited mobility appreciate the convenience of a local shop. Those whose lifestyle choices prioritise ethical trading or sustainable development seek fair trade or recycled goods, while other (or maybe the same) consumers seek material goods of individuality and, some would argue, authenticity. For some the charity shop can be a source of sociability or even a place of sociation, a regular meeting place. It can also be a site of leisure, blending leisure with consumption, as has been noted historically in the case of department stores . . . and more recently associated with the experience of malls . . . and of spectacle in car boot fairs . . .

*

We've got two distinct types of clientele: 75 per cent are the single parents, unemployed, pensioners, low waged – and some dealers; the rest are real yuppies – they spend quite a lot of money, but are more particular about the quality of the goods.

(Manager V, Oxford)

Quite a few come in every day in their lunch break for something to do. Others come in because they're lonely; there are quite a few about. OAPs come in for a chat, have twenty minutes' browse; sometimes they buy but mostly they don't. We try to create a friendly atmosphere; people don't feel afraid to come in and we don't expect everyone to buy.

(Manager Z, Oxford)

The lower working class owner-occupied houses are best [for bag donations], they give all the labels. The smart larger houses in north Oxford give rubbish; it's been good quality, but it's smelling like mad from being worn in the garden and it's full of holes – they've never had to shop in a charity shop, so

they have no idea what to expect. The nouveau riche [*sic*]
who give, give very generously and it's never dirty.

(Manager Q, Oxford)

Regulars come in and say, 'What have you got reduced today,
Maureen?' They know the system: after three weeks, clothes
are reduced to half-price; they look at the ticket and say, 'This
is on its third week, Maureen'. They try to haggle but I only
allow reductions when they go on the £1 rail outside.

(Manager O, Oxford)
Charity Shops: Retailing, Consumption and Society · 2002

SARAH IVENS

*Home shopping: once it was Tupperware parties or Avon; now it's
designer labels and cosmetic surgery.*

There are two things fast-talking Manhattan women love to
do more than anything else – shopping till they drop and gos-
siping with girlfriends, preferably with a cocktail in hand. This
goes some way to explaining why currently the coolest way to
spend a Saturday night in New York is to attend a Switch and
Bitch party. Forget last year's Stitch and Bitch – that's just a
well-marketed knitting circle. The Switch and Bitch is about
fashion, darling.

Any ideas you've absorbed from *Sex and the City* about
how New York women shop are now totally passé. Bergdorf
and Bloomingdale's are still a focus, but the fashion *fatales* of
2006 want to buy their outfits (for dinner at Bette followed
by dancing at Butter, one presumes) in a more intimate setting. These girls cab it to a friend's apartment with Duane
Reade bags full of unwanted clothes to swap for something
else, something they haven't been seen in yet, something a

friend is about to chuck away. . . . 'One girl's trash is another girl's treasure!' . . .

There's nothing like a Switch and Bitch party. You get to gossip, drink and eat delicious things, and possibly come away with a new outfit. I leave with a beautiful Eroto Kritos dress and a rhinestone-studded cowboy shirt I'll live in this winter. Who needs to trudge down the high street in the rain when your friends have already shopped for you?

'Shopping . . . After a Fashion' · 2006

MARKETS AND PEDLARS

MARY WEBB

Webb's love of nature and understanding of human weakness unite her work with Thomas Hardy's.

And indeed I was pleased with the world and all. For there was summat about Lullingford, as if a different air blew there, and as if there was a brighter sun and a safer daylight. I knew not why it was. It was a quiet place, though not near so quiet as now. Folk go off to the cities these days, but when I was young they gathered together from many miles around into the little market towns. Still, it was quiet, and very peaceful, though not with the stillness of Sarn, that was almost deathly, times.

There was one broad street of black and white houses, jutting out above, and gabled, and made into rounded shop windows below. They stood back in little gardens. At the top of the street was the church, long and low, with a tremendous high steeple, well carved and pleasant to see. Under the shadow of the church was the big, comfortable inn, with its red sign painted with a tall blue mug of cider. It had red curtains in the windows, and a glow of firelight in the winter, and it seemed to say, in being so nigh the church, that its landlord's conscience was clear and his ale honest, and that none would get more than was good for him there. But of the last I a little doubt.

Of a Sunday the shops had each a bit of white canvas stuff hung afore the window like an apron, which made it seem very pious and respectable. There were few shops, and only one of each kind, so you could never run from one to another, cheapening goods.

There was the Green Canister, where they kept groceries

and spools and pots and pans, and there was the maltster's, and the butcher's and the baker's, for Lullingford was well up with the times, since it wasna all towns could boast a baker in days when nearly everybody baked at home. Then there was the leather shop, for boots and harness, and the tailor's which was only open in winter, for in summer he travelled round the country doing piecework. There was the smithy too, where the little boys crowded after Dame-School every winter dusk, begging to warm their hands and roast chestnuts and taters. It was a pleasant thing to see the sparks go up, roaring, and to feel the hearty glow about you, warming you to the heart's core, with nothing to pay or to do, like love. Near by the smithy was the row of little cottages where was the weaver's. Like the tailor, he went abroad over the country-side in summer, and sometimes to a village in winter, if it was open weather. But in hard weather he stayed in his snug slip of a house and heard the wind roaring over from the mountains north to the mountains south . . .

The market was in the open, in a paven square by the church. Each had his own booth, and the cheeses stood in mounds between. There were a sight of old women in decent shawls and cotton bonnets selling the same as we had, butter and eggs and poultry. There was a stall for gingerbread and one for mincepies. There was a sunbonnet stall and a toy stall, and one for gewgaws such as strings of coral and china cats, shoe buckles and amulets and beaded reticules. It was a merry scene, with the bright holly and mistletoe, the cheeses yellow in the sun, and the gingerbread as brown and sticky as chestnut buds.

The butcher stood at his door, which gave on to the market-place, shouting his meat, and holding up a long, shining knife, enough to make you think the French were coming. There was a woman selling hot potatoes and pig's fry and a crockman who put up his wares to auction, and every time the clock chimed he broke summat, keeping some 'seconds' in readiness, which served to amuse the people. Then the mummers came along and gave us a treat, and in one corner the beast-leech was pulling teeth out for a penny each, and had a crowd watching. What with them all shouting, and the mummers mouthing their parts, and the crash of broken china, and beasts lowing and bleating from the fair ground close by, and the chimes ringing out very sweet at the half-hours, you may think there was a cheerful noise.

Precious Bane · 1924

JOANNA TROLLOPE

Being market day, Woodborough was full. The country buses brought people in after breakfast and took them away before lunch, their carrier bags bulging with fish from the woman who travelled up from Devon, jeans and T-shirts from the Pakistanis who travelled down from Birmingham and cheese from the man who made his own from herds kept in pastures not five miles from Woodborough. Threading her way among the stalls, Anna bought some vacuum-cleaner bags, a bargain box of soap powder and a punnet of strawberries . . .

She left the market-place and turned down Sheep Street, a narrow street forbidden to traffic . . . Ahead of Anna, a tall young woman was pushing a pram. She stopped outside a newsagent . . . Anna who had not thought of it for years, suddenly remembered her twenty-three-year-old self outside a newsagent in a Bristol suburb, making the abrupt decision not to buy chocolate.

The Rector's Wife · 1991

ANNE HUGHES

14th February 1797

Yesterday we were very busy washing clothes, baking bread and other oddments; later I and John's Mother went to take my butter and eggs to sell. The roads are very muddy so that we bumped a good deal and had a lot of trouble to get along with old Dobbin. I always like to go to the market: it is very nice to get into company sometimes. I sold my butter for sevenpence a pound and sixpence a score for the eggs, which are now dearer, and so adds more money to my stocking. I bought a ribbon for Sarah's hair and a ginger bread man, as well as one for Carter's wife, and a packet of tobacco for John, with various other things we need. Then we went home, it being a dirty day and very cold so we were glad to get back to my warm kitchen, where Sarah had a nice hot meal ready for our return, and a hot noggin of spiced wine to warm our insides.

The Diary of a Farmer's Wife · 1796–7

MOLLIE PANTER-DOWNES

Over the course of her life, Mollie Panter-Downes wrote more than 850 pieces about life in London for the New Yorker. *Her lyrical portrayal of a woman's thoughts over the course of a single day is reminiscent of Virginia Woolf's* Mrs Dalloway.

A cup of coffee, Laura had been thinking while she stood hesitating, and then I can catch the bus home at half-past eleven. The shops, she observed, had a bare, denuded look, as though locusts had descended. Every morning clouds of women came down from the little Georgian houses and snug cottages of Bridbury, they poured in from the surrounding villages, they stripped the counters bare. After eleven, for those in the know, the little town had nothing much to offer. Sorry, the shaken heads would signal to those foolish virgins who came late with their baskets to seek the rare orange, the spotted plaice, the yellow and unyielding bun. But still little Bridbury looked very pretty and prosperous in the sunshine, the new white paint of the Bull glistening, the dark-brown leather and silver bits in the saddler's shop gleaming, and suddenly, round the corner, a drove of sheep being driven to the market, jostling, chins high in panic on each other's dirty woolly backs, filling the air with their country bleating.

Laura's arm ached, for her basket was heavy. She turned thankfully into the coolness of Rosemary's Tea Shoppe where, an hour earlier, she had been queueing for cakes. Now the wire trays on the counter were empty; the locusts had been and gone. About a dozen other women and one or two stray men, who looked uneasy, as though they would have been happier at the Bull, sat about at the small tables, drinking coffee and eating soggy buns. Everything here which was not curly wrought iron was bulbous polished brass or copper, the beams ran whimsically crooked, the window panes distorted the light in greenish spirals. The young woman in the flowered smock advanced, patting her back curls, looking at Laura with pronounced disgust.

'Coffee?'

'Yes, please.'

'Bun or rock keek?'

'Rock cake, I think.'

One Fine Day · 1947

LOUISA MEREDITH

Louisa Meredith moved from Birmingham to Sydney upon her marriage, settling later in Oyster Bay, Tasmania. Artist, botanist and conservationist, she was the first woman to describe life in the region.

[The market in Sydney is] well supplied and . . . held in a large comodious building, superior to most provincial market-houses at home. The display of fruit in the grape season is very beautiful. Peaches also are most abundant, and very cheap; apples very dear, being chiefly imported from Van Diemen's Land, and frequently selling at sixpence each. The smaller English fruits, such as strawberries, etc., only succeed in a few situations in the colony, and are far from plentiful. Cucumbers and all descriptions of melon abound. The large green watermelon, rose-coloured within is a very favourite fruit, but I thought it insipid.

Diary · 1840s

LIZA PICARD

Street vendors each had their accustomed rounds. Perishables were sold by women, often from containers carried on their heads, such as baskets of strawberries, cherries, asparagus and fish, and cans of milk . . .

Men dealt in heavier, longer-lasting commodities such as coal and sand in sacks, water in wooden pails or long hods, and second-hand clothes.

Some goods were frivolous: hobbyhorses and 'fine singing birds' such as canaries, or larks and thrushes from the wilds of Hampstead. Others were more serious. The ink-seller (7d a pint) also provided ready-trimmed quill pens . . .

Shops opened at 6 a.m., or at 8 a.m. in winter, and stayed open until 8 or 9 at night, or nightfall in the winter . . . Some of them seem to have acted as social centres. Elizabeth [Pepys] spent hours at her tailors, whose premises seem to have acted as a club where women could foregather without necessarily buying anything.

Restoration London · 1996

DOROTHY DAVIS

Market rules were strict in medieval Coventry.

Sellers of various different commodities were assigned to particular places and bidden to stay there and not walk about. Cloth sellers were not to spread the stuff out so as to 'obstruct the light'. In the street of the fish sellers, if they chose not to sell from a tub on the ground but to put up a board or trestle it was to be 'holden firm and stable' and to leave what is described as a 'reasonable' space of one yard between it and the house-front for horse or man to pass between. The narrow streets in which the markets were held were lined with tall, narrow houses, oversailing above and open-fronted at street level for they were house, warehouse, workroom and shop in one. Business was done with the customer standing in the street and dealing over the dressing board or counter which at night was pulled up and fastened to act as a shutter.

A History of Shopping · 1966

EVELYN WELCH

Urban and ecclesiastical officials were not always interested in closing down trading. They were also concerned to encourage it. If some days called for abstinence, others called for increased consumption and expenditure. Towns, both small and large, hired trumpeters and criers to announce special shopping opportunities to the widest possible public. Most communities had a dedicated market day or days, often including a Saturday. This day's importance for marketing was invoked when guilds asked to waive their observance of feast days that fell on a Saturday. In fourteenth- and fifteenth-century Venice, peddlers were only permitted into the Rialto from the top of the church of San Giacomo to the stairs known as 'of the Tuscans' on that day and the normally forbidden sale of shoes was also allowed. The right to a space for a Saturday market was highly desirable and attempts to acquire pitches in Piazza San Marco suggest that considerable profits could be made.

Shopping in the Renaissance · 2005

DOROTHY HARTLEY

Dorothy Hartley travelled throughout England in search of
vanishing country customs, which she recorded in two magisterial
works: Food in England *and* Lost Country Life. *The measures*
below would have been used in small shops and at markets.

Goods each had their customary measure: some of them are given here:

Barrel for butter, beer, herrings and other fish (including salmon!), eels, tar, pitch wines, gunpowder.

Bolle for honey and thick liquids.

Bolt for sackcloth, sailcloth and large quantities of haircloth (for straining cider?).

Cartload for hay, straw, faggots and lime, rushes (the rush in smaller quantities was sold by the *shoulderload,* i.e. *creel).*

Chaldron for new coal, salt and quicklime, shells.

Clove for wool.

Cradle for breakable glass (the same word is still used today).

Diker for hurdles, tanned hides, napkins (?), sheepskins, needles (these were also sold by specific quantities).

Dozen for candles (also sold by weight).

Ell(e) for linen and small lengths of haircloth.

Frail for soft fruits.

Firkin for smaller quantities of goods sold in barrels; fish roe.

Gallon for almost anything!

Kilderkin, Puncheon or *Tun* for ale and wines.

There were other curious measures: eels could be bought by the stick (they were slung on to a stick which went through the gills). *Sow* was a term for a large oblong mass of solidified metal, such as might be obtained from a blast- or smelting-furnace. A *pipe* of something (wine, beer, cider, beef, fish and so on) was a large cask with its contents; as a measure of capacity it came to be the equivalent of half a tun – or two *hogsheads*, or four *barrels* (it usually contained a hundred and five imperial gallons). The *pack* was used as a measure of various commodities, including cordwood. The *stone* was usually fourteen pounds avoirdupois – like the petra – but the first could vary with different commodities from eight to twenty-four pounds . . .

The small stalls of the little street markets of London are very similar to mediaeval stalls (and small shops regularly put out a stall in front, extending the window down to the pavement in the same mediaeval fashion). Certain goods could only be sold in certain places and at certain times on certains days, and that was complicated by the ruling that insisted on people selling similar goods all at one place. This ruling gives us the names of our streets: 'Butchers Row', 'Cockspur Street', 'Wood Street', 'Bread Street', 'Petty Cury', 'Poultry', and so on.

Lost Country Life · 1979

Mrs Elizabeth Bonhote

Bonhote was the daughter of a grocer and a contemporary of Fanny Burney and Maria Edgeworth.

'Pedlars'

With what consequence did these people tell to the populace the merits, and the cheapness, of their goods! – With what

rapture did they seem to exult when their eloquence brought
anyone to listen and become a buyer! – Thus the wants of
some confer happiness, and supply the wants of others.
Ambition is not confined to courtiers only – the meanest
mechanics have a portion of it. – I always thought the varieties
of life, and the humours of mankind, from the highest to the
lowest, a most delectable history.

The Rambles of Mr Frankly, published by his sister · 1776

MARGARET PENN

*Penn's autobiographical novel was published as a first-hand account
of working-class life long before the genre became popular. As an
adult she lived in Devon.*

The Talleyman came to Moss Ferry and the surrounding villages regularly every month. He would spread out his huge
shiny black American cloth pack by the kitchen door, talking
all the time, quick and brightly . . . He sold frocks and
pinafores; stays and drawers, chemises and petticoats; men's
working shirts and Sunday shirts and collars; ladies' and children's black woollen stockings; reels of cotton and hanks of
mending wool; coarse roller towels; pins and needles; table-
cloths and collar studs and combs; rolls of red flannel for
weekday, and cream flannel for Sunday, petticoats; sheets and
pillowcases, prints and serges and even pearl bead necklaces.

Manchester Fourteen Miles · 1947

MARGARET H. SPUFFORD

Joan Dant [was] a Quaker chapwoman of London. The tradition concerning her records that she was the wife of a working
weaver of Spitalfields, who was left with little provision on the
dissolution of her marriage. She became a pedlar 'and with

this object in view she provided herself with a well-selected assortment of Mercery, Hosiery, and Haberdashery . . . and set off on her travels with her merchandise on her back'. Her circuit was largely based on Friends' houses. In 1714, at the reputed age of 83, she made her will, in which she disposed of over £9,000, much of it to London Meetings, and to poor Friends. Her inventory and executors' accounts show that her will was no piece of wishful thinking. She was worth £9,150. Her remaining shop goods were all silk, silk stockings, silk gloves, silk and worsted stockings, and raw silk, and her executors had sold them off for £190. 10. 0d. This was a sum which paled the estate of most chapmen into significance . . .

Jane Lewis kept a shop in the village of Llanblethian, west of Cardiff, even though Llanblethian also had a resident pedlar working out from it. She stocked groceries, treacle, oil, dyestuffs, brandy, tobacco pipes, and paper, as well as textiles and clothing. The author of a recent study remarks ruefully that Llanbethian had better shopping facilities in 1698 than either today or in the mid-nineteenth century.

Ursula Thomson of Great Limber in Lincolnshire had the usual predominence of textiles in 1650, followed by haberdashery & ready-made clothing accessories, but she also stocked sugar, treacle, ginger, pepper, soap, hops and tobacco and strong waters.

*

The difficulties of transporting perishables which might squash, slop, spill, stain & rust other goods were obvious. Few men on foot or on horseback attempted it. Yet a small, obstinate minority did. John Carrier of Aby in Lincolnshire broke practically every rule of 'normality'. He jogged round the country in 1619 carrying indigo galls and alum, a piece of a sugar-loaf, pepper, cloves, mace, saffron, nutmeg, and 'cinnamen in a paper'. He also had starch 'in a leather bag', two firkins of soap, and spectacles. Since he did not carry books, perhaps these were an aid to the use of the knitting needles and sewing materials he also sold. John Bibbie of Manchester in 1661 had an odd and very unusual assortment of garden seeds and 'spice fruit'.

The Great Reclothing of Rural England · 1984

MARI TOMASI

Novelist, poet, editor and journalist, Tomasi focused on Italian immigration to New England, and especially Vermont. Both of her parents were from northern Italy.

Hardly a season rolls by the Wincoski valley without the homely appearance of Peddler Jenny. In sleet, snow, rain, or scorching sun, few have not heard her high-pitched, nasal chant. 'You buy something today?' she sings. 'A spool of tread, maybe? Everybody need tread to home. Black tread for the men's suits, white tread for the ladies and babies. You buy today, hah?'

She came ploughing down the business street, her rubber-soled, canvas shoes scuffing the slush. She was an ageless, brown, dumpy creature in yards of ankle length, printed calico, and she pushed an antique wicker baby carriage that was piled high with wares. A rusty safety pin held together the collar of faded coat sweater, the lower half gaped over her soft abdomen. A scarf, the brown of her skin, bound her head to skull-smoothness, and the powdery November snow that was falling progressed unhampered from crown to face. The snow clung for a moment to the hairy upper lip and the creases of her pudgy nostrils, and then subdued by skin-heat it settled to splotches of shiny wet. The carriage wheels creaked to a stop.

She wiped her moist cheeks and nose with green mittened hands, and pressed the woolen palms for a little time to the dark puffs that encircled her black eyes.

She bargained: 'You buy one spool of black tread, one white, and one blue. I make four cents profit and I talk to you all you want. You don't lose nothing anyway – everybody got to need tread to home sometime. All right?' . . .

'Tomorrow I go to Montpelier. I got streets there I don't go near, like here in this town. The rich houses I stay away from. They look at me and my carriage like we are dirt. Years ago I used to stay in this town longer than in other places. I used to go to the houses up on the hill where the quarries are. I make a little more money then. The women up there always used to buy from me. They don't come down to town so much then, and they were glad to see a peddler. They used to buy a lot. Now they got cars. They come to town to buy. I don't blame them. If I have a car I would like to ride around the country all the time. It's better than to stay at home. Me, I don't like to be in four walls like a jail. I got to be out. I got to be on the road. That's why I like to peddle. I earn my money on the road.'

'Peddler Jenny' · *c.* 1930s

Marianne Baillie

Buenos Ayres
June 30th, 1821
The shops here are so inconveniently appointed, that the task of shopping becomes nearly impossible to females in the higher classes of society.

There are women who answer the description of female pedlars, who are frequently employed both by shopkeepers and ladies, and who run about the town retailing goods of various kinds, gaining a profit both from the purchaser and the tradesman. These very often unite the trade of smuggling to their other occupations, and are then called 'Contrabandistas.' I am told, that they abound both in this country and in Spain. The manufactories are still in a state of infancy, or of very inferior pretensions; they chiefly consist of silks, earthenware, snuff, and glass; but the importations from Germany have of late years more than rivalled the productions of the latter.

Lisbon in the Years 1821, 1822, and 1823 · 1824

SAYO MASUDA

Sent to work as a nursemaid at the age of six and sold at twelve to a geisha house, Masuda worked for much of her life as a no-frills prostitute at a remote rural hot-springs resort. Her true story is a startling and unsentimental corrective to the portrayal of the pampered geishas in Arthur Golden's bestselling novel, Memoirs of a Geisha.

Before long I heard from a neighbor that you could make money by going out to the countryside to buy food and then reselling it in town. I went to see Elder Sister Karuta in Goi to borrow some start-up money and had myself included in the group.

But at that time you couldn't just go and buy a train ticket whenever you wanted; the whole business required extraordinary effort. First you would sleep squatting on the street with your arms around your knees; in the morning you'd finally get hold of a ticket and get on the first train; then you'd go way out into the country where no one else went, looking for things, walking for miles. You'd come back loaded with rice and your arms full of sweet potatoes and drive your weary body to Asakusa and Ochanomizu, where you'd make the round selling the things you'd brought back. I'll never forget the price of sweet potatoes: you'd buy them for 8 yen and sell them for 12. My little brother would look after me when I came home exhausted. Sometimes it would be as late as nine or ten at night, but he'd always be waiting up with something prepared for dinner . . .

The strain of working too hard finally took its toll, and in March of the year after I'd begun foraging in the countryside, I took to my bed for a week. I don't remember clearly what happened after that. At any rate, foraging for food to sell was heavy physical work; it was obvious that my body couldn't take it any longer.

One day when I was walking through the grounds of Chiba Shrine, I ran into Matsumura-san, a Korean I knew slightly, so I asked him if there wasn't some way I could make a bit of money. I felt like I was grasping at straws, but I got him to let me sell soap. In the grounds of the shrine was a lively outdoor black market, and most of the stall operators were Koreans. I fell in with them.

'Right this way! Right this way! Top-class luxury soap for sale! Gentle to your hands! Look how rich and foamy it is!' I'd cry out, stopping people in their tracks and showing them how it foamed up. At first I found it hard to get my voice out. And although I claimed it wouldn't hurt your skin, in fact it did, so badly that it peeled off in sheets. It was terrible stuff that turned to mush in the space of three days. I bought it for 15 yen and sold it for 20.

The market was right on the border between heaven and hell. If you failed to grab a spot right in the center but were a little off to the side, you'd find yourself square in the middle of hell. It fairly teemed with terrifying goings-on such as you'd never see on the right side of the world.

Autobiography of a Geisha · 2004

MARGARET BAKER

A pedlar, I:
Who'll buy, who'll buy?
Come, good my masters, maidens shy;
I've fancies spun of cob-web cloth,
As light as down from back of moth;
I've dreams of summer moonbeams' making,
Whims the rainbow's colours taking;
Elfin ware I cry.
Who'll try?
Who'll try?

Pedlar's Ware · 1925

SHOPPING ABROAD

Rule No 1: never buy anything near the big square (Jemaa el Fna). *Rule No 2:* if you see something you really like, buy it, wherever you are. And whatever you do, don't look as though you really like it.

This advice comes from . . . a . . . personal shopper, but spend any time in the jumbled alleys of the old city in Marrakesh and you hear plenty more, no less baffling, counsel – depending on who you ask and what they are selling.

The last time I found myself in this dusty pink city, seven years ago, the bargaining codes got the better of me. The more time I spent in the souks the less I felt like doing battle with shopkeepers. I became a master at waving away the touts. Which was all very well until I got home without a pouf or a pair of babouches to show for my troubles. As the only person ever to leave Marrakesh without pointy slippers, I felt incomplete.

And so I have returned, with three days and one aim: to fill my rucksack with goodies. My only restriction comes in the form of my boyfriend, Gervase, not known to be an enthusiastic shopper. He does, however, come into his own when preventing rash purchases . . .

What seems at first to be total chaos – sheep heads next to leather belts, lizards and tortoises lying in cages next to trays of spices – starts to take on a coherent pattern and we navigate the souks with growing confidence . . .

My slipper mission is complete, but I'm hungry for more. And that's the problem with shopping in Morocco – what you take home is never enough. A couple of lanterns and a pair of

slippers transplanted into your living room will not magic up
the spirit of the Maghreb. For that you need hundreds of everything. Pink dappled sunlight and a backdrop of the Atlas
Mountains wouldn't go amiss either.

'Souks you, madam . . .' · 2006

LILIAN BELL

*Lilian Bell confessed to reading a book a day, and rewriting her own
chapters or paragraphs sometimes twenty times or more. She was
said to have 'glorious eyes'.*

Shopping in Constantinople is not shopping as we Americans
understand it, unless you happen to be an Indian trader by profession. I am not. Therefore, the system of bargaining, of going
away from a bazaar and pretending you never intended buying,
never wanted it anyhow, of coming back to sit down and take
a cup of coffee, was like acting in private theatricals. By nature
I am not a diplomat, but if I had stayed longer in the Orient, I
think I would have learned to be as tricky as Chinese diplomacy.

We were given, by several of our Turkish friends, two or
three rules which should govern conduct when shopping in
the Orient. One is to look bored; the second, never to show
interest in what pleases you; the third, never to let your robber
salesman have an idea of what you really intend to buy. This
comes hard at first, but after you have once learned it, to go
shopping is one of the most exciting experiences that I can
remember. I have always thought that burglary must be an
exhilarating profession, second only to that of the detective
who traps him. In shopping in the Orient, the bazaars are dens
of thieves, and you, the purchaser, are the detective. We found
in Constantinople little opportunity to exercise our new-found

knowledge, because we were accompanied by our Turkish friends, who saw to it that we made no indiscreet purchases. On several occasions they made us send things back because we had been overcharged, and they found us better articles at less price. Of course we bought a fez, embroidered capes, bolero jackets, embroidered curtains, and rugs, but we, ourselves, were waiting to get to Smyrna for the real purchase of rugs, and it was there that I personally first brought into play the guile that I had learned of the Turks . . .

Abroad with the Jimmies · 1900

ELISABETH RUSSELL TAYLOR

I loved the market. I loved its moods. Lying low beside the river, it could be misty, it could be translucent. No chalky dust hung about the stalls. I was introduced to an art form that did not exist in England. I had gone, as the doctor had ordered, where I could feast my senses. Polished pyramids of apples and pears, still-life arrangements of humble carrots and potatoes, hillocks of pale butter topped with parsley trees, cut flowers in superannuated tins green-painted – and a cast of salesmen who in England would have found employment only once a year, in pantomime. I watched the butcher with particular fascination. Holding a joint of beef before him on an outstretched arm, he would wave his free hand over its surface in a gesture approaching a mystical rite, conferring upon the excellence of his merchandise a value far in excess of what the none-too-prosperous housewives of Reine hoped to pay.

'*Mesdames! Regardez-vous bien!* What quality! And where on the face of this earth would you find such an exceptional price? Such value . . .' . . .

In winter the chestnut-seller installed himself at the edge of the market. While he fanned his charcoal-burner with bellows he gossiped to a gaggle of old women who gathered to warm themselves around his patch. He knew everyone, and their business, and he made it his.

Pillion Riders · 1993

AMELIA B. EDWARDS

Edwards lived and travelled widely with a woman companion in an age when men were considered not only desirable but essential as chaperones. As far as was possible, the two women did without male guides, revelling in the sense of freedom and adventure. When she died, Edwards left her library of Egyptology and Egyptian antiquities to University College, London, along with a bequest of £2,500 to establish the first chair in Egyptology.

It chanced to be market-day; so we saw Minieh under its best aspect, than which nothing could well be more squalid, dreary, and depressing. It was like a town dropped unexpectedly into the midst of a ploughed field; the streets being mere trodden lanes of mud dust, and the houses a succession of windowless mud prisons with their backs to the thoroughfare. The Bazaar, which consists of two or three lanes a little wider than the rest, is roofed over here and there with rotting palm-rafters and bits of tattered matting; while the market is held in a space of waste ground outside the town. The former, with its little cupboard-like shops in which the merchants sit cross-legged like shabby old idols in shabby old shrines – the ill-furnished shelves – the familiar Manchester goods – the gaudy native stuffs – the old red saddles and faded rugs hanging up for sale – the smart Greek stores where Bass's ale, claret, curaçoa, Cyprus, Vermouth, cheese, pickles, sardines, Worcester sauce, blacking, biscuits, preserved meats, candles, cigars, matches, sugar, salt, stationery, fireworks, jams, and patent medicines can all be bought at one fell swoop – the native cook's shop exhaling savoury perfumes of Kebabs and lentil soup, and presided over by an Abyssinian Soyer blacker than the blackest historical personage ever was painted – the surging, elbowing, clamorous crowd – the donkeys, the camels, the street-cries, the chatter, the dust, the flies, the fleas, and the dogs, all put us in mind of the poorer quarters of Cairo. In the market, it is even worse. Here are hundreds of country folk sitting on the ground behind their baskets of fruits and vegetables. Some have eggs, butter, and buffalo-cream for sale, while others sell sugar-canes, limes, cabbages, tobacco, barley, dried lentils, split beans, maize, wheat, and dura. The women go to and fro with bouquets of live poultry. The chickens scream; the sellers rave; the buyers bargain at the top of their voices; the dust flies in clouds; the sun pours down floods of light and heat; you can scarcely hear yourself speak; and the crowd is as dense as that other crowd which at this very moment, on this very Christmas Eve, is circulating among the alleys of Leadenhall Market.

The things were very cheap. A hundred eggs cost about fourteen-pence in English money; chickens sold for fivepence each; pigeons from twopence to twopence-halfpenny; and fine live geese for two shillings a head. The turkeys, however, which were large and excellent, were priced as high as three-and-sixpence; being about half as much as one pays in Middle and Upper Egypt for a lamb. A good sheep may be bought for sixteen shillings or a pound. The M. B.'s, who had no dragoman and did their own marketing, were very busy here, laying in store of fresh provision, bargaining fluently in Arabic, and escorted by a bodyguard of sailors.

A Thousand Miles Up the Nile · 1891

ISABEL BURTON

To her mother, Isabel wrote: 'I want a wild roving vagabond
life . . . I wish I were a man. If I were I would be Richard Burton;
but, being only a woman, I would be Richard Burton's wife'. The
following extract suggests an appetite for shopping to equal that for
vagabonding.

After a long residence in Damascus, I always say to my friends,
'If you have two or three days to spare, follow the guide books;
but if you are pressed for time come with me, and you shall see
what you will best like to remember, and you shall buy the
things that are the most curious . . .' . . .

Before we enter the bazars, look at that Afghan sitting
under yonder tree. If you like to invest in a little brass or silver
seal, he will, for a few piastres, engrave your name upon it in
Arabic. We will then enter the sadlery bazar, where you can
buy magnificent trappings for a pony or donkey for the children at home. This is a pretty S·k. There are saddle-cloths of
every colour in cloth, embossed with gold, holsters, bridles of
scarlet silk, with a silken cord – a single rein, which makes you
look as if you were managing a fiery horse by a thread, and the
bridle is effectively covered with dangling silver and ivory
ornaments. There are mule and donkey trappings of every
colour in the rainbow, mounted with little shells . . .

We should do wisely to go into the shoemakers' bazar. You
see how gaudy the stalls look. I want you to buy a pair of
lemon-coloured slippers, pointed at the toe, and as soft as a kid
glove. The stiff red slippers and shoes are not so nice, and the
red boots with tops and tassels and hangings, are part of the
Bedawi dress, and that of the Shaykhs generally. Why must
you buy a pair of slippers? Because you must never forget at
Damascus that you are only a 'dog of a Christian,' that your

unclean boots must not tread upon sacred ground, and that if you wish to see anything you must be prepared at any moment to take off the impure Giaour things, put on these slippers, and enter reverently; all around you will do that same for that matter . . .

We will now inspect the marqueterie bazar, where we shall find several pretty things inlaid with choice woods, mother-of-pearl, or steel; the former are the best, if finely worked. These are the large chests which form part of the bride's *trousseau*. Those ready made are generally coarse, but you can order a beautifully fine and very large one for about five napoleons. There are tables, and the clogs used by the harìm in marble courts. You will likewise find toilette hand-glasses, but they are far better at Jerusalem or Bethlehem. Now we will go to the smithy-like gold and silver bazar, where they sit round in little pens, hammering at their anvils. Each seems to have a strong-box for his treasures. All this is the greatest possible rubbish for a European to wear, but you will pick up many barbarous and antique ornaments, real gold and real stones, though unattractive. You may buy all sorts of spangling things as ornaments for your horse; you will find very beautiful Zarfs, or filigree coffee-cup-holders; you may order, on seeing the pattern, some very pretty raki cups of silver, inlaid with gold, very minute, with a gold or silver fish trembling on a spring, as if swimming in the liqueur . . .

We will now pass down a narrow lane joining two bazars. A wretched wooden stall with shelves, filled with dirty bottles, and odds and ends of old china, here attracts your eye, and squatting on the counter a shrivelled little old man sits under his turban, with his palsied chin shaking like the aspen leaves. You see how smilingly he salutes me: out of those unwashed bottles he is looking for his finest atr (ottar) and his best sandalwood-oil. Being fond of ladies' society, he will saturate our handkerchiefs and clothes with his perfumes, and we shall be traceable for a week to come – it is not easy to divest yourself of ottar when it has once touched clothes. He has long ago given me all his confidence. He is not so poor as he looks. He has sold ottar and sandalwood-oil all his life, some 95 years; he has 15 wives and 102 children, and he would still like, he says, to marry again. I reprove him for having married eleven more than allowed by the Kor·n.

Now we will repair to another bazar, and likewise to a khan. You must see both before choosing an abba – a large, loose, square robe worn by Shaykhs, of the richest silk, powdered with gold. The ground may be black, scarlet, sky-blue, rose-coloured, or what you please. It will make a fine smoking dress for your husband, or a *sortie de bal* for yourself. The other articles are Damascus silks, and carpets – a kufiyeh, which is a large coloured and tasselled handkerchief of pure silk, or more generally of mixed silk and cotton, also gold-powdered. The Bedawin wears it on his head, falling about the shoulders, fastened by a fillet (aghal) of camel's hair. How anybody can travel in any other head-dress I don't know . . .

You can also buy an iz·r, to walk about the bazars *incognita*, like a native. It covers all, except your face, from head to foot, like a shroud. It is pure silk, and you can choose your own colours; they are mostly brilliant, but I care only for black. Some are worked beautifully in gold. If you wish to pass for a Christian, you may expose your face, or wear an apology for a covering; but as Moslemahs we must buy mandìls, white handkerchiefs, or coloured, with flowers and figures so thickly laid on that no one can recognize our features. If you have one of the black and gold or coloured iz·rs, you will be a great personage. If you want to pass unobtrusively, you must wear a

plain white linen sheet, with a thick mandìl, and in that costume you might walk all day with your own father and not be
known except by the voice . . .

I will also recommend you to invest in an embroidered
jacket (damr), of gold-embroidered cloth, with long flying
open sleeves, to be worn over a white muslin bodice; it will be
very effective in red, blue, or black. You must not forget to buy
a few pure silk towels; they are very pleasant – likewise an
embroidered towel or two, worked with gold. The latter is
slung over the shoulder of the servant who hands you the sherbet, and you wipe your mouth with it . . .

You see there is every kind of *bric-à-brac*. Persian enamel,
coffee-cups, jewellery, bits of jade, eastern inkstands, incense
burners, rose-water stoups, brass trays, china, and what not.
Those little bottles of silver, with crescents and chains, contain
the kohl for the toilette. It is finely powdered antimony, and is
put into these little bottles . . .

'Now, O Shaykh! What do you want for all this?'

'O lady! Allah knows that if his servant gives them to thee
for 1,000 francs it will be like a gift, and may they bring thee a
blessing!'

'Thou art mad, O Shaykh! I will give thee one hundred
francs.' (I know they are worth between three and four hundred.)

The blood is rising in his face, but he struggles to keep it
down, and to cool his temper walks away for a little, as if it
were not worth his while to do any business with *me* . . .

Now you see he has returned quite coolly, and offers us
more sweetmeats as a peace offering. We will now go up 50
francs at every mouthful, because it is near sunset; we have
three quarters of an hour's ride to Salahìyyeh, and the gates
will be shut. If you give me *carte blanche*, I will stop at 500

francs. I have made a mental calculation whilst I have been talking. They will be well paid for at 460 francs, and 500 will give him something over. He will have every reason to be sat-isfied, and so will you, for they are really worth the money, and in Europe they would fetch a much higher price – at the same time, none but English would give him that sum here, and their travelling dragoman would cheat him of half of it. So now I have told him, and also that we wish him a cordial good day, and blessings upon his house. We will mount our donkeys, leaving a Kawwass to pick up the goods and load a boy with them; the Shaykh attends us to his gate, swearing that we have ruined his prospects for ever . . .

I dare say you feel quite tired. We will go home, and you shall go to your room and wash your hands for dinner at once; I will go round to the stable and see that the animals are all right, and be with you in ten minutes.

'A Day's Shopping in the Bazars' · 1875

ANONYMOUS

All the best shops in St. Petersburg are kept by foreigners; articles of clothing are very dear, especially those imported, which I was informed was mainly caused by the very great duty imposed on them, and by the unwise restrictions of the government. The Russian shops are almost all confined to the Gostinoi Dwor, a kind of bazaar, situated in the centre of the town. It is a square building, surrounded by a piazza, and con-tains an immense number of warehouses. We never passed through it without being reminded of the London ''prentices' in Walter Scott's 'Nigel,' who formerly in Cheapside saluted the passers by with 'What do ye lack?' Just the very same thing may be heard in Moscow and St. Petersburg: for at the door of each shop either the master or a servant takes his station, and endeavours to draw the stranger's attention to his goods: 'What do you wish, Sudarina? beautiful ribbons, laces, collars, handkerchiefs?'

Another calls out, 'Warm boots, shoes, slippers!' A third assails one with 'Fine bonnets of the newest fashion; velvet, silk, satin, whatever you wish!' A fourth with 'brooches, rings, scissors, knives (real English), bracelets.' All this is pronounced with inconceivable volubility which at the first hearing, seems to be some interminable word peculiarly Russian. The shops that strike a foreigner most forcibly are those filled with pictures of the saints, household gods, and crosses. Here a St. Anthony or St. Serge, a Virgin and Child, or a Catherine, as the purchaser may require, can be bought at any price, from sixpence to fifty guineas. These portraits are highly ornamented with an immense quantity of gold and pearls, or tinsel, according to the sum the buyer may wish to give for his patron and guardian angel, and make a glittering show in the warehouse.

Having arrived at the shop to which the stranger has been directed, the purchase is made somewhat in this fashion: – Lady. 'I wish, if you please, to look at some French ribbons.' Shopman. 'Horro sha, Sudarina' (very well, lady). The shopman takes down a box, the contents of which are undeniably Russian manufacture.

L. 'These are not French – I want French ribbons.'

S. 'These are real French: they are from Paris.'

L. 'No, I am sure they are not.'

S. (After again most energetically repeating his assertion) 'Well! how much do you want?'

L. 'Show me the ribbons, and then I will tell you.'

S. 'How many arsheens did you say!'

L. 'Show me the French ribbons.'

The shopman unblushingly puts back the box which he has so recently declared contained the real article, and takes down another, which is filled with ribbons really of French fabrication.

L. 'How much is this an arsheen?'

S. (With a most graceful inclination) 'Seventy copecks.'

L. 'Seventy copecks! Why the price is only fifty, and that is all I will give you.'

S. (Quite indignant) 'Fifty! they cost us more than that; you shall have it for sixty-five.'

L. 'Fifty.'

S. 'Bosja-moia! No! I can't think of fifty – say sixty.'

L. 'Not a copeck more than fifty.'

S. 'By Heaven! I can't sell it for that price; you shall have it for fifty-five.'

L. 'Will you take fifty or not?'

S. 'I can't indeed.' (He shuts up the box and puts it back into its place) 'You shall have it for fifty-three.'

The purchaser refuses to be cheated of even three copecks an arsheen, and walks out of the shop; she has perhaps gone half-a-dozen yards, when the shopkeeper's voice is heard calling out, 'Barishna, Barishna! come back, if you please !'

L. 'Not a copeck more than fifty.'

S. (Having persuaded her to re-enter the warehouse, says in a confidential manner) 'You shall have it for fifty-one.'

L. 'I said fifty, and I will give you no more.'

S. 'Well! say fifty and a half!'

L. 'If you don't like to take what I said, I will go to the next shop.'

S. (Finding that his customer will not be cheated) 'Horro sha, Mosjna! well, you may have it; how much do you want?'

L. 'Six arsheens.' He proceeds to measure the ribbon, and she

takes out her purse, and gives him, perhaps, a five-rouble note
to change. The shopkeeper's hopes of cheating begin to revive
at the sight of the note, for he can't find the amount of the balance due to his customer by two or three copecks.

L. 'You must give me three copecks more; this is not right.'

S. (With a very low bow) 'Isvenete veno vat, I beg your
pardon, I am in fault.' The remaining three copecks are
slowly produced, and the customer at last walks away with
her ribbon. In this senseless manner do the Russian shopkeepers waste their own time and that of the purchaser. One
would think that the minutes thus lost would be of more
value than the consideration of the profit of a few copecks
more.

The Englishwoman in Russia by A Lady · 1855

JOANNA ROBERTSON

Hurrying up Via del Pie' di Marmo – the Street of the Marble
Foot. It is four days before Christmas, and the Roman air is ice
blue. On the corner of Piazza Collegio Romano, nestled
behind an unruly stack of semi-parked, semi-flung *motorini*, is
a large, plain shop window hung with port-wine velvet curtains drawn protectively against a pool of still-strong winter
sunlight.

Through a gap in the heavy cloth can be glimpsed a fat
copper vat filled to its capacious brim with plump, brown,
sugar-encrusted chestnuts; Christmas *marrons glacés*, gently
cooling.

Numbers 21 to 22 Via del Pie' di Marmo is a perfect sweet
shop, La Confetteria Moriondo and Gariglio.

The brass door handle wobbles unsteadily, the shop bell
rings, and a thick warm scent of chocolate laps out into the
winter air, wafting past a doorstop of a lean dachshund cast in

iron, his savouring nose outstretched in a never-ending, rapturous sniff.

Pull the door closed, and step into a quietness of rustling foil wrappers, shuffling paper cases, a sighing of closing chocolate-box lids, and a soft laughing chatter flowing out from the tiny humming and bubbling sweet-kitchen.

In the centre of the shop, at a round occasional table, a young girl sits in a scarlet overall. She is wrapping chocolates in vibrant coloured foil, which she has neatly cut into small squares with a pair of battered kitchen scissors.

Around the walls, shelves bursting with sweets and knick-knacks reach right up to the stuccoed ceiling. There are stacks of pretty straw baskets, tangles of gay satin ribbons, and expectant piles of the shop's signature scarlet chocolate boxes in squares and rectangles, both shallow and deep, in all kinds of sizes. There are fat, old-fashioned blown-glass sweet-jars filled with dark chocolate-coated coffee beans or sun-baked raisins, smooth wedding-white sugared almonds, and glistening jellied fruits. Orderly rows of no-nonsense, rubber-sealed preserving pots belie their succulent, decadent contents; *marrons glacés* lurk within, lying in thick, dark, sugary wait for tooth enamel and tastebuds.

Behind a broad, heavy old glass and mahogany counter, the clock stands eternally at not quite half-past eight amidst a jumbled parade of miniature Christmas trees hung with assorted chocolates in pale pink, turquoise, Quality Street green, St Nicholas red, gold, silver and midnight blue. An antique silver dish blushes with brazen ripe pomegranates, and bottles of blackcurrant-scented Vino Novello wine rest becalmed amidst a shoal of beribboned chocolate fish.

To and fro goes the Signora Piemina Mimeli – the proprietress – her dark hair twisted loosely into a bun, her well-worn crepe-soled shoes bulging a little at the shop-hardened corns. She has a wise smile in a face aged kindly with sweet secret recipes.

The Signora's chocolates, in either *latte* or *fondente* – milk or plain – are flavoured with amaretto liqueur, coconut, orange oil, raspberry, coffee, pineapple, pistachio, strawberry, or marsala *zabaglione*. Next to them lie sticky rows of jellied quince, orange, lemon, pineapple, strawberry, raspberry and tangerine, in thick slices or small delicious lumps. Chocolate hearts are stacked next to chocolate stars, chocolate Christmas trees next to a treasure of golden-wrapped chocolate coins.

Signora Mimeli's great-grandfather, Signor Marcello Proietti, was an inspirational grand maestro chocolatier from the northwestern city of Turin in the Piedmont region of Italy. In 1886, he journeyed south to Rome, bringing with him the great chocolate tradition of his famous hometown, and founded his shop at the Street of the Marble Foot, a few minutes away from the glittering Palazzo Doria Pamphili.

When the then King of Italy, Umberto II, wed Maria José in 1924, it was Signor Proietti who dreamed up the matrimonial sweets, creating elegant Parisian-style chocolates and sophisticated delectable confections that were a revelation to the southern capital.

Now it is Signora Mimeli who carries her family's art to and fro across the shop, in and out of the sweet-kitchen door; she and her son, Attilio, who grew up amidst the copper pans of bubbling sugar syrup, pungent rich cocoa solids, and thick boiling cream. He now works away each day with his mother in that very same kitchen, re-creating his great-great-grandfather's sublime confectionery – over eighty varieties of chocolates, pralines, fondants, jellied fruits, truffles and caramelised nut confections.

In the shop, golden trays of sweets are laid out under the glass-topped counter, where napkins sit to wipe one's mouth after tasting.

'Try this, and this, and what about these? Signora, I assure you, your little daughter will love them . . .'

Sugar-crystallised drops of rose water – tiny balls in pink, white, violet and mint-green, tasting delicately of a summer garden. Signora Mimeli wraps them in paper cone, adding some *lingue di gatto* – cats' tongues – dark chocolates shaped like old-fashioned ice-cream sticks, each marked with a kitten's face, and then, just to goad them, she pops in a little *gianduja* puppy-dog.

The shop bell rings once more. The rapturous dachshund sniffs farewell. Out on the street, face-to-face with the stack of inelegant *motorini*, the air is no longer ethereal, warm and sweet but earthbound – sharp, plain and rather cold.

La Confetteria Moriondo e Gariglio · 2006

ELIZABETH MARY LEVESON GOWER GROSVENOR

Wednesday, 22nd

Belgrave called on Monsieur Tschumaya, a Greek merchant, to whom he had a letter from Mr. Bulgakow at Petersburg, and who immediately came down to walk with us, and to go shopping. We went to look for shawls, and begun by a Bokharian, who, after some solicitation, took us mysteriously upstairs, to their living rooms, over the warehouses, and produced a beautiful white Cashmere shawl, with all possible borders and corners; for this they asked five thousand roubles. M. Tschumaya lifted up his hands and eyes, and begun to argue, and in five minutes the price was four thousand; that was still, however, much too dear, and M. Tschumaya continued bargaining, screaming and gesticulating for near an hour, when the price became near two thousand. We, however, went away, and before we had gone twenty yards, one of the Bokharians followed, asking if we would give two thousand one hundred; but when we went back, the other had changed his mind, and would not take it. So away we went, and saw some others, which M. Tschumaya talked and reasoned over in the same manner; but as we intended to see more the next day, we concluded nothing. We begun, however, by going to a fur shop, where, with Monsieur Tschumaya's assistance, we bought eight parcels of ermine skins, made up; each parcel of forty skins costing twelve roubles each. We also bought two parcels of squirrel skins for linings for pelisses. After passing a long time in looking after these purchases, we returned home to dinner. Mr. Foottil dined with us at seven. After the first day, Gartner cooked our dinner in the kitchen of the house. I should have mentioned that we saw again to-day, on the finger of a Bokharian, a beautiful turquoise ring. We had asked the owner what he would take for it the day before; he said two hundred roubles; but Monsieur Tschumaya argued to-day till the price came down to fifty roubles, when Belgrave carried it off in triumph. We also bought, under Monsieur Tschumaya's auspices, some engraved cornelians, and some Turkish pastilles of different kinds.

Diary of a Tour in Sweden, Norway and Russia in 1827,
with Letters · 1879

SARA JEANNETTE DUNCAN

Duncan was the first woman employed full time by the Toronto Globe. Her columns were initially unsigned, but she soon adopted the pen name Garth Grafton. A round-the-world journey in 1888 resulted in the novel from which this extract is taken and a husband, whom she met in Calcutta. She died in London in 1921.

I don't know that I ought to say that we are going 'shopping'. The term is improper and impertinent in the Mikado's empire, but no appreciative person with a sense of commercial niceties has yet invented a better one. You don't 'shop' in the accepted sense in Japan. Shopping implies premeditation, and premeditation is in vain there. If you know what you want, your knowledge is set aside in a moment, in the twinkling of an eye, and your purchases gratify anticipations that you never had – to be entirely paradoxical. The taint of vulgarity which great and noisy 'emporiums' have cast upon the word is also absent there. So is the immorality of competing prices. To shop in Japan is to perform an elaborate function which operates directly on the soul; its effect upon the pocket is an ulterior consideration which does not appear at all until three days later, when one's first ecstasy is overpast. Then, perhaps, psychical luxuries strike one as being a little expensive.

And you never fully know the joy of buying until you buy in Japan. Life condenses itself into one long desire, keener and more intense than you have ever had before – the desire of paying and possessing. The loftiest aims are swallowed up in this; the sternest scientist, or political economist, or social theorist that was ever set ashore at Yokohama straightaway loses life's chief end among the curio shops, and it is at least six weeks before he finds it again. And as to the ordinary individual, like you and Orthodocia and me, without the guidance of superior aims, time is no more for her, nor things temporal; she is lost in contemplation and the eternal in the art of Nippon; and she longs to be a man that she might go to the unspeakable length of pawning her grand-aunt's watch, or selling her own boots in order to carry it off with her to the extent of the uttermost farthing within her power. At least, that is the way Orthodocia said she felt. Don't imagine you ever experienced anything like it in a Japanese shop in London, where the prices give you actual chills, and the demeanour of the ladies-in-waiting lowers the temperature further. Japan can't be exported with her *bric-à-brac*, and, after all, it is Japan you succumb to first, and her bronzes and porcelains afterwards . . .

One sees nothing, anywhere else in the world, like the wonders that tempt us to ruin in this other sort of shopping in Japan. As a nation, she measures us, and manufactures to suit what she believes to be our taste; and these things she sends us and no other. For the best Japanese art we must go to Japan. It does not leave the country as merchandise . . .

Ivory wonders – *takusan*! The loveliest is a maiden, Japanese, slightly idealised, as the heroine of a romance might be. She holds a bird-cage in her hand, empty; and her head is turned in the direction of the truant tenant's flight. The soft dull white of the ivory is not vexed by any colours, but fine lines and patterns of the most unobtrusive blacks and browns, that shade away into it delicately. The folds of her dress are exquisitely long and thin and graceful – she stands there an ephemeral thing caught imperishably, and her price is five hundred and fifty dollars, height ten inches. At your elbow is a tiny teapot, value five cents. Orthodocia buys the teapot and longs for the maiden. As she cannot have the maiden she buys another teapot.

A Social Departure · 1890

CLARA FITZROY KELLY BROMLEY

To Sir Fitzroy Kelly, M.P.   *October 1853*

I have also profited by this comparatively idle day, by doing a little Mexican shopping; that is to say, I intended to do so, but unfortunately I find, on examination, that the prices of the articles I particularly desired were quite beyond my *portée*. The principal object of my ambition, in the way of personal deco-ration, was a genuine Spanish mantilla made of blonde, either black or white, such as I see *les grandes dames* of Mexico are in the habit of wearing; but on selecting one which pleased me, and inquiring its price, I heard, to my consternation, that it amounted to 200 dollars, *i.e.* upwards of 40*l*. So, as anything like that sum was out of the question, I ceased to think any more about it. I have, however, succeeded in obtaining two very handsome specimens of the Mexican 'serape,' which I shall send to you the first opportunity, or, if none presents itself, I shall keep and bring home with me. They are, at all events, uncommon, and not to be seen every day. The only thing against them is, that though they will make capital rail-way wraps, and effectually preserve you from both dust and cold, they are so singular in form, and the colours so many and so brilliant, that I almost fear you might render yourself liable to be taken up, or mistaken for the Pope or the Sultan, or some equally mischievous person.

1853

FRANCES HODGSON BURNETT

Born in Manchester in 1849, Frances moved with her family to the United States after her father's death. She is best remembered for her children's fiction.

To an English shopkeeper the American has, of late years, rep-resented the spender – the type which, whatsoever its rank and resources, has, mysteriously, always money to hand over coun-ters in exchange for things it chances to desire to possess. Each year surges across the Atlantic a horde of these fortunate per-sons, who, to the sober, commercial British mind, appear to be free to devote their existences to travel and expenditure. This contingent appears shopping in the various shopping thoroughfares; it buys clothes, jewels, miscellaneous attractive things, making its purchases of articles useful or decorative with a freedom from anxiety in its enjoyment which does not mark the mood of the ordinary shopper. In the everyday purchaser one is accustomed to take for granted, as a factor in his expenditure, a certain deliberation and uncertainty; to the travelling American in Europe, shopping appears to be part of the holiday which is being made the most of. Surely, all the neat, smart young persons who buy frocks and blouses, hats and coats, hosiery and chains, cannot be the possessors of large incomes; there must be, even in America, a middle class of middle-class resources, yet these young persons, male and female, and most frequently unaccompanied by older persons – seeing what they want, greet it with expressions of pleasure, waste no time in appropriating and paying for it, and go away as in relief and triumph – not as in that sober joy which is clouded by afterthought. The salespeople are sometimes even vaguely cheered by their gay lack of any doubt as to the wisdom of their getting what they admire, and rejoicing in it. If America always buys in this holiday mood, it must be an enviable thing to be a shopkeeper in their New York or Boston or San Francisco. Who would not make a fortune among them? They want what they want, and not something which seems to them less desirable, but they open their purses and – frequently with some amused uncertainty as to the differences between sovereigns and half-sovereigns, florins and half-crowns – they pay their bills with something almost like glee. They are remarkably prompt about bills – which is an excellent thing, as they are nearly always just going somewhere else, to France or Germany or Italy or Scotland or Siberia.

Those of us who are shopkeepers, or their salesmen, do not
dream that some of them have incomes no larger than our
own, that they work for their livings, that they are teachers,
journalists, small writers or illustrators of papers or magazines,
that they are unimportant soldiers of fortune, but, with their
queer American insistence on exploration, and the ignoring of
limitations, they have, somehow, managed to make this exul-
tant dash for a few daring weeks or months of freedom and new
experience. If we knew this, we should regard them from our
conservative standpoint of provident decorum as improvident
lunatics, being ourselves unable to calculate with their odd
courage and their cheerful belief in themselves. What we do
know is that they spend, and we are far from disdaining their
patronage, though most of them have an odd little familiarity
of address and are not stamped with that distinction which
causes us to realise the enormous difference between the
patron and the tradesman, and makes us feel the worm we
remotely like to feel ourselves, though we would not for worlds
acknowledge the fact. Mentally, and in our speech, both
among our equals and our superiors, we condescend to and
patronise them a little, though that, of course, is the fine old
insular attitude it would be un-British to discourage. But, if we
are not in the least definite concerning the position and
resources of these spenders as a mass, we are quite sure of a
select number. There is mention of them in the newspapers, of
the town houses, the castles, moors, and salmon fishings they
rent, of their yachts, their presentations actually at our own
courts, of their presence at great balls, at Ascot and
Goodwood, at the opera on gala nights. One staggers sometimes before the public summing-up of the amount of their
fortunes. These people who have neither blood nor rank, these
men who labour in their business offices, are richer than our

great dukes, at the realising of whose wealth and possessions
we have at times almost turned pale.

'Them!' chaffed a costermonger over his barrow. 'Blimme, if
some o' them blokes won't buy Buckin'am Pallis an' the 'ole
R'yal Fambly some mornin' when they're out shoppin'.'

The Shuttle · 1907

LILIAN BELL

*Early in her career Lilian Bell was invited to deliver a lecture on
literary women of Germany in the Middle Ages. She couldn't find
enough material but, nothing daunted, agreed to speak. Her lecture
was praised for its erudition and dramatic interest, whereupon Bell
confessed to having made it up.*

In going to Europe timid persons often cover their real design
by claiming the intention of taking German baths, of 'doing'
Switzerland, or of learning languages. But everybody knows
that the real reason why most women go abroad is to shop.
What cathedral can bring such a look of rapture to a woman's
face as New Bond Street or what scenery such ecstasy as the
Rue de la Paix? . . .

When I first went to Europe I had all of the average
American woman's timidity about asserting herself in the
face of a shopgirl or salesman. Many years of shopping in
America had thoroughly broken a spirit which was once
proud. I therefore suffered unnecessary annoyance during my
first shopping in London, because I was overwhelmingly
polite and affable to the man behind the counter. I said
'please,' and 'If you don't mind,' and 'I would like to see,'
instead of using the martial command of the ordinary
Englishwoman, who marches up to the show-case in flat-
heeled boots and says in a tone of an officer ordering

'Shoulder arms,' 'Show me your gauze fans!' I used to listen to them standing next me at a counter, momentarily expecting to see them knocked down by the indignant salesman and carried to a hospital in an ambulance . . .

I consider shopping in Paris one of the greatest pleasures to be found in this vale of tears. The shops, with the exception of the Louvre, the Bon Marché, and one or two of the large department stores of similar scope, are all small – tiny, in fact, and exploit but one or two things. A little shop for fans will be next to a milliner who makes a specialty of nothing but gauze theatre bonnets. Perhaps next will come a linen store, where the windows will have nothing but the most fascinating embroidery, handkerchiefs, and neckware. Then comes the man who sells belts of every description, and parasol handles. Perhaps your next window will have such a display of diamond necklaces as would justify you in supposing that his stock would make Tiffany choke with envy . . .

As long as these shops are all crowded together and so small, to shop in Paris is really much more convenient than in one of our large department stores at home, with the additional delight of having smiling interested service. The proprietor himself enters into your wants, and uses all his quickness and intelligence to supply your demands. He may be, very likely he is, doubling the price on you, because you are an American, but, if your bruised spirit is like mine, you will be perfectly willing to pay a little extra for politeness . . . I defy any woman to walk down one of these brilliant shop-lined streets of Paris for the first time, and not want to buy every individual thing she sees . . .

Vienna fashions are very elegant. Being the seat of the court, there is a great deal of dress. There is wealth, and the shops are magnificent. Personally, I much prefer the fashions of

Vienna to those of Paris. Prices are perhaps a little more moderate, but the truly Paris creation generally has the effect of making one think it would be beautiful on somebody else. I can go to Worth, Felix, and Doucet, and half a dozen others equally as smart, and not see ten models that I would like to own. In Vienna there were Paris clothes, of course, but the Viennese have modified them, producing somewhat the same effect as American influence on Paris fashions. To my mind they are more elegant, having more of reserve and dignity in their style, and a distinct morality. Paris clothes generally look immoral when you buy them, and feel immoral when you get them on . . .

It was the brightest, most brilliant Mediterranean sunshine which irradiated the scene the morning on which we arrived at Smyrna. A score of gaily clad boatmen, whose very patches on their trousers were as picturesque as the patches on Italian sails, held out their hands to enable us to step from one cockle-shell to another, to reach the pier. In the way the boats touch each other in the harbour at Smyrna, I was reminded of the Thames in Henley week. We climbed through perhaps a dozen of these boats before we landed on the pier, and in three minutes' walk we were in the rug bazaars of Smyrna. Such treasures as we saw!

We were received by the smiling merchants as if we were long-lost daughters suddenly restored, but we practised our newly acquired diplomacy on them to such an extent that their faces soon began to betray the most comic astonishment. These people are like children, and exhibit their emotions in a manner which seems almost infantile to the Caucasian. Alas, we were not the prey they had hoped for. We sneered at their rugs; we laughed at their embroideries; we turned up our noses at their jewelled weapons; we drank their coffee, and walked out of their shops without buying. They followed us into the street, and there implored us to come back, but we pretended to be returning to our ship. On our way back through this same street, every proprietor was out in front of his shop, holding up some special rug or embroidery which he had hastily dug out of his secret treasures in the vain hope of compelling our respect. Some of these were Persian silk rugs worth from one to three thousand dollars each. Although we would have committed any crime in order to possess these treasures, having got thoroughly into the spirit of the thing, we turned these rugs on their backs and pretended to find flaws in them, jeered at their colouring, and went on our way, followed by a jabbering, excited, perplexed, and nettled horde, who recklessly slaughtered their prices and almost tore up their mud floors in their wild anxiety to prove that they had something – anything – which we would buy. They called upon Allah to witness that they never had been treated so in their lives, but would we not stop just once more again to cast our eyes on their unworthy stock?

Having had all the amusement we wanted, and it being nearly time for luncheon, we went in, and in half an hour we had bought all that we had intended to buy from the first moment our eyes were cast upon them, and at about one-half the price they were offered to us three hours before. Now, if that isn't what you call enjoying yourself, I should like to ask what you expect . . .

In truth, some of my richest experiences have been in exploring with Jimmie tiny second-hand shops, pawn-shops, and dark, almost squalid corners, where, amid piles of rubbish, we found some really exquisite treasures. Mrs. Jimmie and Bee would have been afraid they would catch leprosy if they had gone with us on some of our expeditions, but Jimmie and I trusted in that Providence which always watches over children and fools, and even in England we found bits of old silver, china, and porcelain which amply repaid us for all the risk we ran. We often encountered shopkeepers who spoke a language utterly unknown to us and who understood not one word of English, and with whom we communicated by writing down the figures on paper which we would pay, or showing them the money in our hands. Perhaps we were cheated now and then – in fact, in our secret hearts we are guiltily sure of it, but what difference does that make?

When you get to Cairo, it being the jumping-off place, you naturally expect the most curious admixture of stuffs for sale that your mind can imagine, but, after having passed through the first stages of bewilderment, you soon see that there are only a few things that you really care for. For instance, you can't resist the turquoises. If you go home from Egypt without buying any you will be sorry all the rest of your lives. Nor ought you to hold yourself back from your natural leaning toward crude ostrich feathers from the ostrich farms, and to bottle up your emotion at seeing uncut amber in pieces the size of a lump of chalk is to render yourself explosive and danger-ous to your friends. Shirt studs, long chains for your vinaigrette or your fan, cuff buttons, antique belts of curious stones (gen-erally clumsy and unbecoming to the waist, but not to be withstood), carved ostrich eggs, jewelled fly-brushes, carved brass coffee-pots and finger bowls, cigar sets of brilliant but rude enamel, to say nothing of the rugs and embroideries, are some of the things which I defy you to refrain from buying. To be sure, there are thousands of other attractions, which, if you are strong-minded, you can leave alone, but these things I have enumerated you will find that you cannot live with-out . . .

With all this cumulative experience, as Jimmie says, 'of how to misbehave in shops,' we got back to London, where I could bring it into play, and in a manner avenge myself for past slights.

I was so grateful to Jimmie for the King Arthur that he gave me at Innsbruck that I decided to surprise him by something really handsome on his birthday.

When we got to Paris, there seemed to be an epidemic of gun-metal ornaments set with tiny pearls, diamonds, or sapphires. Of these I noticed that Jimmie admired the pearl-studded cigar-cases and match-safes most, but for some reason I waited to make my purchase in London, which was one of the most foolish things I ever have done in all my foolish career, and right here let me say that there is nothing so unsatisfactory as to postpone a purchase, thinking either that you will come back to the same place or that you will see better further along, for in nine cases out of ten you never see it again.

When we got to London, Bee and I put on our best street clothes and started out to buy Jimmie his birthday present. We searched everywhere, but found that all gun-metal articles in London were either plain or studded with diamonds. We couldn't find a pearl. Finally in one shop I explained my search to a tall, heavy man, evidently the proprietor, who had small green eyes set quite closely together, a florid complexion, and hay-coloured side-whiskers. His whiskers irritated me quite as much as the fact that he hadn't what I wanted. Perhaps my hat vexed him, but at any rate he looked as though he were glad he didn't have the pearls, and he finally permitted his annoyance, or his general British rudeness, to voice itself in this way:

'Pardon me, madame,' he said, 'but you will never find cigar-cases of gun-metal studded with pearls, no matter how much you may desire it, for it is not good taste.'

I was warm, irritated, and my dress was too tight in the belt, so I just leaned my two elbows on that show-case, and I said to him:

'Do you mean to have the impertinence, my good man, to tell two American ladies that what they are looking for is not in good taste, simply because you are so stupid and insular as not to keep it in stock? Do you presume to express your opinion on taste when you are wearing a green satin necktie with a pink shirt? If you had ever been off this little island, and had gone to a land where taste in dress, and particularly in jewels, is understood, you would realise the impertinence of criticising the taste of an American woman, who is trying to find something worth while buying in so hopelessly British a shop as this. Now, my good man,' I added, taking up my parasol and purse, 'I shall not report your rudeness to the proprietor, because doubtless you have a family to support, and I don't wish to make you lose your place, but let this be a warning to you never to be so insolent again,' and with that, I simply swept out of his shop. I seldom sweep out. Bee says I generally crawl out, but this time I was so inflated with an unholy joy that I recklessly cabled to Paris for Jimmie's pearls, and to this day I rejoice at the way that man covered his green satin tie with his large hairy red hand, and at the ecstatic smiles on the faces of two clerks standing near, for I *knew* he was the proprietor when I called him 'My good man.' . . .

[T]he custom in several large department stores of never returning your money if you take back goods, but making you spend it, not in the store, but in the department in which you have bought, makes shopping for dry goods excessively annoying to Americans.

I took back two silk blouses out of five that I bought at a large shop in Regent Street much frequented by Americans, which carries on a store near by under the same name, exclusively for mourning goods. To my astonishment, I discovered that I must buy three more blouses, or else lose all the money I paid for them. In my thirst for information, I asked the reason for this. In America, a lady would consider the reason they gave an insult. The shopwoman told me that ladies' maids are so expert at copying that many ladies have six or eight garments sent home, kept a few days, copied by their maids and returned, and that this became so much the custom that they were finally forced to make that obnoxious rule.

I have heard complaints made in America by proprietors of large importing houses that women who keep accounts frequently order a handsome gown, wrap, or hat sent home on approval, wear it, and return it the next day. If this is the custom among decent self-respecting American women, who masquerade in society in the guise of women of refinement and culture, no wonder that shopkeepers are obliged to protect themselves.

There is nowhere that the saying, 'the innocent must suffer with the guilty,' obtains with so much force as in shopping, particularly in London.

It is a characteristic difference between the clever American and the insular British shopkeeper that in America, when a thing such as I have mentioned is suspected, the saleswoman or a private detective is sent to shadow the suspect, and ascertain if she really wore the garment in question. In such cases, the garment is returned to her with a note, saying that she was seen wearing it, when it is generally paid for without a word. If not, the shop is in danger of losing one otherwise valuable customer, as she is placed on what is known as the 'blacklist,' which means that a double scrutiny is placed on all her purchases, as she is suspected of trickery . . .

But shopkeepers all over Europe are quick to anticipate all your wants, to suggest tempting things which have not occurred to you to buy, and to offer to have things made, if nothing in stock suits you. I suppose I am naturally slow and stupid. Bee says I am, but having been brought up in America, in the South, where nothing is ever made, and where we had to send to New York for everything, and where even New York has to depend on Europe for many of its staples, my surprise overpowered me so that it mortified Bee, when they offered to have silk stockings made for me in Paris.

Like most Americans, I am in the habit of turning away disappointed, and preparing to go without things if I cannot find what I want in the shops, but in London and Paris they will offer of their own accord to make for you anything you may describe to them, from a pair of gloves to a pattern of brocade. This is one and perhaps the only glory of being an American in Europe, for, as my friend in Naples, of the firm of Ananias, Barabbas, and Company, said to me:

'Behold! you are an American, and by Americans do we not live?'

Abroad with the Jimmies · 1900

SARA JEANNETTE DUNCAN

[H]ow oddly different London is from an American city to go shopping in. At home, the large, important stores are pretty much together, in the business part of the city, and anybody can tell from the mere buildings what to expect in the way of style and price. In London you can't tell at all, and the well-known shops are scattered over square miles of streets, by twos and threes, in little individual towns, each with its own congregations of smaller shops, and its own butchers and bakers and news-stands, and post-office and squares and 'places', and blind alleys and strolling cats and hand organs; and to get from one to another of the little towns it is necessary to make a journey in an omnibus. Of course, I know there are a few places pre-eminent in reputation and 'form' and price – above all in price – which gather in a few well-known streets; but life in all these little centres which make up London would be quite complete without them. They seem to exist for the benefit of that extravagant element here that has nothing to do with the small respectable houses and the little domestic squares, but hovers over the city during the time of year when the sun shines and the fogs are not, living during that time in notable localities, under the special inspection of the 'Morning Post'. The people who really live in London – the people of the little centres – can quite well ignore these places; they have their special shop in Uxbridge Road or St. Paul's Churchyard, and if they tire of their own particular local cut, they can make morning trips from Uxbridge Road to the High Street, Kensington, or from either to Westbourne Grove. To Americans this is very novel and amusing, and we get a great deal of extra pleasure out of shopping in London in sampling, so to speak, the different submunicipalities.

An American Girl in London · 1891

LADY MARY RHODES CARBUTT

We arrived in Mexico at 7.15 next morning, and drove at once to the hotel for breakfast. We spent the whole day shopping and packing.

The plaza was full of booths and hawkers selling sweets, candied fruits, toys of all kinds, and great paper boxes of curious shapes, meant to be filled with bonbons, and hung up at

Christmas parties as a kind of Aunt Sally, to be shied at. When broken, of course the sweets fall all over the floor, and the children scramble for them. Some were ballet-girls, some devils, balloons, fish, and the prettiest of all were ships in full sail. There was a great crowd, and numbers of boys with baskets, anxious to be hired to carry home purchases. A lady told me that on the Jour des Morts there was a similar market, but all the wares represented skeletons, coffins, death's-heads, or something pertaining to death or burial. Children were sucking sugar skulls, and the stall-keepers cried, 'Fresh skeletons!' She gave me a skeleton ice-seller, wonderfully made in paper, for which she had paid a real.

Five Months Fine Weather in Canada, Western U.S.,
and Mexico · 1889

ROSE GEORGINA KINGSLEY

Rose was the daughter of novelist and social reformer Charles Kingsley. When she visited her brother Maurice in Colorado Springs, he built her a shanty from which she wrote letters which were eventually published in book form as South by West. *The similarity of parts of her narrative below to Frances Calderon de la Barca's* Life in Mexico *suggest that she had read that work, published some forty years earlier.*

The 'Mantequero', lard merchant, is an important person, for in Mexico lard is used instead of butter in all kitchens. He stalks along all in grey, grey shirt, short drawers, and strip of grey cloth round his waist like a short petticoat, carrying the tub of lard piled up in a white pyramid on his head.

The 'Galopinas', kitchen maids, go out to market each morning to get the provisions for the day's consumption – nothing is bought in large quantities. Their plain dark brown or blue stuff gowns and blue rebozos look dingy, though respectable: and one is glad of a bit of bright colour in the dress of some of the other women in the city, who wear the universal white shift, embroidered round the neck, and a full petticoat which is of some bright red stuff three quarters of its length, while the upper part is bright yellow.

But after all, the most interesting of all the Indios are the bird-sellers, who bring their 'huacals', or packs of birds, up from the Tierra Caliente, and sit in crowds in the Plaza outside the cathedral. They bring 'Sen sotiles' or mocking-birds; clarines, with their quiet grey plumage and ringing metallic voices; pito real, or royal whistler, a green and blue bird the size of a thrush, dirty and greedy when kept in confinement, devouring an unbelievable amount of 'moscas', small black flies, which are found, I believe, near the Lake of Tezcoco, and sold by the pint measure; 'cardinals', with brilliant red plumage; and the lovely 'canario di siete colores', or nonpareil as it is called in the southern States, a canary with seven different colours on its tiny body; parrots and paroquets from Vera Cruz and Oaxaca; and sometimes, I grieve to say, a cage of little humming-birds, lovely as the flowers put at the bottom of their cage, who generally beat themselves to death in a few hours.

In the evening, the streets, though deserted by these traders, are anything but quiet. Their place is taken by more noisy vendors, who rend the air with cries of 'Tomales con puerco', a very uninviting hot and greasy kind of sausage-roll. And one woman about 9 P.M. every night chanted in piercing tones a long recitation, of which I could only distinguish the words – 'Hot ducks, O my soul! O hot ducks!'

South by West: or, Winter in the Rocky Mountains
and Spring in Mexico · 1874

LADY BARKER

*Jamaica-born Lady Barker was by her own admission 'an ugly, tall,
thin, tomboy of a child'. After the death of her first husband, she
married toyboy Frederick Napier Broome – he was 22 to her 33 –
on one of his visits home from New Zealand and left her sons
behind to live with him for three years on his sheep farm before
returning to England. Station Life was the first of Barker's many
books, and is thought to have been based on actual letters to her
younger sister Jessie.*

You know that I have travelled a good deal in various parts of
the world, but I have never seen anything at all like
Melbourne. In other countries, it is generally the antiquity of
the cities, and their historical reminiscences, which appeal to
the imagination; but *here*, the interest is as great from exactly
the opposite cause. It is most wonderful to walk through a
splendid town, with magnificent public buildings, churches,
shops, clubs, theatres, with the streets well paved and lighted,
and to think that less than forty years ago it was a desolate
swamp without even a hut upon it. How little an English
country town progresses in forty years, and here is a splendid
city created in that time! I have no hesitation in saying, that
any fashionable novelty which comes out in either London or
Paris finds its way to Melbourne by the next steamer; for
instance, I broke my parasol on board ship, and the first thing
I did on landing was to go to one of the best shops in Collins
Street to replace it. On learning what I wanted, the shopman
showed me some of those new parasols which had just come
out in London before I sailed, and which I had vainly tried to
procure in S—, only four hours from London . . .

I have been already to a shop where they sell skins of birds,
and have half ruined myself in purchases for hats. You are to

have a 'diamond sparrow,' a dear little fellow with reddish brown plumage, and white spots over its body (in this respect a miniature copy of the Argus pheasant I brought from India), and a triangular patch of bright yellow under its throat . . .

We admired the fine statue, at the top of Collins Street, to the memory of the two most famous of Australian explorers, Burke and Wills, and made many visits to the Museum, and the glorious Free Library; we also went all over the Houses of Legislature – very new and grand. But you must not despise me if I confess to having enjoyed the shops exceedingly: it was so unlike a jeweller's shop in England to see on the counter gold in its raw state, in nuggets and dust and flakes; in this stage of its existence it certainly deserves its name of 'filthy lucre,' for it is often only half washed. There were quantities of emus' eggs in the silversmiths' shops, mounted in every conceivable way as cups and vases, and even as work-boxes: some designs consisted of three or five eggs grouped together as a centre-piece. I cannot honestly say I admired any of them; they were generally too elaborate, comprising often a native (spear in hand), a kangaroo, palms, ferns, cockatoos, and sometimes an emu or two in addition, as a pedestal – all this in frosted silver or gold. I was given a pair of these eggs before leaving England: they were mounted in London as little flower-vases in a setting consisting only of a few bulrushes and leaves, yet far better than any of these florid designs; but the emu-eggs are very popular in Sydney or Melbourne, and I am told sell rapidly to people going home, who take them as a memento of their Australian life, and probably think that the greater the number of reminiscences suggested by the ornament the more satisfactory it is as a purchase . . .

Our day came to an end all too soon, and we re-embarked for Wellington, the most southern town of the North Island.

The seat of government is there, and it is supposed to be a very thriving place, but is not nearly so well situated as Nelson nor so attractive to strangers. We landed and walked about a good deal, and saw what little there was to see. At first I thought the shops very handsome, but I found, rather to my disgust, that generally the fine, imposing frontage was all a sham; the actual building was only a little hut at the back, looking all the meaner for the contrast to the cornices and show windows in front. You cannot think how odd it was to turn a corner and see that the building was only one board in thickness, and scarcely more substantial than the scenes at a theatre.

Station Life in New Zealand · 1870

LADY MARY WORTLEY MONTAGU

To Lady Mar, *Rotterdam, 3 August 1716*
I walked almost all over the town yesterday, incognito, in my slippers, without receiving one spot of dirt, and you may see the Dutch maids washing the pavement of the street with more application than ours do our bedchambers. The town seems so full of people, with such busy faces, all in motion, that I can hardly fancy that it is not some celebrated fair, but I see it is every day the same. 'Tis certain no town can be more advantageously situated for commerce. Here are seven large canals, on which the merchant ships come up to the very doors of their houses. The shops and warehouses are of a surprising neatness and magnificence, and so much cheaper than what we see in England I have much ado to persuade myself I am still so near it . . . The common servants and the little shop women here are more nicely clean than most of our ladies, and the great variety of neat dresses (every woman dressing her head after her own fashion) is an additional pleasure in seeing the town . . .

You see I have already learnt to make a good bargain, and that it is not for nothing I will so much as tell you that I am your affectionate sister.

The Turkish Embassy Letters · 1763

ELIZABETH MISSING SEWELL

Our party separated in the course of the morning. Lady H – wished to take a drive by the side of the lake, and two or three of us, myself included, determined to go with her; so we turned back to the hotel, intending, on our way, to buy a quantity of fruit and some cakes which we might carry with us on our journey to Innsbruck. Soap also was an article much needed, for it is never provided at the hotels; and Como being a famous place for soap, we thought it well to lay in a stock. It was amusing enough, and very like England, to see a quantity of common yellow soap brought out, but it was not at all cheap.

In consequence of the festival, shopping was not as easy as it might have been at other times. Half the people in the place were at church, or gone on some excursion. We purchased grapes and cakes; but when we required a basket to put them in, we found that we were in a difficulty. None were to be seen in the windows; and we only procured one at last by the favour of a woman in a grocer's shop, who sent a message to a neighbour to say what we wanted. Then, indeed a man appeared, who led us across the street, unlocked and unbarred a door, and gave us entrance into a basket warehouse, where we had a choice of baskets, very much the same as we might have had in England.

*

I scarcely ever remember to have been more anxious for a new ribbon and a clean bonnet cap. But shopping in Innsbruck is not a very easy matter. A plain straw bonnet was a treasure not to be purchased at any price. There were some, – fine, flimsy, and open-worked, brought, we were told, from Vienna; but we could not meet with anything more substantial, except the peasants' caps. Matching ribbon was equally difficult, though the colour required was a common dark purple. I ordered a new stick for my parasol, which was broken; and when it was brought home it was like a long, stout, little walking-stick; very strong, undoubtedly, as the woman reminded me with great satisfaction when she held it up to be admired, but not quite what we are accustomed to carry about with us in England. As for pins, they were a perpetual torment; but I believe bad pins are not peculiar to Innsbruck, but are common everywhere abroad. I bought a paper of very large ones, thinking they would be serviceable, and they were no sooner put into my dress than they bent like pieces of wire.

'Journal of a Summer Tour' · 1852

ELIZABETH ELLIS

The editor of Wayward Women: A Guide to Women Travellers, *described Ellis's as 'one of the funniest travel books ever written'.*

We stopped at Port Said for four hours. During the first two hours I was charmed with the place; it seemed just like a big exhibition, everything was so strange and unreal. The donkeys were delightful, the Turkish traders so amusing, and shopping, when one has to bargain twenty minutes over every article, and then toss up about the price, is certainly a new experience.

During the third hour I found that the heat, dust, and endless noise and chatter were far from unreal. I had bought every conceivable thing that I could not possibly want, and paid three times the proper price for it. The Arabs ceased to be amusing; I was bored to tears . . .

My one attempt at shopping by gesture in the bazaar was not an unqualified success. I selected an aged and kindly looking stall keeper, and proceeded to collect together in a heap the few small articles I desired to purchase. During this proceeding she watched my actions with astonishment and some suspicion, but the later feeling was set at rest when I produced a rupee and offered it to her. She took it, and while she sought the change, I pocketed my purchases.

But when she returned, her face expressed the greatest consternation, and she burst into a torrent of Burmese. Quite at a loss to understand her, I hurriedly offered her more money, but she refused it with scorn, and continued her explanations and entreaties, in which the numerous spectators of the scene presently joined, laughing as though it were the greatest joke in the world.

Presently the old lady picked up a bobbin of cotton, such as I had just bought, and waved it frantically in my face; I mechanically took it and pocketed it also. At this action on my part the spectators became still more hilarious, but the old lady looked annoyed, evidently considering the matter was getting beyond a joke.

At last, in desperation, I pulled out all my purchases and flung them on the stall. To my astonishment this proved to be precisely what she desired; the good lady beamed with satisfaction, gathered them together with her own fair hands, and returned them, and my change, to me with many bows and smiles. I do not know to this day what was the reason for her excitement.

An English Girl's First Impressions of Burmah · 1899

FRANCES CALDERON DE LA BARCA

'Fanny' Calderon de la Barca was born in Edinburgh and grew up
in Normandy and the United States. She married her Spanish
husband, Don Angel Calderon de la Barca, the same year he was
appointed Minister to Mexico, and five years later published Life in
Mexico, *which may have served as a template for the Mexican part*
of Rose Kingsley's South by West. *Under the guise of a German*
diplomat, Fanny wrote another book attacking the U.S.
government. She died a marchesa in Spain.

Of course I could not leave Havana without devoting one
morning to shopping. The shops have most seducing names –
Hope, Wonder, Desire, etc. The French modistes seem to be
wisely improving their time, by charging respectable prices for
their work. The shopkeepers bring their goods out to the
volante, it not being the fashion for ladies to enter the shops,
though I took the privilege of a foreigner to infringe this rule
occasionally. Silks and satins very dear – lace and muslin very
reasonable, was, upon the whole, the result of my investiga-
tion; but as it only lasted two hours, and that my sole purchases
of any consequence, were an indispensable mantilla, and a
pair of earrings, I give my opinion for the present with due dif-
fidence . . .

There are an extraordinary number of street-cries in
Mexico, which begin at dawn and continue till night, per-
formed by hundreds of discordant voices, impossible to
understand at first, but Señor — has been giving me an expla-
nation of them, until I begin to have some distinct idea of
their meaning. At dawn you are awakened by the shrill and
desponding cry of the Carbonero, the coalmen, 'Carbon,
Señor?' which, as he pronounces it, sounds like 'Carbosiu?'
Then the grease-man takes up the song, 'Mantequilla! lard!

lard! at one real and a half.' 'Salt beef! good salt beef!' ('Cecina buena!') interrupts the butcher in a hoarse voice. 'Hay cebo-o-o-o-o-o?' This is the prolonged and melancholy note of the woman who buys kitchen-stuff, and stops before the door. Then passes by the *cambista*, a sort of Indian she-trader or exchanger, who sings out 'Tejocotes por venas de chile?' a small fruit which she proposes exchanging for hot peppers. No harm in that.

A kind of ambulating pedler drowns the shrill treble of the Indian cry. He calls aloud upon the public to buy needles, pins, thimbles, shirt-buttons, tape, cotton-balls, small mirrors, etc. He enters the house, and is quickly surrounded by the women, young and old, offering him the tenth part of what he asks, and which, after much haggling, he accepts. Behind him stands the Indian with his tempting baskets of fruit, of which he calls out all the names, till the cook or housekeeper can resist no longer, and putting her head over the balustrade, calls him up with his bananas, and oranges, and granaditas, etc.

A note of interrogation is heard, indicating something that is hot, and must be snapped up quickly before it cools. 'Gorditas de horna caliente?' 'Little fat cakes from the oven, hot?' This is in a female key, sharp and shrill. Follows the mat-seller. 'Who wants mats from Puebla? mats of five yards?' These are the most matinal cries.

At midday the beggars begin to be particularly importunate, and their cries, and prayers, and long recitations, form a running accompaniment to the other noises. Then above all rises the cry of 'Honey-cakes!' 'Cheese and honey?' 'Requeson and good honey?' (*Requeson* being a sort of hard curd, sold in cheeses.) Then come the dulce-men, the sellers of sweetmeats, of meringues, which are very good, and of all sorts of candy.

'Caramelos de esperma! bocadillo de coco!' Then the lottery-men, the messengers of Fortune, with their shouts of 'The last ticket yet unsold, for half a real!' a tempting announcement to the lazy beggar, who finds it easier to gamble than to work, and who may have that sum hid about his rags.

Towards evening rises the cry of 'Tortillas de cuajada?' 'Curd-cakes?' or, 'Do you take nuts?' succeeded by the night-cry of 'Chestnuts hot and roasted!' and by the affectionate vendors of ducks; 'Ducks, oh my soul, hot ducks!' 'Maize-cakes,' etc., etc. As the night wears away, the voices die off, to resume next morning in fresh vigour.

Life in Mexico · 1843

AUGUSTA DE WIT

There are several flower-markets in Batavia. But I have taken a particular fancy to the one held at Tanah Abang. Its site is a somewhat singularly chosen one for the purpose, near the entrance to the cemetery and in the shadow of the huge old gateway, the super scription on which dedicates the place to the repose of the dead, and their pious memory. In its deep, dark arch, as in a black frame, is set a vista of dazzling whiteness, plastered tombstones, pillars, and obelisks huddled into irregular groups, with here and there a figure hewn in fair white marble soaring on out stretched wings, and everywhere a scintillation as of molten metal – the colour, intolerable glare, to which the fierce sunlight fires the corrugated zinc of the roofs protecting the monuments. But on the other side of the gateway there are restful shadows and coolness. Some ancient gravestones pave the ground, as if it were the floor of an old village church – bluish-grey slabs emblazoned with crests and coats-of-arms in worn away bas-relief. Heraldic shapes are still faintly discernible on some; and long Latin epitaphs, engraved in the curving characters of the seventeenth century, may be spelt out, recording names which echo down the long corridors of time in the history of the colony; and, oddly latinized, the style and title bestowed on the deceased by the Lords Seventeen, rulers of the Honourable East India Company – the Company of Far Lands, as in the olden time it was called. Hither, before the sun is fairly risen, come a score of native flower-sellers, shivering in the morning air, who spread squares of matting on the soil, and, squatting down, proceed to arrange the contents of their heaped-up baskets. The bluish-grey gravestones, with the coats of arms and long inscriptions, are covered with heaps of flowers: creamy Melati as delicate and sharply-defined in outline as if they had been carved out of ivory; pink and red Roses with transparent leaves, that cling to the touch; Tjempakah-telor, great smooth globes of pearly whiteness; the long calixes of the Cambodja-blossom, in which tints of yellow and pink and purple are mixed as in an evening sky; the tall sceptre of the Tuberose, flower-crowned; and 'pachar china', which seems to be made out of grains of pure gold. Some who know the tastes of the 'orang blandah' have brought flowering plants to market, mostly Malmaison Roses and tiny Japanese Lilies, just dug up, the earth still clinging to their delicate roots; or they sit binding wax-white Gardenias, violet Seabiosa, and leaves as downy and grey as the wings of moths, into stiff clumsy wreaths; for they have learnt that the white folks choose flowers of these dull tints to lay upon the tombs of their dead. And there is one old man, brown, shrunken, and wrinkled, as if he had been made out of the parched earth of the cemetery, who sells handfuls of plucked-out petals, stirring up now and then, with his long finger, the soft, fragrant heap in his basket – thousands of brilliantly-coloured leaflets. About seven o'clock, the customers, almost exclusively women, arrive, fresh from their bath in the neighbouring river. They form picturesque groups on the sunny road, those slender figures in their bright-hued garments, pink, and red, and green, their round brown faces and black hair, still wet and shining, framed in the yellow aureole of the payong which they hold spread out behind their head. And the quiet spot in the shadow of the cemetery gate is alive with their high-pitched twittering voices, as they go about from one flower-seller to another, bargaining for Jessamines, Orange-blossoms, and tiny pink Roses, which, with deft fingers, they twist into the glossy coil of their 'kondeh'.

Java: Facts and Fancies · 1905

ANNA HARRIETTE LEONOWENS

Leonowens's fictionalised memoir of the six years she spent as governess at the Royal Palace of Bangkok inspired the famous Broadway musical, The King and I, *as well as two Hollywood films.*

Morning dawned fair on the river, the sunshine flickering on the silver ripples, and gilding the boats of the market people as they softly glide up or down to the lazy swing of the oars. The floating shops were all awake, displaying their various and fantastic wares to attract the passing citizen or stranger . . .

Yet one more bend of the tortuous river, and the strange panorama of the floating city unrolls like a great painted canvas before us,–piers and rafts of open shops, with curious wares and fabrics exposed at the very water's edge . . .

Bangkok, the modern seat of government of Siam, has

(according to the best authorities) two hundred thousand floating dwellings and shops . . .

The Meinam itself forms the main avenue, and the floating shops on either side constitute the great bazaar of the city, where all imaginable and unimaginable articles from India, China, Malacca, Birmah, Paris, Liverpool, and New York are displayed in stalls . . .

The streets are few compared with the number of canals that intersect the city in all directions. The most remarkable of the former is one that runs parallel with the Grand Palace, and terminates in what is now known as 'Sanon Mai,' or the New Road, which extends from Bangkok to Paknam, about forty miles, and crosses the canals on movable iron bridges. Almost every other house along this road is a shop, and at the close of the wet season Bangkok has no rival in the abundance of vegetables and fruits with which its markets are stocked . . .

The raw silk, elephants' tusks, and other rare products of Siam, are highly prized by the Mohammedan traders, who compete one with another in shipping them for the Bombay markets. They are usually put up at auction; and, strange to say, the auctioneers are women of the royal harem, the favorite concubines of the First King. The shrewd Moslem broker, turning a longing eye upon the precious stores of the royal warehouses, employs his wife, or a trusty slave, to approach this Nourmahal or that Rose-in-bloom with presents, and promises of generous premium to her whose influence shall procure for the bidder the acceptance of his proposal. By a system of secret service peculiar to these traders, the amount of the last offer is easily discovered, and the new bidder 'sees that' (if I may be permitted to amuse myself with the phraseology of the Mississippi bluff-player) and 'goes' a few ticals 'better.' There are always several enterprising Stars of the Harem ready to vary the monotony by engaging in this unromantic business; and the agitation among the 'sealed' sisterhood, though by no means boisterous, is lively, though all have tact to appear indifferent in the presence of their awful lord.

The English Governess at the Siamese Court · 1870

ISABELLA L. BIRD

A broad-paved avenue, only open to foot passengers, leads from this street to the grand entrance, a colossal two-storied double-roofed mon, or gate, painted a rich dull red. On either side of this avenue are lines of booths – which make a brilliant and lavish display of their contents – toy-shops, shops for smoking apparatus, and shops for the sale of ornamental hair-pins predominating. Nearer the gate are booths for the sale of rosaries for prayer, sleeve and bosom idols of brass and wood in small shrines, amulet bags, representations of the jolly-looking Daikoku, the god of wealth, the most popular of the household gods of Japan, shrines, memorial tablets, cheap ex votos, sacred bells, candlesticks, and incense-burners, and all the endless and various articles connected with Buddhist devotion, public and private. Every day is a festival-day at Asakusa; the temple is dedicated to the most popular of the great divinities; it is the most popular of religious resorts; and whether he be Buddhist, Shintoist, or Christian, no stranger comes to the capital without making a visit to its crowded courts or a purchase at its tempting booths. Not to be an exception, I invested in bouquets of firework flowers, fifty flowers for 2 sen, or 1d., each of which, as it slowly consumes, throws off fiery coruscations, shaped like the most beautiful of snow crystals. I was also tempted by small boxes at 2 sen each, containing what look like little slips of withered pith, but which, on being dropped into water, expand into trees and flowers . . .

[Nikko] These villages are full of shops. There is scarcely a house which does not sell something. Where the buyers come from, and how a profit can be made, is a mystery. Many of the things are eatables, such as dried fishes, 1.5 inch long, impaled on sticks; cakes, sweetmeats composed of rice, flour, and very little sugar; circular lumps of rice dough, called mochi; roots boiled in brine; a white jelly made from beans; and ropes, straw shoes for men and horses, straw cloaks, paper umbrellas, paper waterproofs, hair-pins, tooth-picks, tobacco pipes, paper mouchoirs, and numbers of other trifles made of bamboo, straw, grass, and wood. These goods are on stands, and in the room behind, open to the street, all the domestic avocations are going on, and the housewife is usually to be seen boiling water or sewing with a baby tucked into the back of her dress . . .

I have had to do a little shopping in Hachiishi for my journey. The shop-fronts, you must understand, are all open, and at the height of the floor, about two feet from the ground, there is a broad ledge of polished wood on which you sit down. A woman everlastingly boiling water on a bronze hibachi, or brazier, shifting the embers about deftly with brass tongs like chopsticks, and with a baby looking calmly over her shoulders, is the shopwoman; but she remains indifferent till she imagines that you have a definite purpose of buying, when she comes forward bowing to the ground, and I politely rise and bow too. Then I or Ito ask the price of a thing, and she names it, very likely asking 4s. for what ought to sell at 6d. You say 3s., she laughs and says 3s. 6d.; you say 2s., she laughs again and says 3s., offering you the tabako-bon. Eventually the matter is compromised by your giving her 1s., at which she appears quite delighted. With a profusion of bows and 'sayo naras' on each side, you go away with the pleasant feeling of having given an industrious woman twice as much as the thing was worth to her, and less than what it is worth to you! . . .

Lacquer and things curiously carved in wood are the great attractions of the shops, but they interest me far less than the objects of utility in Japanese daily life, with their ingenuity of contrivance and perfection of adaptation and workmanship. A seed shop, where seeds are truly idealised, attracts me daily. Thirty varieties are offered for sale, as various in form as they are in colour, and arranged most artistically on stands, while some are put up in packages decorated with what one may call a facsimile of the root, leaves, and flower, in water-colours. A lad usually lies on the mat behind executing these very creditable pictures – for such they are – with a few bold and apparently careless strokes with his brush. He gladly sold me a peony as a scrap for a screen for 3 sen. My purchases, with this exception, were necessaries only – a paper waterproof cloak, 'a circular', black outside and yellow inside, made of square sheets of oiled paper cemented together, and some large sheets of the same for covering my baggage . . .

To-morrow I leave luxury behind and plunge into the interior, hoping to emerge somehow upon the Sea of Japan . . .

Unbeaten Tracks in Japan · 1911

ROSE MACAULAY

What is this foolish, this unconsidered mercery, this itch for having, this covetous desire for alien trifles, that mads the brain in foreign climes, emptying purse and bursting suitcases?

Personal Pleasures · 1935

GOING POSTAL

*Good Housekeeping printed this article detailing women's
shopping misdemeanours and the unusual postal requests received
by shops.*

A man writes from Siberia asking a New York department
store to buy him a special kind of dogs and send them out. A
woman writes from a far wilderness in Alaska, to which mail
and express penetrate but twice a year. She sends a one hundred dollar bill and asks for a complete supply of clothing (not
itemized) to be sent to her. These orders are filled, of course,
though at what cost of time and thought can well be imagined.

Funny letters drift in occasionally from simple, quiet spots
in the old South or the new West. A masterpiece of quaint
trust was a letter from a gentle old lady in the Middle West,
who wrote, some time ago, describing in detail a hat that she
wanted. It must be 'just so,' and to insure its perfect taste she
graciously requested 'Mr Wanamaker' to turn the matter of
selection over to Mrs Wanamaker. 'She will know just what I
want,' concluded the writer, confidently.

'When Woman Buys' · 1909

India Knight

In recent years, I have . . . become obsessed with the magic of
online shopping. You have to kiss a lot of frogs, but eventually
you find a real prince of a shop . . . You sit there in your pyja-
mas, click a few buttons with your wee mouse, and a few days
later a wonderful, thrilling parcel arrives. There is such a special delight in opening a parcel, tearing through the cardboard,

feeling like you've got a fabulous, perfect present from someone who knows you really well. Which, in fact, you have.
Only yesterday a lovely pistachio-and-violet-coloured suede
backgammon board arrived from an online shop (*and* it was
cheap), which probably explains my good mood today. Hell
being other people, you don't get a mood like that from schlep-
ping up and down Oxford Street on a Saturday afternoon.

The Shops · 2003

ANONYMOUS

Montgomery Ward was the first and the oldest U.S. mail-order
catalogue, but Sears, Roebuck and Co.'s Big Book and Christmas
Wish Book fuelled the dreams of thousands of rural customers. In
Britain, Freemans entered the mail order industry in 1905 and
Littlewoods in 1932.

1964 Plain Black India Linen
29 inches wide. $0.10

7396 *Hell up to Date*
The journey of R. Polasco Drant, newspaper correspondent, through the Infernal Regions, as reported by
himself. Illustrated by Art Young.
Retail price . . . . $1.00 Our price $0.75

7500 Marriage Certificates
Episcopal form on white heavy paper, with monogram
and description, spaces for names and dates. Size 11 x
14 Each . . . . $0.07 Per doz $0.75

8431 Solid Comfort Baby Bib
with black rubber nipple lace edge and honey comb
cloth.
Each . . . . $0.10 Per doz $1.10

10950 Madame Schack's Dress Reform Abdominal and Hose Supporter

Where shapeliness, comfort and health are desired it is indispensable – recommended to reduce corpulency and to all who suffer from weakness of their sex. Size, 28 to 44. Measure tightly around the fleshy part of the hips, *deducting two inches* to get the size wanted. Postage 10c. extra. Each $2.00

12534 Men's Plain White Handkerchiefs

Each . . . . $0.04 Per doz $0.40

13630 Turkey Feather Dusters

10 inches Each . . . . $0.22 Per doz. $2.25

16341 Poker Chips

ivory finish, warranted not to chip or warp, 1¼ inches in diameter, 100 in box assorted as follows: 50 white, 25 red, 25 blue. Weight, packed, 25 oz. Per box of 100 . . . . $0.30

17709 Full Beards

on wire. $1.00

17713 ventilated $2.00

21300 Beautiful Cake Basket

Height, 10 inches Each. $1.50

23511 Bi-Focal Spectacles

double convex, all numbers, upper lens focused for distance, lower lens for reading. Very convenient and popular. Good steel frame. Each $0.50

24308 Whisson's Improved Pig Forceps

has points of excellence which make it a most practical instrument, and may be used upon either small or large sows with equal satisfaction. Will not tear the sow or otherwise injure the animal in operation. Price. $1.00

24614 Baltimorean Hand Inking Press, No. 5.
Will print a form 1¾ x 3⅛ in. Weight of press and
outfit, 7 pounds. Price, including press complete, one
font type, package of cards, ink and furniture. . $1.75

24873 Rubber Snakes
natural color and shape; you can have more fun with
them than with a basket of monkeys.
Large size, each $0.40

25643 Violin Cases
Papier Mache, French, violin shape, lined with baize,
lock, handle and clasps. Each $2.50

31534 Cow Boys' Sombrero Hats
'Ranch King,' Mexican style. Color: Belly nutria,
silver tinsel cord band, no binding, soft crown, stiff
brim, crown 6½ inches, brim, 5 inches, weight, 8 oz.
Each . . . . $6.00 Per dozen $64.80

37002 Single Russet Pony Harness
Single strap; imitation hand sewed; bridle, ½ inch, box
loops, round winker stay, layer on crown; breast collar,
weight, per set, wrapped in paper, 11 lbs. Per set $10.00

37660 Deodorized Goat Robes
Gray Japanese Goat Robe, deodorized, lined with
medallion felt, scalloped border, size 48x60 inches.
Weight, about 6½ lbs. Each $3.30

48118 Eight-ball Croquet Set
mallets and balls of neat design, painted and striped, 2
large fancy stake, heavy coppered arches. An excellent
set at a low price $1.75

53831 First Prize Dog Power
This power can be operated by a dog, goat or sheep;
yields 25 per cent more power from a given weight of
animal than any other, and with adjustable bridge to

regulate the required power and motion, a 30 pound animal will do the churning; if you keep a dog make him 'work his passage.' The power can be connected to any churn sold by us. Price $15.00

72163 Commode

Affords all the conveniences of the most elaborate water-closet, without deadly sewer gas. Absolutely necessary where there are no sewers. The effect on health is so great and expense so little that every family should have one. Weight, 40 pounds. Price, complete $10.75

74402 Lady's Reed Rocker

has hardwood frame and side arms; very showy. Weight, 11 pounds. Natural reed, only $2.25
New shellac finish $2.65

Catalogue No. 57, Montgomery Ward & Co. · 1895

JANE WELSH CARLYLE

To Miss Stodart,
22 George Square,
Edinburgh.

Craigenputtoch.
Monday, July 29th, 1828

My dear, dear Angel Bessy!!!,

What a world of trouble is in these words announced to you! In fact, my tea is done, and my coffee is done, and my sugar, white and brown; and without a fresh supply of these articles my Husband would soon be done also. It might be got at Dumfries – but bad; and so I have bethought myself of your kind offer to do my commissions as of old, and find it come more natural for me to supply *you* in this way than another.

To proceed then, at once, to business, that so I may afterwards proceed with freedom to more grateful topics. Will you order for me at Polland's, in North Hanover Street (nearly opposite Miss Grey's), two stones of brown sugar at 8d. and one stone, very brown, at 6½d.; as also a small loaf of white at 12d., with five pounds of ground rice. Then, Angel Bess, you must not go home by the Mound, but rather along the Bridges, that you may step into the new tea establishment in Waterloo Place, and get me four pounds of tea at five and four pence per pound, two pounds at seven shillings, and two pounds of ground coffee at two shillings: this the Cockneys must be instructed to wrap in strong paper and carry to Polland's addressed to Mrs. Carlyle, Cragen etc., etc., and you will have the goodness to tell Polland beforehand that such a parcel will be sent to him to forward along with his sugar, and that he must pack the whole nicely up in a box and send it to the first Dumfries carrier, addressed to me, to the care of Mr. Aitken, Academy Street, Dumfries. Now one thing more, thou Archangel Bessy; you will pay these things (somewhere about 4 pounds, as I calculate) in the trembling hope of being repaid by the earliest opportunity, and unless it goes hard with me I will take good care that you are not disappointed. The truth is I have no five pound note to send you, and four small ones would make rather a bulky letter. And here you may draw your breath, as I do mine; for I have nothing farther to trouble you with (except, on recollection, half a pound of Dickson's mustard), not even a longwinded apology for the trouble already given . . .

Ever truly your friend,

J.W. Carlyle.

Letters · 1828

ANONYMOUS

Paris Shopping Service for Soldiers
Established by
Four of the Big Stores From Home

FOUR *big stores from home have established a Paris Shopping Branch expressly for the Service of Soldiers in the American Forces: 'Filene's' of Boston, 'Horne's' of Pittsburg, 'Bamberger's' of Newark and 'Scruggs' of St. Louis.*

TWO American women who have lived over here for years are in charge of this joint Paris Shopping Service; they are Miss Anne Evans and Miss Faith Chipperfield. They are experienced buyers and know Paris so well they often can obtain things Americans need and don't know where to find.

Things soldiers want and can't get in camp, sweets like jam and honey, smokes, both cigarettes and makings, delicious freshly-roasted chickens or potted ham or tongue, these the Shopping Service will send you anywhere in France.

Toilet articles (not in bottles), shaving things, needed drugs, etc. – ask the Shopping Service for them.

Wrist watches, fountain pens and other things get out of order. Send them along and the Shopping Service will have them repaired.

NO charge at all, except actual cost of packing and shipping. The Four Big Stores place the Paris Shopping Branch freely at your disposal. Prices, of course, the lowest obtainable in Paris.

Order by mail anything you want and can't get where you are and enclose money order for what you wish to spend. If it is too little, you will be asked to make up the difference. If too much, balance will be promptly returned to you. If things don't suit, return them for exchange, or price refund. Just the same broad guarantees stand behind the Paris Branch as in the big home Stores you all know!

Write for 'Mutt and Jeff' comics cut from American papers, and our bulletin of merchandise available this month in Paris shops. Mention the name of the Store below nearest your home town in America.

Address:
PARIS SHOPPING SERVICE FOR SOLDIERS.
208 Rue de Rivoli, Paris,
Representing

Wm. Filene's Sons Company, BOSTON, MASS.

L. Bamberger & Company, NEWARK, NEW JERSEY

Joseph Home Company, PITTSBURG, PENN.

Scruggs, Vandervoort, Barney ST. LOUIS, MO.

The Stars and Stripes · 1918

LISA SNOWDON

Love shopping. Love it. I've been shopping online like a freak. Net-a-Porter, My-Wardrobe, Coco Ribbon, those are the best websites . . . And it's like a little present to myself, pretty much every day at the moment. A good day for me is, I wake up, the sun's shining, ding dong: it's the man from DHL with a nice little package! I love textures, I love fabrics, and buying things online gives me the same thrill, the same fix as actual shopping does. Plus I feel less guilty about buying online.

interviewed for the *Observer* · 2006

LANDMARKS

CHRISTINE JONES

The first time I set foot in Peter Jones, the Sloane Square department store landmark, I was both baffled and delighted. It was my second or third visit to London, and I was in no doubt that there was a vast amount I didn't understand about English culture – but, I reckoned, as a born-and-bred American suburban girl I *did* understand one thing: shopping – and, more particularly, department stores.

I'd spent years of my life in department stores, long trips with my mother as a tiny child standing impatiently while she shopped: examining seams and buttons in Women's Casuals or Formal Wear with the concentration of a jeweller; picking up and minutely re-positioning translucent porcelain plates in Fine Tableware – I was always hoping, not very silently, for a trip to the toy section, or an ice cream in the top floor restaurant, legs swinging. My mother rarely bought anything – she was always on the hunt, just in case – for exactly the right *thing*: an object with some mystical combination of quality, value and desirability which would sing, just for her.

Later, I worked in a department store, glorying in the title of 'floater'. In these same years that I was loudly and gracelessly (if inevitably) trying to reject all that my mother had taught me, I would find solace as I moved from Lingerie to Plus Sizes to Teen Girl, every Monday, Thursday and Saturday. The changing soap operas in each department were always entertaining, but it was the constant care of the merchandise, the folding, the hanging, the smoothing, the stacking that gave me the most pleasure. I knew the labels that were 'quality' and could see at twenty paces which goods wouldn't make it home before losing their glow.

And it was a number of Top Floor restaurants which provided the setting for my sometime ceasefires with my mother, all around us other mothers and daughters, sisters, friends sipping their French onion soup, murmuring, piles of shopping bags at their tired feet. My mother would treat me to a glass of wine, and I flushed as much from the grown-up treatment, which I didn't in the least deserve, as I did from the wine. We would talk – about Christmas shopping (was it done yet? by October, it usually was), shoes, handbags, the importance of a good coat – but, also, sometimes, about my life, and where it was going.

So when I went to Peter Jones, having been directed there by every single person to whom I mentioned my search for a wedding present, I thought I'd be in a familiar setting, albeit in a different country. And, I wasn't wrong, exactly, but as I browsed through beautiful wicker picnic hampers, complete with china plates, linen napkins and tiny glass salt and pepper shakers, I realised the next aisle offered washing-up brushes, clothes pegs and kitchen bins. What I loved in the department stores I had previously known – that everything one could possibly need was there – was here taken to a whole new level. I spent several hours there on that first visit, going from floor to floor – the school uniform department was particularly curious – marvelling at the treasure trove on offer. The Egyptian cotton sheets, the jewel-coloured damask curtains, the bolts and bolts of beautiful fabrics (the fabrics alone made me want to cry), the cut flowers, the baby equipment, the closet organisers, the ribbons, the chandeliers, the carpets, the gift wrap. It wasn't the biggest department store I'd ever seen, nor the most exclusive. But it had *that glow*. Even before

I saw an impeccably dressed English woman of a certain age, shopping with her Yorkshire terrier on a red velvet lead.

I live in London now, and in the years since my first visit I have gone back to Peter Jones countless times. I've bought tiny vests as I impatiently awaited the arrival of my children, a black wrought iron lamp and mirror which were about all we had to furnish our first house, a set of poppers that I could hammer on to my son's duvet cover (no seamstress, I was thrilled to do something so practical when the original ones had fallen off); every major appliance in our home, the dress for my daughter to wear at her aunt's wedding, my niece's silver monogrammed napkin ring.

I've also realised that I am far from alone – Peter Jones holds a particular place in the hearts of many women, for the quality of the staff as much as the quality of the merchandise. The recent refurbishment was the topic of concerned conversation – would it somehow steal the spirit? It hasn't (except you can no longer take your dog, a shame).

My daughter has accompanied me on my PJ forays since she was three weeks old and she loves it as much as I do. I look at her swinging her legs in the Top Floor restaurant, tired from our latest quest for *exactly the right thing*, and we smile.

'Me and Peter Jones' · 2006

MARY CANTWELL

Mary Cantwell wrote and edited for Mademoiselle *and* Vogue, *and also sat on the editorial board of the* New York Times. *She lived most of her life – and did much of her shopping – in Greenwich Village.*

I remember Bloomingdale's as I would paradise . . .

I have never known the name of a plant that has long stems

and round leaves and that, dried, smells of spices and pepper. Antique dealers love it. So do the owners of 'country' shops. But Bloomingdale's was the first place I ever smelled those leaves. Smell them now and I have just traversed the Directional couches and the rosewood room dividers to join the shoppers who, barred from entrance by a velvet rope, are viewing the model rooms.

Even when they were supposed to evoke the South of France or a corner of Tuscany or somebody's Maine hideaway, the model rooms evoked New York. It was their scale and their extravagance and sometimes the sheer nonsense of them. All I ever bought at Bloomingdale's, besides white-sale linens, were lamps with black paper shades and cheeses from the delicacy department, but I returned again and again to those rooms. None of them, really, were to my sober, strait-laced taste. Still, I was proud of them, even proprietary. 'You don't see raisin bread like this at home,' a visiting friend of my mother's said one day when I gave her tea and toast. You didn't see rooms like these, either.

Once in a while a salesman would unhook the rope and escort a customer inside. The customer was always a woman, always thin, always ash blond, and almost always, I assumed, from out of town. She and the salesman would pause over a fruitwood armoire, a terra-cotta urn deep enough to hide a thief, an enormous Rya rug. He would whip out his order book; the viewers' eyes would shift to the right, where a discreet sheet of plastic-covered paper listing items and prices hung on the wall. God! That woman had just spent $500 on – oh, let's say a beaten copper tray from Morocco.

Together they emerged, the woman flushed with the pride of someone who can spend $500 on foolishness, the salesman saying something about delivery in ten days. The line of viewers parted to let them through, then moved slowly on to the next room. No one spoke; we were too busy inhaling opulence.

Dreamily I would descend the escalators and eventually the stairs to the basement. Lackadaisically I would make my way to the subway and the Fourteenth Street stop of the West Side IRT. Emerging at Twelfth Street and Seventh Avenue, I was still sedated – by the scent of the dried round leaves and the rip-rip of sales slips being torn from order books. A few blocks south, a few yards west, and I was unhooking the gate into the areaway, as refreshed as if I had been hours in deep sleep. I had not spent a cent. I had not wanted to. The bustle was sufficient, and the traffic and the noise, and above all the Lethe that was Bloomingdale's fifth floor.

Manhattan, When I Was Young · 1995

SHARON ZUKIN

Betsy, with her marketing job at Ralph Lauren, has been transformed by the aesthetic experience of shopping in the company's flagship store on Madison Avenue.

'It's an old mansion,' she says about the store. 'It's incredible. You walk in there, and you understand how [Ralph Lauren] can sell clothes like that, that cost that much. There's beautiful mahogany, chandeliers, carpets on the floors. Everyone is super nice.

'In the mansion, you feel like what you're buying is really worth something. You know it's good, that it won't fall apart on you. It really conjures up an image.

'It's very hard to shop elsewhere now, to look at things when your eye has been trained by such beauty. You get jaded.'

Before she worked for Ralph Lauren, Betsy was a bargain shopper. 'I'd go to Loehmann's, or Filene's Basement, or

Century 21,' she says. 'I'd never just walk into any store and buy something. Now I do almost all my shopping at Ralph Lauren . . . It's a whole lifestyle.'

Point of Purchase · 2004

MARILYN BENDER

Mrs. Dalloway opens with Clarissa setting out to buy flowers for her party. She crosses Victoria Street, heading for St. James Park. Later in the day, her daughter Elizabeth will shop for petticoats and have tea with Miss Doris Kilman at the Army and Navy Stores further up Victoria Street. Woolf herself, a dowdy dresser, patronized the plain vanilla emporium as did several of her characters. The Stores are still there, greatly expanded though hardly chic. 'I'd say it's a place for a bloke like me,' a taxi driver said when I asked him for an assessment. I found it to be a trove for Christmas stocking stuffers.

Virginia Woolf's London · 1999–2006

LADY CYNTHIA ASQUITH

'Beb' was Lady Cynthia's nickname for her husband, Herbert, the future Prime Minister, then serving in the Royal Field Artillery, while 'Bib' was her younger sister Lady Irene Charteris. The Rt Hon. Harold Trevor Baker appears as 'Bluetooth', and Michael, her shopping companion, was her second son. The book she mentions hunting down was a collection of poems by her husband, newly published in 1915.

Friday, 16th April 1915

I got up to London just before twelve and had a hellish morning in pursuit of my summer tweed from Harrods. I went to Selfridges first, took back a hat which made a trench in my forehead and found a pretty black-and-white one instead.

Sharp skirmish with Harrods on telephone about my skirt. Had hair waved at Emile. Went to Harrods – found it closed and skirt just despatched to fictitious address in Conduit Street. Lunched in neighbouring A.B.C. shop off two poached eggs and rusks and butter. Returned to Harrods and finally ran down skirt.

Friday, 7th May 1915
Tried on white skirt at Prince's. Went to Bumpus and ordered tiny Shakespeares to send out to Beb. Ordered a cake at Buzzards and then went to Downing Street . . .

Elizabeth took me out in motor and we did various shattering shoppings together for two hours, finally killing ourselves at Selfridges. Margot told me to order things in her name at Fortnum and Mason, so I selected delicious comforts for Beb – cigarettes, chocolate, bottled fruit, chicken galantine, and so on.

Saturday, 15th May 1915
I went by myself to Prince and told him he must do something to my white coat and skirt to make me look less like Queen Mary. He is having trouble with the police as the order for internment has just gone forth. He says he is a Russian, but hasn't got his papers to prove it. Bussed from Oxford Circus to Harrods Stores and walked back home to Cadogan.

Wednesday, 1st December 1915
Basil and I went into the Wallace Collection and then to the Grosvenor Gallery to see a wax bust of Lady Cunard by the Serbian sculptor Mestrovic – ludicrous. We lunched at Selfridges. I behaved outrageously, complaining of the smell of oysters and being overheard by the oyster eater, and insisting on opening a window. The rain poured in on a fat customer

and she said with dignity, 'I'm eating *hot* food'. I thought it very funny and the window had to be shut.

Thursday, 30th December 1915
I went out to Selfridges early and did some masterly shopping – I asked for *The Volunteer*. They had had it, but it was sold out. I also went to The Times Book Club and ordered a copy – about three were lying in a little pile. They said they had sold a good few, but the saleswoman was not forthcoming, and I hadn't the nerve to press for numbers. I felt my name was written on my forehead.

Thursday, 20th April 1916
I went off and scoured the bargain basement at Selfridges . . .

Monday, 22nd January 1917
The Professor and I went to Selfridges – in an emporium I am with excitement, as he aptly said, 'like a dog in a rabbit warren'. It is bitter, penetratingly cold and the pavements are covered with icicles of slime. Walking is beastly.

Wednesday, 21st March 1917
Bitter cold again. Intermittent falls of snow. Claud sent me a ghastly newspaper photograph of myself headed 'Helping the lads' with 'There's one here who needs you'. I got up after necessary writing and telephoning. Bussed to Selfridges and spent practically all my poker earnings on boots, torch, socks, and comestibles for Beb.

The Diaries of Lady Cynthia Asquith · 1915–18

CATHERINE HELEN SPENCE

Though born in Scotland, Spence lived most of her life in southern Australia, where she was an active feminist. Her 1854 Clara Morison *was the first novel about Australia written by a woman.*

In the following work she projected 100 years into the future – a
time now decades in the past (1988).

'Now,' said Mr. Oliphant, as we departed, 'you should see a
large co-operative distribution store.'

'I have seen such things, and read about them a great deal.
The Civil Service and the Army and Navy stores were quite
great establishments.'

'Oh! these were cheap-selling stores, not saving stores, like
those established by the Rochdale pioneers, and copied all
over the North of England. Even these were not true to their
original traditions. I shall take you to one which the Owen
Home deals at – proprietary stores, where all those who buy
and all those who sell have a vested interest.'

I was taken to this great Emporium, and noted how little
was expended for show either in the building or the get-up of
the goods. All goods were bought first-hand at the lowest
remunerative prices. There were no show-cases, no useless
decorations, no fancy boxes with colored pictures, of more or
less merit, to make the contents attractive. I priced several
articles, and while I noted that many necessary and useful
things were cheaper, a great many of the minor conveniences
and little luxuries of life were dearer. I did not regret to see that
lucifer matches – for which there was now a limited demand –
were much more expensive than they were, so that they would
not be so wastefully and recklessly used. It was the endeavor of
the London manufacturers to compete with the cheap production of Sweden that brought down the price, while the
miserable match-box makers lived in rags and dirt in London
slums and the unhealthy fumes shortened the lives of the
matchmakers themselves.

There must have been great displacement of industry

everywhere. The girls who earned a living by making fancy boxes, and by drawing and designing pictures for them, had no successors now-a-days. Christmas and birthday cards, too, had gone out. I understood that everything was to be had at the stores, from a needle to an anchor, from a dancing shoe to a ton of coals, but when I asked for birthday cards, the shopman stared at me.

A Week in the Future · 1888

LUCY SIEGLE

The shopping mecca for WAGs – wives and girlfriends of football stars – is the Liverpool boutique Cricket.

Wag style has even spawned its own verbs. Going out? Then you get 'Cricketed up'. If you're used to the minimal interiors preferred by most retailers of luxury goods, where a £700 handbag is displayed on a lit plinth, Cricket is a bit of a shock. Chloë and Balenciaga bags appear to be everywhere, following the 'pile 'em high' retail maxim, while Missoni, Cavalli, Balenciaga, McQueen, Biba and Matthew Williamson for Pucci jostle for rail space. But the really striking thing is the volume of customers making a pilgrimage up the hallowed stairs . . . The changing rooms are like revolving doors and I can honestly say I've seen slower Saturdays at Top Shop. Shoes and boots are mixed in with a Juicy Couture children's range, and Juicy dog beds in powder blue peek out from beneath the rails. One after another, children, ordinary girls, *Emmerdale* starlets and even grandmothers leave clutching their distinctive carrier bag (you'll find these on sale on eBay for £25 a pop).

'The Liver Birds' · 2006

MOLLY HARRISON

[G]radually an entirely new type of retailer appeared – the chain store, which was essentially based on selling the products of a wide variety of different trades. This form of trading had started in the 1890s with the Penny Bazaars which Michael Marks first established in Manchester, and with the first British branch of Woolworths in Liverpool in 1909. Before 1914 put a check on further development, chain stores spread very quickly: men's outfitting, chemists' goods, tobacco, and stationery were the main lines involved.

Marks and Spencer's established an important position among chain stores, but they retained for a number of years features which had been characteristic of the market place and the market hall: open display, easy accessibility of goods, and self-selection. The typical Marks and Spencer bazaar before and during the First World War had a gangway running its entire length, with a horseshoe counter running round the three internal walls. On both sides of the entrance were counters opening onto the street, which were accessible to passers-by and could be closed at night by roll-top shutters. For a long time the bazaars displayed a sign 'Admission Free'.

People and Shopping · 1975

KATE FOX

The M&S Test

If you want to get an idea of the convoluted intricacy of shopping class-indicators, spend some time observing and interviewing the shoppers in Marks & Spencer. In this very English high-street chain, you trip over invisible class barriers in every aisle. M&S is a sort of department-store, selling clothes, shoes, furniture, linen, soap, make-up, etc. – as well as food and drink – all under its own brand name.

- The upper-middle classes buy food in the very expensive but high-quality M&S food halls, and will also happily buy M&S underwear and perhaps the occasional plain, basic item such as a t-shirt, but will not often buy any other clothes there, except perhaps for children – and certainly not anything with a pattern, as this would identify it as being from M&S. They would never buy a party dress from M&S, and are squeamish about wearing M&S shoes, however comfortable or well made they may be. They will buy M&S towels and bed-linen, but not M&S sofas, curtains or cushions.

- The middle-middles also buy M&S food, although those on a lower budget would not do their entire weekly shop here. They complain a bit (to each other, not to M&S) about the high prices of M&S food, but tell themselves it is worth it for the quality, and buy their cornflakes and loo paper at Sainsbury's. They will buy a much wider range of clothes from M&S than the upper-middles, including things with prints and patterns, and they are happy to buy M&S sofas, cushions and curtains. Their teenage children, however, may turn up their noses at M&S clothes, not for class reasons but because they prefer the more youthful, fashionable high-street chains.

- Lower-middles and some upwardly mobile upper-workings buy M&S food, but usually only as a special treat – for some, particularly those with young children, an M&S 'ready-meal' is an alternative to eating out at a restaurant, something they might have as an indulgence, maybe once a week. They cannot afford to food-shop here regularly, and regard anyone who does as extravagant and quite possibly 'stuck-up'. 'My sister-in-law buys all her veg and washing-up liquid and everything from Marks, stupid cow,' a middle-aged woman told me, with a disdainful, disapproving sniff.

Watching the English · 2004

BARBARA TAYLOR BRADFORD

One night, towards the end of the week, [Emma] . . . was working feverishly at her desk when she had a sudden and quite irresistible urge to go down into the store. At first she dismissed the idea as the silly whim of an old woman who was feeling vulnerable, but the thought so persisted that she could not ignore it. She was literally overcome with an inexplicable desire, a *need*, to walk through those vast, great halls below, as if to reassure herself of their very existence. She rose slowly. Her bones were afflicted with an ague and the pain in her chest was ever present. After descending in the lift and speaking to the security guard on duty, she walked through the foyer that led to the ground-floor departments. She hesitated on the threshold of the haberdashery department, regarding the hushed and ghost-like scene that spread itself out before her. By day it glittered under the blaze of huge chandeliers, with their globes and blades of crystal that threw off rays of prismatic light. Now, in the shadows and stillness of the night, the area appeared to her as a petrified forest, suspended in time and space, inanimate, frozen and lifeless. The vaulted ceiling, cathedral-like in its dimensions, was filled with bluish lacy patterns, eerie and mysterious, while the panelled walls had taken on a dark purple glaze under the soft, diffused flow which emanated from the wall sconces. She moved noiselessly across the richly carpeted floor until she arrived at the food halls, a series of immense, rectangular rooms flowing into each other through high-flung arches faintly reminiscent of medieval monastic architecture.

To Emma, the food halls would always be the nucleus of the store, for in essence they had been the beginning of it all, the tiny seed from which the Harte chain had grown and flowered to become the mighty business empire it was today. In contrast to the other areas of the store, here at night, as by day, the full supplement of chandeliers shone in icy splendour, dropping down from the domed ceilings like giant stalactites that filled the adjoining halls with a pristine and glistening luminosity. Light bounced back from the blue and white tiled walls, the marble counter tops, the glass cases, the gleaming steel refrigerators, the white tiled floor. Emma thought they were as clean and as beautiful and as pure as vast and silent snowscapes sparkling under hard, brilliant sun. She walked from hall to hall, surveying the innumerable and imaginative displays of foodstuff, gourmet products, delicacies imported from all over the world, good wholesome English fare, and an astonishing array of wines and liquors, and she was inordinately proud of all she observed. Emma knew there were no other food halls, in any store anywhere in the world, which could challenge these, and she smiled to herself with a profound and complete satisfaction. Each one was an extension of her instinctive good taste, her inspired planning and diligent purchasing; in the whole hierarchy of Harte Enterprises, no one could lay claim to their creation but she herself . . .

When she came to the charcuterie department, a sudden mental image of her first shop in Leeds flitted before her, at once stark and realistic in every detail. It was so compelling it brought her to a standstill. That little shop from which all this had issued forth; how unpretentious and insignificant it had been in comparison to this elegant establishment that exuded refinement and wealth! She stood quite still, alert, straining, listening, as if she could hear sounds from long ago in the silence of this night. Forgotten memories, nostalgic and poignant, rushed back to her with force and clarity. Images, no longer nebulous and abandoned, took living form. As she ran her hands over the rich polished oak counter it seemed to her that her fingers touched the scrubbed deal surface of the counter in the old shop. She could smell the acrid odour of the carbolic soap she had used to scrub the shop every day; she could hear the tinny, rattling clink of the old-fashioned secondhand cash register as she joyfully rang up her meagre sales.

Oh, how she had loved that poor, cramped little shop, filled to overflowing with her own homemade foods and jams, bottles of peppermints, and stone jars of pickles and spices.

'Who would have thought it would become *this*?' Emma said aloud, and her voice echoed back to her in the silence of the empty hall where she stood.

A Woman of Substance · 1979

JOAN DIDION

They float on the landscape like pyramids to the boom years, all those Plazas and Malls and Esplanades. All those Squares and Fairs. All those Towns and Lands. Stonestown. Hillsdale. Valley Fair, Mayfair, Northgate, Southgate, Eastgate, Westgate. Gulfgate. They are toy garden cities in which no one lives but everyone consumes, profound equalizers, the perfect fusion of the profit motive and the egalitarian ideal, and to hear their names is to recall words and phrases no longer quite current. Baby Boom. Consumer Explosion. Leisure Revolution. Do-it-Yourself Revolution. Backyard Revolution. Suburbia. 'The Shopping Center,' the Urban Land Institute could pronounce in 1957, 'is today's extraordinary retail business evolvement . . . The automobile accounts for suburbia, and suburbia accounts for the shopping center.' . . .

I was living in New York, working for *Vogue*, and taking, by correspondence, a University of California Extension course in shopping-center theory. This did not seem eccentric to me at the time. I remember sitting on the cool floor in Irving Penn's studio and reading, in *The Community Builders Handbook*, advice from James B. Douglas on shopping-center financing. I recall staying late in my pale-blue office on the twentieth floor of the Graybar Building to memorize David D. Bohannon's parking ratios. My 'real' life was to sit in this office and describe life as it was lived in Djakarta and Caneel Bay and in the great châteaux of the Loire Valley, but my dream life was to put together a Class-A regional shopping center with three full-line department stores as major tenants.

That I was perhaps the only person I knew in New York, let alone on the Condé Nast floors of the Graybar Building, to have memorized the distinctions among 'A,' 'B,' and 'C' shopping centers did not occur to me (the defining distinction, as long as I have your attention, is that an 'A,' or 'regional,' center has as its major tenant a full-line department store which carries major appliances; a 'B,' or 'community,' center has as its major tenant a junior department store which does not carry major appliances; and a 'C,' or 'neighborhood,' center has as its major tenant only a supermarket): my interest in shopping centers was in no way casual. I did want to build them. I wanted to build them because I had fallen into the habit of writing fiction, and I had it in my head that a couple of good centers might support this habit less taxingly than a pale-blue office at *Vogue*.

'On the Mall' · 1979

LAURA INGALLS WILDER

Little House in the Big Woods *was the first book in the Little House series. In the posthumously published* The First Four Years, *Wilder describes the perils of debt and buying on credit.*

Right on the edge of the lake, there was one great big building. That was the store, Pa told her. It was not made of logs. It was made of wide, gray boards, running up and down. The sand spread all around it . . .

There was a wide platform in front of the store, and at one end of it steps went up to it out of the sand. Laura's heart was beating so fast that she could hardly climb the steps. She was trembling all over . . .

The store was full of things to look at. All along one side of it were shelves full of colored prints and calico. There were beautiful pinks and blues and reds and browns and purples. On the floor along the sides of the plank counters there were kegs of nails, and kegs of round, gray shot, and there were big wooden pails full of candy. Here were sacks of salt, and sacks of store sugar.

In the middle of the store was a plow made of shiny wood, with a glittering bright plowshare, and there were steel ax heads, and hammer heads, and saws, and all kinds of knives – hunting knives and skinning knives and butcher knives and jack-knives. There were big boots and little boots, big shoes and little shoes.

Laura could have looked for weeks and not seen all the things that were in that store. She had not known there were so many things in the world.

Little House in the Big Woods · 1932

BEHIND THE COUNTER

RUTH LEIGH

In a retail store, you have a wonderful chance to study human beings. Don't you think it is interesting to look at men and women and to wonder about them? Who are they? What are their chief characteristics? Why do they act and talk as they do? Where are they going? For what purposes do they buy various articles?

This does not mean that you must be 'nosey'. It simply means that as an alert individual you must study people.

It is the most absorbing game in the world, even more interesting than reading stories or novels. You are dealing with all types of individuals. Each one talks and acts differently. Why?

*

[Y]our expression must be an indication of your attitude and personality . . .

No matter how tired you are, smile pleasantly at the approach of a customer. Do not smirk or give a bored smile of duty, but smile in a sincere, engaging way that will make a customer feel that she is welcome in the store. Unfortunately, however, salespeople's smile can be overdone; they can make or break sales.

The Human Side of Retail Selling · 1921

EDNA FERBER

Ferber won the Pulitzer Prize in 1924 for her novel So Big, *but it was the book behind the musical* Showboat *that made her famous. Fanny's mother runs the Brandeis Bazaar in this story of a young girl growing up Jewish in a small midwestern town.*

You could not have lived a week in Winnebago without being

aware of Mrs. Brandeis. In a town of ten thousand, where every one was a personality, from Hen Cody, the drayman, in blue overalls (magically transformed on Sunday mornings into a suave black-broadcloth usher at the Congregational Church), to A. J. Dawes, who owned the waterworks before the city bought it. Mrs. Brandeis was a super-personality. Winnebago did not know it. Winnebago, buying its dolls, and china, and Battenberg braid and tinware and toys of Mrs. Brandeis, of Brandeis' Bazaar, realized vaguely that here was some one different.

When you entered the long, cool, narrow store on Elm Street, Mrs. Brandeis herself came forward to serve you, unless she already was busy with two customers. There were two clerks – three, if you count Aloysius, the boy – but to Mrs. Brandeis belonged the privilege of docketing you first. If you happened in during a moment of business lull, you were likely to find her reading in the left-hand corner at the front of the store, near the shelf where were ranged the dolls' heads, the pens, the pencils, and school supplies.

You saw a sturdy, well-set-up, alert woman, of the kind that looks taller than she really is; a woman with a long, straight, clever nose that indexed her character, as did everything about her, from her crisp, vigorous, abundant hair to the way she came down hard on her heels in walking. She was what might be called a very definite person. But first you remarked her eyes. Will you concede that eyes can be piercing, yet velvety? Their piercingness was a mental quality, I suppose, and the velvety softness a physical one. One could only think, somehow, of wild pansies – the brown kind. If Winnebago had taken the trouble to glance at the title of the book she laid face down on the pencil boxes as you entered, it would have learned that the book was one of Balzac's, or, perhaps,

Zangwill's, or Zola's. She never could overcome that habit of snatching a chapter here and there during dull moments. She was too tired to read when night came.

There were many times when the little Wisconsin town lay broiling in the August sun, or locked in the January drifts, and the main business street was as silent as that of a deserted village. But more often she came forward to you from the rear of the store, with bits of excelsior clinging to her black sateen apron. You knew that she had been helping Aloysius as he unpacked a consignment of chamber sets or a hogshead of china or glassware, chalking each piece with the price mark as it was dug from its nest of straw and paper.

'How do you do!' she would say. 'What can I do for you?' And in that moment she had you listed, indexed, and filed, were you a farmer woman in a black shawl and rusty bonnet with a faded rose bobbing grotesquely atop it, or one of the patronizing East End set who came to Brandeis' Bazaar because Mrs. Brandeis' party favors, for one thing, were of a variety that could be got nowhere else this side of Chicago. If, after greeting you, Mrs. Brandeis called, 'Sadie! Stockings!' (supposing stockings were your quest), you might know that Mrs. Brandeis had weighed you and found you wanting.

There had always been a store – at least, ever since Fanny could remember. She often thought how queer it would seem to have to buy pins, or needles, or dishes, or soap, or thread. The store held all these things, and many more. Just to glance at the bewildering display outside gave you promise of the variety within. Winnebago was rather ashamed of that display. It was before the day of repression in decoration, and the two benches in front of the windows overflowed with lamps, and water sets, and brooms, and boilers and tinware and hampers. Once the *Winnebago Courier* had had a sarcastic editorial about what they called the Oriental bazaar (that was after the editor, Lem Davis, had bumped his shin against a toy cart that protruded unduly), but Mrs. Brandeis changed nothing. She knew that the farmer women who stood outside with their husbands on busy Saturdays would not have understood repression in display, but they did understand the tickets that marked the wares in plain figures – this berry set, $1.59; that lamp, $1.23. They talked it over, outside, and drifted away, and came back, and entered, and bought.

She knew when to be old-fashioned, did Mrs. Brandeis, and when to be modern. . . .

[Fanny] developed a surprising knack at selling. Yet it was not so surprising, perhaps, when one considered her teacher. She learned as only a woman can learn who is brought into daily contact with the outside world. It was not only contact: it was the relation of buyer and seller. She learned to judge people because she had to. How else could one gauge their tastes, temperaments, and pocketbooks? They passed in and out of Brandeis' Bazaar, day after day, in an endless and varied procession – traveling men, school children, housewives, farmers, worried hostesses, newly married couples bent on house furnishing, business men.

She learned that it was the girls from the paper mills who bought the expensive plates – the ones with the red roses and green leaves hand-painted in great smears and costing two dollars and a half, while the golf club crowd selected for a gift or prize one of the little white plates with the faded-looking blue sprig pattern, costing thirty- nine cents. One day, after she had spent endless time and patience over the sale of a nondescript little plate to one of Winnebago's socially elect, she stared wrathfully after the retreating back of the trying customer.

'Did you see that? I spent an hour with her. One hour! I showed her everything from the imported Limoges bowls to the Sevres cups and saucers, and all she bought was that miserable little bonbon dish with the cornflower pattern. Cat!'

Mrs. Brandeis spoke from the depths of her wisdom.

'Fanny [. . .] it isn't only a matter of plates. It's a matter of understanding folks. When you've learned whom to show the expensive handpainted things to, and when to suggest quietly the little, vague things, with what you call the faded look, why, you've learned just about all there is to know of human nature . . .'

Fanny Herself · 1917

EMILY DICKINSON

I asked no other thing –
No other – was denied –
I offered Being – for it –
The Mighty Merchant sneered –

Brazil? He twirled a Button –
Without a glance my way –
'But – Madam – is there nothing else –
That We can show – Today?'

Poem 621 · *c.* 1890

ELISABETH WYNHAUSEN

The 'Manly' in the title of Wynhausen's memoir comes from the school she attended near Sydney, Australia.

That week, or the next, Dad started as a salesman at David Jones and, as soon as we dared, we dressed up to go to the David Jones emporium on George Street, in the city, just to see him at work. The department store was an enchanted realm that tempted all the senses. Aromatic smells from the food hall in the basement wafted through the ground floor. Packages mysterious with newness were piled up on the counters. Clasped firmly by the hand, Jules and I dug in by the elevator, never having seen its like before, and confirmed our astonishment in each other's faces as Mum hurried us off to the tie department.

'Look, look,' we whispered, unwilling to draw attention to ourselves, unsure how to contain the excitement of seeing Dad in so remote and significant a role, 'there he is . . .' He stood talking to an important-looking man who wore a white carnation in his buttonhole. We couldn't take our eyes off him, but Mum pretended to be a customer, holding up some ties until at last he saw us and came over. Worried about our getting him into trouble, I kept glancing around, but it was all right, because Mum appeared to be consulting him about a dark red tie, and we left in a minute or two without anyone having noticed.

On the way back along George Street, we were caught in the eddy of a crowd waiting for a tram . . .

'Ah, here is Paps . . .'

'We saw you at work, Papa,' I said.

'In there,' added Jules, wriggling around in Dad's arms to point. The interior of the department store was deserted. Dustsheets thrown over the counter shone white in the gloom.

My mother had glanced around at the sound of the post office clock. 'In fifteen minutes, the shops will all be dark and the streets will be empty.'

'Empty?' I said wonderingly. The crowd had flowed out around us.

'Completely empty . . .'

Manly Girls · 1989

DOROTHY DAVIS

It was in the smart shops of Cheapside that the practice grew up of having the tradesmen's wives sitting in seats 'built-a-purpose' at the doors of the shops to engage passers-by in conversation and entice them into making purchases . . . These talkative ladies developed a famous line in badinage with the men-about-town who idled up and down that length of street and showed off to their friends by allowing themselves to be teased into making extravagant bargains. The wit and beauty of these Cheapside wives became something of a legend.

A History of Shopping · 1966

WILLA CATHER

Across the river stretched the level land like the top of an oven. It was a country flat and featureless, without tones or shadows, without accent or emphasis of any kind to break its vast monotony. It was a scene done entirely in high lights, without relief, without a single commanding eminence to rest the eye upon. The flat plains rolled to the unbroken horizon vacant and void, forever reaching in empty yearning toward something they never attained . . .

Near the river was a solitary frame building, low and wide, with a high sham front, like most stores in Kansas villages. Over the door was painted in faded letters, 'Josiah Bywaters, Dry Goods, Groceries and Notions'. In front of the store ran a straight strip of ground, grass grown and weedy, which looked as if it might once have been a road. Here and there, on either side of this deserted way of traffic, were half demolished buildings and excavations where the weeds grew high, which might once have been the sites of houses. For this was once El Dorado, the Queen City of the Plains, the Metropolis of Western Kansas, the coming Commercial Centre of the West.

Whatever may have been there once, now there were only those empty, windowless buildings, that one little store, and the lonely old man whose name was painted over the door. Inside the store, on a chair tilted back against the counter, with his pipe in his mouth and a big gray cat on his knee, sat the proprietor. His appearance was not that of the average citizen of western Kansas, and a very little of his conversation told you that he had come from civilization somewhere. He was tall and straight, with an almost military bearing, and an iron jaw. He was thin, but perhaps that was due to his diet. His cat was thin, too, and that was surely owing to its diet, which consisted solely of crackers and water, except when now and then it could catch a gopher; and Solomon valley gophers are so thin that they never tempt the ambition of any discerning cat. If Colonel Bywaters's manner of living had anything to do with his attenuation, it was the solitude rather than any other hardship that was responsible. He was a sort of 'Last Man'. The tide of emigration had gone out and had left him high and dry, stranded on a Kansas bluff. He was living where the rattlesnakes and sunflowers found it difficult to exist . . .

He rose at six, as he had always done, ate his meagre breakfast and swept out his store, arranged his faded calicoes and fly-specked fruit cans in the window, and then sat down to wait. Generally he waited until bedtime. In three years he had not sold fifty dollars' worth. Men were almost unknown beings in that region, and men with money were utterly so. When the town broke up, a few of the inhabitants had tried to farm a little, – tried until they had no grain to sow and no horses to plough and no money to get away with. They were dead, most of them. The only human faces the Colonel ever saw were the starved, bronzed countenances of the poor fellows who sometimes passed in wagons, plodding along with their wives and children and cook stoves and feather beds, trying to get back to 'God's country'. They never bought anything; they only stopped to water their horses and swear a little, and then drove slowly eastward. Once a little girl had cried so bitterly for the red stick candy in the window that her father had taken the last nickel out of his worn, flat pocketbook. But the Colonel was too kind a man to take his money, so he gave the child the money and the candy, too; and he also gave her a little pair of red mittens that the moths had got into, which last she accepted gratefully, though it was August.

'El Dorado: A Kansas Recessional' · 1901

LADY DUFF GORDON, 'LUCILE'

Lady Duff Gordon survived the sinking of the Titanic, the scandal of sister Elinor Glyn's 'racy' novels, and her own 1888 divorce. In 1894 she set up a dressmaking establishment on Old Burlington Street, and from 1910 to 1922 she wrote a syndicated fashion page for the Hearst Newspapers. Maison Lucile became world famous and Lady Duff Gordon enormously wealthy, but she died in straitened circumstances after the collapse of her business.

I was particularly anxious to have a department for beautiful underclothes, as I hated the thought of my creations being worn over the ugly nun's veiling or linen-cum-Swiss embroidery which was all that the really virtuous woman of those days permitted herself. With the arrogance which success was beginning to give me I vowed to change all that, and made plans for the day of chiffons and laces, of boudoir caps and transparent nightdresses.

So I started making underclothes as delicate as cobwebs and as beautifully tinted as flowers, and half the women in London flocked to see them, though they had not the courage to buy them at first. Those cunning little lace motifs let in just over the heart, those saucy velvet bows on the shoulder might surely be the weapons of the woman who was 'not quite nice'? But slowly one by one they slunk into the shop in a rather shame-faced way and departed carrying an inconspicuous parcel, which contained a crepe-de-chine or a chiffon petticoat, and although one or two returned to bring the new purchases back because a Victorian husband had 'put his foot down', the majority came back to order more.

Discretions and Indiscretions · 1932

ANONYMOUS

Women were beginning to read newspapers in the 19th century,
and Miss Caley was one of the first shopkeepers to take advantage
of this by placing an advert in her local paper. Her husband later
adopted his wife's business name.

M. Caley, Milliner, Dress-Maker & Haberdasher, late of Thames Street Windsor, begs leave to inform the Ladies of Windsor, Eton, and their Environs, that the above business will in future be carried on in Castle-street, in conjunction with her Sister, Mrs Noke. M.C. takes this Opportunity of returning the most grateful Thanks for the numerous and distinguished Favours hitherto so liberally conferred: and (jointly with her Sister) most respectfully solicits a Continuance of the same.

Windsor and Eton Express · October 1813

ANNETTE AUSTIN

Many women derive much the same sensation from being a party to a business transaction as a child gets out of masquerading in grown-up's clothes – a sense of being mysteriously exalted into a sphere of dignity where they don't belong, and where all their attempts to sustain the role will be looked upon with loving indulgence . . .

Now, the department stores have every reason in the world to cater to the trade of women. The manufacture and sale of clothing and household goods occupies five-sixths of the working population of the world. The buyer, the consumer of all this production, is the woman.

The remark of an official of one of the large Broadway department stores of New York, that women buy five-sixths of what they see and one-sixth of what they want, explains in a nutshell the reason that the trade can afford to put up with the peculiarities of women, as long as they show a disposition to fall victims to the gorgeousness of their displays . . .

'Woman is a tremendous factor in trade today,' declared a member of a New York firm which caters to the most refined trade among women. 'And we have in our business to take into consideration all her whims, as well as her likes and dislikes. We have made a deep study of all this and our policy of regarding the customer as always right, no matter how wrong she may be in any transaction in the store, is the principle that builds up the trade. She is wrong, of course, lots of times. She takes advantage of privileges accorded her; she is inconsiderate of the earnest efforts of sales people; she causes delay and loss through carelessness or ignorance, but it all goes down in the budget of expenses for running the store and is covered, like other expenses, in the price of the goods.' . . .

It is the 'lady' shopper who offends. The poor woman goes to a store only when she actually means to buy something she needs. She goes in a hurry, and even if the thing she sees is not just what she wants, she will 'make it do,' somehow. But the woman of leisure and pocket money shops for the pleasure of shopping. Shopping in this sense requires neither cash nor credit, only eyes and hands and – a large Chicago house asserts – a natural disposition to annoy. It is the shopper with time to spare or to burn who trails critically around the counters, haggling for a bargain or seeking to bully the store into giving her something for nothing.

A typical instance of this sort of abuse is related by a Sixth Avenue store, whose custom is among the millionaires as well as the masses. . . . 'Not long ago [said the manager of the store], a lady – one of our wealthy customers, by the way – came in here and purchased a necklace, just before starting on a trip down South to visit her relatives. She had the necklace altered to fit her neck and bought it with the express understanding that it could not be exchanged. Two months later she returned with the necklace, which, she said, had not reached her house until after her departure, and she wanted it credited. The necklace bore unmistakable signs of wear. She denied this stoutly, became highly indignant that we should doubt her word, shrilly declared that she would take her custom away from the store if we refused to receive it back and, in the end, won her point. She probably thinks to this day that we do not know she wore the necklace; or she takes a pride in having been able to bully the store into compliance. That woman would probably repudiate fiercely the insinuation that she would steal.

'There are well-known types of people who try to impose upon the stores,' continued this manager. 'There is, for instance, the woman whose baby has outgrown its crib – and she wants the crib "exchanged." She is not at all an uncommon visitor. There was even a woman in here recently who wanted her baby's carriage robe taken back because the baby was "in heaven now and didn't need a robe" – that's the literal truth! She employed the same tactics as the lady of the necklace, vowed she'd never spend another cent in the store if we didn't give her the money back on that blanket. What did we do with her? Why, our clever saleswoman finally persuaded her that it would be a more worthy action – one favorable in the sight of heaven – if she would give the robe to some little poor baby in memory of her own. And she did.

'The lady who has won a prize at a card party and comes in to get the cash on it is another well-known character. Sometimes, it is a Christmas gift or a birthday present, and I've even known them to want the cash on a wedding present.'

The loss resultant on returned goods in this store was estimated, so the manager said, at twenty-five per cent of the day's sales.

'When Woman Buys' · 1909

SONIA KEPPEL

The personality of Mr Reville always intrigued me as, apart from being an expert dress designer, he was also an expert on Chinese art. As one came into the shop, a large part of the left side of it was divided off by curtains, sumptuously embroidered with Chinese dragons, behind which one had an occasional tantalizing glimpse of a large gilt Buddha and walls draped in black. Wild rumour had it that, behind the Buddha, Mr Reville had an opium den and Mamma told me never to accept an invitation from him to go behind the curtains.

Edwardian Daughter · 1958

MRS M.E. BRADDON

Mr Dowden's hot-houses were the draper's chief pride. He had more glass than his partner Plowden, and prettier daughters; but the Plowdens, who lived in Bayswater, gave themselves more airs, and cultivated professional society. The Plowdens revolved in a circle of other shop-keepers and their families, keeping company with jewellery and fur, with silver and plated goods, with books and stationery, but not with butcher's meat, pastry, or poultry; and in this commercial circle there had sparkled occasional stars from the professional sphere – a barrister not over-proud, a genial young doctor, a journalist, something of a Bohemian, whose wit had kept the Clapham table in a roar.

The Rose of Life · 1905

MARGARETE BÖHME

Department stores were thrillingly new at the beginning of the twentieth century, and staff were still learning how to cope with the masses swarming through their cavernous halls. This soapy novel predates Fritz Lang's 1927 film Metropolis *but shares some of its feverish mood. In the tragic conclusion to the following scene, a shoplifter commits suicide in the store after being apprehended – and an employee scam is uncovered.*

The almost daily apparition of Fraülein Iversen in Müllenmeister's shop struck the employees, but they did not long puzzle over it . . . people scarcely noticed her presence. In her dun-coloured, cheap gown, with the dark sailor hat and withered face beneath it, she was just 'somebody or other' to be seen, forgotten, and seen again unrecognized the next moment.

To-day she was strolling languidly, like someone who has

much time to look and little money to spend, by the counters, now and again standing still to examine the wares and then wandering further. Her rather dull grey eyes were following furtively but attentively a stout dark-haired woman, who was moving along unconcernedly between the tables towards the silk department. At one moment, Iversen collided, accidentally as it seemed with an elderly man, apparently belonging to the lower middle class. He murmured an apology and hastened by. Only a very shrewd and close observer could have seen that, in the chance encounter, he moved his lips, and exchanged a quick, significant glance with Iversen. She went quietly onwards. Nobody noticed her inward excitement . . . She had now been for nearly five months in the secret service of the firm, and had not yet succeeded in furnishing a proof of her qualifications for the new post.

What she had at first done reluctantly in obedience to her urgent need, had gradually become a kind of passion. The at first detested tracking and spying, listening and watching, had slowly, to her own surprise, grown to be second nature; she no longer thought there was anything 'unfair' in it. The instincts of the blood-hound had wakened in her, and now she was following with eager zest the long-sought trail she had at last scented.

The Department Store · 1912

MARY LOU QUINLAN

Quinlan is a well-known brand consultant in the United States.

[W]ith higher-ticket, longer-term decisions such as cars, durable goods, and financial services, women determine whether they have a trusting relationship with the seller. With apparel and household needs, however, women want results more than a relationship. They are in too much of a hurry for the obligations of a relationship . . .

[But] women . . . get annoyed when the shopping experience is purely transactional. For instance, with high-end skin care, women said that they expected the beauty advisor at the counter to 'put the product on my face – that personal touch is what I'm paying for' . . .

- *Make a good impression; she is watching.* Remember that women are paying attention to every detail and nuance of your store, even when they are in a stressed-out hurry. Women have amazing peripheral audio and visual abilities. Call it eavesdropping. Call it spying. But know that it is happening, and clean up your act . . .

- *When she is ready to check out, she is already checked out –* *hurry!* Once a woman has given you her precious time, her first thought is the lengthy to-do list that is constantly scrolling in her head. She has somewhere else to go, and you tarnish a great in-store shopping experience if you ruin the checkout moment . . . She did her job by shopping. Now it is your turn.

Just Ask a Woman: Cracking the Code of What Women Want
and How They Buy · 2003

LISTS

MARGARET PASTON

The medieval housewife Margaret Paston wrote to her husband
John from Norwich, asking him to buy things for her in London and
giving him very precise instructions. Another of her letters is just as
exacting about fabric prices and the fit of her wooden pattens, or
shoes.

I pray that you will . . . buy some frieze to make your child's
gowns. You shall have best cheap and best choice of Huy's
wife as it is told me. And that you will buy a yard of broad-
cloth of black for an hood for me at 3/8 or 4/- a yard, for there
is neither good cloth nor good frieze in this town.

*

[B]uy me three yards of purple schamlet price to the yard 4/-; a
bonnet of deep murrey, price 2/4; a hose-cloth of yellow carsey
of an ell, I trow it will cost 2/-; a girdle of plunket ribbon,
price 6d.; 4 laces of silk, two of one colour, and two of another,
price 8d.; 3 dozen points with red and yellow, price 6d.; three
pair of pattens . . . I was wont to pay but 2½d. for a pair, but I
pray you let them not be left behind though I pay more. They
must be low pattens; let them be long enough and broad upon
the heel.

The Paston Letters · 1400s

SUSANNAH TOWSEY

Sisters Susannah and Elizabeth Towsey ran a millinery and
haberdashery shop in Chester which became Browns and Chester
when Susannah married Mr Brown, a druggist. The sisters
carefully chose their stock from City wholesalers because of the
prestige of London and Paris fashions. The following were

Susannah's instructions to her forewoman for the first day of a visit
to London.

In the first place call at Steward Spavold and Smiths, where
settle our accounts and look at modes of all sorts, at the
white silk, the blue and green. Do not buy any. Ask if they
have any black . . . coat, as had last at 62s. Then go to Harris
and Penny, pay their bill, and just look at what kind of fancy
gloves they have to sell. Tell them that the gloves they called
maid were most of them small girls, that they were too dear,
that as their account was a small one it had indeed been
almost forgot, that I had advised Weatherall people we
should draw them in favour of Harris and Co., but in hurry of
business we had quite forgot it. Next place you may call at
Moores, or not, as you will have a good deal to do and the
morning will be pretty far advanced. You may then go to
Bread Street. Just call in at Adams, and if they have any
pretty fancy ribbons, pick out a few. Get the bill made out
and take it with you to Drury's which is just by there. Perhaps
they may not have sent out the goods last ordered. Get to
look at the order whether they have or not, and you will be
able to judge what is wanted of those kind of things. And be
sure to get some white souflee or tippets as we have some
bespoke for next week. If they have none done, as I do not
suppose they have, they may perhaps let you have a yard or
two of some that may be done for other customers, which we
shall be obliged if they will let us have. A small quantity
must be had at any rate to send on Wednesday.

You may call at Tibets and see if there is anything particularly pretty in the ribbon way there. As Barton and Simpson
live in the same street call and balance their account, then go
to Price and Cook who live in the same street, balance their

account, look over their gloves, ask the prices of different sorts. If there is anything particularly nice you may look them out and order them to Drury's as the parcel from there will not be a large one . . .

Go either to Tooly Street or Will Weaver, which is most convenient, where I fancy you will be glad to rest.

Letter from Susannah Towsey to her forewoman · *c.* 1780s

SUE TOWNSEND

Sue Townsend once worked as a shop assistant, but found fame with her hilarious Adrian Mole diaries.

Wednesday September 9th
Grandma phoned, she has found out about Doreen and Maxwell going to Skegness. She is never speaking to my father again.

Here is my shopping list:

Blazer	£29.99
2 pairs grey trousers	£23.98
2 white shirts	£11.98
2 grey pullovers	£7.98
3 pairs black socks	£2.37
1 pair PE shorts	£4.99
1 PE vest	£3.99
1 track suit	£11.99
1 pair training shoes	£7.99
1 pair football boots and studs	£11.99
1 pair football socks	£2.99
Football shorts	£4.99
Football shirt	£7.99
Adidas sports bag	£4.99

1 pair black shoes	£15.99
1 calculator	£6.99
Pen and pencil set	£3.99
Geometry set	£2.99

My father can easily spare a hundred pounds. His redundancy payment must have been huge, so why he is lying on his bed moaning I don't know. He is just a mean skinflint! He hasn't paid with *real* money anyway! He used his American Express card.

Pandora admired me in my new uniform. She says she thinks I stand a good chance of being made a prefect.

The Secret Diary of Adrian Mole, Aged 13¾ · 1985

ANNA ADAMS

All pocket archaeologists
    digging for railcards, coins and keys,
find superseded shopping lists:
    torn shards of petty histories.

In shorthand jottings, all of life
    is hinted at on strips of scrap:
rye bread, red wine (all drunk), minced beef,
    pig-liver for the cat (now dead, poor chap).

Go to the bank: pay in, draw out;
    Greengrocer: beansprouts, fruit, courgettes;
Fish Barrow: mackerel or trout;
    a dozen eggs for omelettes.

Cornfields come with the brown bread rolls,
    orchards with apples, and the sea

heaves, vast, around the herring shoals,
    and China swims in Lapsang Souchong tea.

Wine glasses, green, recycled ones,
    potscourer, Persil, margarine—
implying fields of petalled suns,
    great crowds of holy fellahin.

Post Office, pension, porridge-oats;
    pay garage bill, buy *Radio Times*—
implying music, (storms of notes),
    and News of ghastly human crimes.

These cancelled litanies of stuff
    consumed, excreted, day by day,
can never say the word 'Enough'
    though they suggest futility,

but, join the dots, they sketch a place
    and time, with dreams that come and go,
now passed to endless outer space—
    digested days that nourish Now.

'Shopping Lists' · 1996

ELIZABETH PUREFOY

May the 1st 1737
I am forced to give Mr. Robotham this trouble, having been
called upon for some Quit Rent which is to be paid in
Cummin seed – so pray send me seven pound of Cummin
seed done up in single pounds; you are to have it at the
Drugsters. Send it with the rest of the things and let us
know the newest fashioned hats the ladies wear. My son

and self join in our service to you and Mrs. Robotham and
I am

Your humble friend
Elizabeth Purefoy

To Mrs. Price senior
   at Whitfield
   February 8th 1743

This desires Mr. Belchier to send mee a round neat light
mahogany folding table with four legs, two of them to draw out
to hold up the folds. It must be four foot two inches wide.
Send it (with the price thereof) by Mr. Zachary Meads the
Bucks carrier who sets out of London on Monday nights and
Friday nights. This will oblige

Your humble servant
Elizabeth Purefoy

P.S. My son's service waits on you. Pray a letter by post when
you send it.

   for Mr Belchier
      A cabinet maker at the Sun. The
      South Side of St. Paul's in St. Paul's
      Churchyard, London.

The Purefoy Letters · 1737, 1743

ISABELLA D'ESTE

*Isabella d'Este was famous for indulging her whims, regardless
of cost, and the first of the letters below from the seventeen-year-old
Marchioness of Mantua was addressed to a member of the court at
Ferrara as he prepared to go to France. Somewhat later, in 1496,
Isabella wrote to a Mantuan in Venice to order some fabric.*

To Girolamo Zigliolo

I am sending you a hundred ducats and wish you to understand that you are not to return the money if any of it is left,
after buying the things that I want, but are to spend it in
buying some gold chain or anything else that is new and elegant. And if more is required, spend that too, for I had rather
be in your debt so long as you bring me the latest novelties.
But these are the kind of things that I wish to have –
engraved amethysts, rosaries of black, amber and gold, blue
cloth for a *camora*, black cloth for a mantle, such as shall be
without a rival in the world, even if it costs ten ducats a
yard; as long as it is of real excellence, never mind! If it is
only as good as those which I see other people wear, I had
rather be without it!

To Giorgio Brognolo

We wish to have six to eight *braccia* of Rhenish linen that is so
fine and beautiful that it is beyond comparison because we
already have a good quantity of the ordinary type. We wish you
to search all of the warehouses in Venice to find the most
beautiful and have it shown to your wife who will understand
these things better than you. If you cannot find this amount of
excellent material, send out a left-over scrap of two or three
braccia and do not spare the expense because even if it costs a
ducat a *braccia* we do not care.

Letters of Isabella d'Este · late 1400s – early 1500s

DOROTHY OSBORNE

*Dorothy Osborne and Sir William Temple fell in love when they
met in 1648. The dating of Osborne's letters is difficult to establish,
but the one below was probably written before they married.*

??Sunday
April 10th, 1653

Sir

When you go into the Exchange, pray call at the great shop above, 'The Flower Pott'. I spoke to Heams, the man of the shop, when I was in town, for a quart of orange-flower water; he had none that was good then, but promised to get me some. Pray put him in mind of it, and let him show it you before he sends it me, for I will not altogether trust to his honesty; you see I make no scruple of giving you little idle commissions, 'tis a freedom you allow me, and that I should be glad you would take. The Frenchman that set my seals lives between Salisbury House and the Exchange, at a house that was not finished when I was there, and the master of the shop, his name is Walker, he made me pay 50s. for three, but 'twas too dear . . .

Yrs.

1653

ALESSANDRA STROZZI

In the name of God.   8 May 1469

Fiammetta tells me I should tell you that she'd like to make herself a cloak of black Milanese twill, and that you should tell Lorenzo to buy it. She really needs it because it's not the season for wearing gowns with a hood, and [with such a hood] she'll be able to wear a lighter gown. You should arrange it so she can make it and have it soon, because it seems to me she needs it. Nothing more for now; may God keep you from harm. From your Allesandra Strozzi in Florence.

Letter from Alessandra Strozzi to her son Filippo · 1469

Sara Hutchinson

Mr Monkhouse, Mr Bush's – 29 Pudding Lane, London
Gallow Hill, nr Wykeham, Malton, Yorkshire
                                        8 Augt 1800

George will thank you to go immediately upon the receipt of this to Mr Idle's & purchase two Hats one is for him & the other for Mr Dickson – they must be handsome fashionable but not round tops and sent by the coach directed as you address your letters . . . You may either pay for the Hats or leave them for Mr R. Dickson to pay when he comes to Town or in any other way you may advise – I suppose Miss W. has left Town before this – she behaved very shabbily not to call here – if she did not bring Mary's Shakespear send it along with the Hats . . . I am Dr John yours affty S. Hutchinson.

I will thank you to purchase for me at your friend the Chip Hat house a Chip Hat or bonnet of the very *newest* fashion – I would have it cold *pea-green* else lilac I would prefer – a useful size that is one to shade the face but not too large as you know that would be out of proportion, but I have a small head . . . you can order it to be sent to the Idles who will pack it carefully up – mind no flowers or kick-shaws about it let it be very modest – not hemmd with Ribband or any thing but simply the Hat itself don't give an extravagant [price?] – I will repay you . . . for the Book when I return to S . . . with thanks. Don't be angry at the trouble we give you.

The Hats must be 23 inches round the outside of the crown.

Mr Monkhouse, Mr Bush's – Pudding Lane, London
Gallow Hill, Augt 23rd [1800]

My dr John,

I think it is almost necessary for me to pay the postage of my letters as I shall be an expensive correspondent to you if I contrive to write at this rate but as the hats are not arrived I am afraid we shall lose them without some enquiry is made after them – they might have been half a dozen times down from London since I wrote and I apprehend they are laying at York or Malton – I will therefore trouble you once more to enquire what coach they were sent by, to what Inn at York and the Innkeeper's name . . .

I have opened my Letter to say that should you not have got my last letter (which is rather improbable) that this will be a perfect riddle to you – I had desired you to send two Gentleman's hats fashionable & hansome but not round tops 22 inches round the outside of the crown to be bought of Mr Idle – one for Mr Dickson the other for George – a chip hat also for myself but as it is so late in the season it is of little consequence – you need not trouble yourself – the other hats you must forward immediately – one here the other to George at Stockton.

Miss Monkhouse, Hindwell, nr new Radnor
Grasmere, April 19th [1809]

My dear Mary

We are rejoiced to find that you are all so much pleased with Hindwell; but it is a sad tale that you tell about the maid Servants – I know not what you will do – I should be tempted to send you one if I could hear of one that was *unexceptionable* . . .

I have ordered your Pots – the crate will cost more than

£4 which our's did – because as I knew you would want every thing – I desired that 6, instead of 2, Ewers & Basons, 8, instead of 2, Chambers, & some more Jugs – and some Egg cups might be added – but they are cheaper than any common pots *bought at a pot shop* – as to the Churn I can do nothing for you – the one Mr Taylor recommended was Beetham's (*patent* Churn I believe) . . . Mr Taylor's only churn 12 lb – and a churn of that shape to churn nearly a firkin would be very awkward – I saw one advertized in the Courier yesterday; but it was a patent one also – & made only in Lancashire – J. Woods Ormskirk – 'It is worked by a lever with a weight & grit & performs more work wth it than 2 women in the same time without it' – but then they give no account *how* it is worked – & what is very suspicious he offers to sell the right of making them for 5 Gs & has many on hand price £2. 12. 6. – What kind of Churns are used in the Country? . . . The nicest model of a churn I ever saw was in 'Barrow's account of the interior of Africa' . . .

>   *Thomas Monkhouse Esqre, Budge Row, London*
>   *Sunday Eveng [16 May, 1813]*

My dear Cousin
[William Wordsworth] is now returned and it is determined that a Turkey carpet must be had for the dining-room – the dimensions of which are 19.4 by 13.4 – The proper measurement for the Study Carpet, which room is to serve also for drawing room, you will find on the other side. This *you say* must be Brussels – we should be very well contented with the old-fashioned Wilton, if it is to be had at a cheaper rate – only we must confine you to colour and pattern – the pattern to be as *small as possible* without regarding the fashion; and the colour to be of drabs, and a light yellow; which last is the

colour of the window hangings. I have also a commission for Mary Addison in connection with this last part of my direction to you in which she will be greatly assisted by your procuring her a patch of the carpet for the study. We are quite ashamed to give you such troublesome jobs – but we hope you will sometime have the satisfaction of seeing how smart you have made us – But nature has done more for us than we can all do – for surely this is the most beautiful and gay place you ever beheld. I wish you could at this moment behold the splendor of Winandermere which lies before my eyes illuminated by the setting sun with the lovely green veil of Ambleside between us and it. – But I have forgotten part of my commission which was that you would be so good as buy for William 2 pair of Pantaloons, of the knit kind, – such as you got him before when he was in Town – one grey & the other drab. The money for all these things including Mary Addison's you must get at Staple Inn to be placed to account.

Kendal Penny Post
My 19, 1813

My dear Mary
I leave it to T[om] M. to make my apologies for troubling you with a commission – which is to procure me 5 shades of drab rug worsted from the darkest drab nearly black to white included – 2 pounds of each shade; and 6 pounds of a *lightest* bright yellow. T.M. has to get a Carpet with these colours in & he will perhaps be able to shew you the colour. Also 16 yards of Canvas not coarse rug canvas neither the finest kind used for Tent Stitch but proper for cross stitch rather open.

Our best remembrances to your Mother Aunt and all your brothers. God bless you very truly. Your's S.H.

Letters · c. 1800, 1809, 1813

ANGELA BANNER

*If you try shopping online for the delightful Ant and Bee series of
1960s children's books, you will find some editions now priced at
over $1,000 because the publisher doesn't think they're worth
keeping in print.*

One day Ant and Bee had to make a shopping list *because Ant
and Bee had asked Kind Dog to come to supper*! Ant and Bee wrote
their shopping list on a piece of paper that was square and flat.
Ant and Bee cut the square and flat piece of paper into two
pieces. Then Ant had half of the square and flat piece of shopping list. And Bee had half of the square and flat piece of
shopping list. Ant and Bee said they would buy ONLY what was
written on their shopping list: Apple Pie, Grapes, Nuts, Ball (for
Kind Dog), Cake, Bananas, Crisps, Biscuit bone (for Kind Dog).

Then Ant and Bee went to their money banks. Ant had a
money bank that was square and fat. Bee had a money bank
that was round and fat. Ant took five round and flat money
coins out of his square and fat money bank. Bee took five
round and flat money coins out of his round and fat money
bank. Then Ant and Bee put the two halves of the square and
flat shopping list inside their shopping basket. The basket had
a balloon that was round and fat. Then OFF flew Ant and Bee
to the shops!

Suddenly! Ant and Bee saw a NEW shop! The shop was
square and round and fat and flat!!!! Before Ant and Bee went
inside the shop <u>Bee told Ant that they must buy only what was
written on their shopping list</u> because . . . Bee told Ant that
they only had enough money to buy what was written on
their shopping list. BUT Ant tried to buy things that were
not on his shopping list . . . SO Bee told Ant to put all his
wrong shopping back at once!

Then Ant did all the shopping that was written on his piece of shopping list: an apple pie, grapes, nuts, a ball for Kind Dog. Most of the things that Ant bought were round. Then Bee did all the shopping that was written on his piece of shopping list: a cake, bananas, crisps, a biscuit bone for Kind Dog. All the things that Bee bought were *different* shapes! And all the things that Ant and Bee bought . . . cost Ant and Bee all this money! Ant and Bee had spent nine round and flat money coins! The only money Ant and Bee had left was . . . one round and flat money coin!

Then Bee said they must spend their last round and flat money coin on a pink square shopping bag. But Ant said the pink square shopping bag was not as good as their old shopping basket. But Bee *wanted* the pink square shopping bag.

Ant said NO Bee said YES Ant said NO Bee said YES

Then Ant said YES. So Ant . . . and Bee bought the pink square shopping bag with their last round and fat money coin.

And then Ant and Bee put all their shopping inside the pink square shopping bag. Then Bee flew home . . . with Ant. BUT when Ant and Bee were home from shopping they saw that a most terrible thing had happened.

All the shopping was SQUASHED! Because the pink, square shopping bag was not so good for carrying shopping as the old shopping basket.

When Kind Dog came to supper Ant and Bee were still crying. So Kind Dog made Ant and Bee better. Then Kind Dog said they could have a nice supper party with *squashed food*! The squashed food looked very funny but Kind Dog said it tasted very nice!

After supper Kind Dog said something IMPORTANT. Kind

Dog asked Ant and Bee to go shopping with him the *next day*! Kind Dog said he wanted to give Ant and Bee a *happy* shopping time.

Ant and Bee said YES!

THE NEXT DAY Kind Dog came to take Ant and Bee out shopping. Kind Dog said the Zoo Man had given him ten round and flat money coins for them to spend! Kind Dog told Ant and Bee that they would buy CHOCOLATES and FRUIT and CAKES.

So Ant and Bee made a new shopping list on a new square and flat piece of paper. Ant and Bee cut the square and flat piece of paper into three pieces. Then Ant and Bee and Kind Dog each had a piece of shopping list. Then Kind Dog took Ant and Bee shopping . . . to the shop that Kind Dog liked best!

Bee told Ant that he must NOT buy things that were *not* on the shopping list . . . and Kind Dog said they must go and choose some cakes. There were so many cakes to choose from that Ant and Bee and Kind Dog all wanted *different* cakes. Ant chose a round and flat cake. Bee chose a square and fat cake. Kind Dog chose a round and square and fat and flat cake made for dogs!

Then Ant and Bee began to worry that their cakes would get squashed even in their shopping basket. But Kind Dog said the shop would pack their cakes into square and fat empty boxes *so that the cakes would not get squashed*. Then Ant and Bee and Kind Dog went to choose some fruit. *And Ant and Bee and Kind Dog all chose* . . . plums! And the shop packed up the plums into empty boxes *so that the plums would not get squashed*. Then Ant and Bee and Kind Dog went to choose some chocolates! Ant chose a chocolate mountain! Bee chose chocolate beans! Kind Dog chose a chocolate bone! And the shop packed up the chocolates into empty boxes *so that the chocolates would not get squashed.*

Ant and Bee and Kind Dog looked at the shopping list. CAKES ✓ FRUIT ✓ CHOCOLATES ✓ All the shopping was done! The shopping cost six round and flat money coins. There were four round and flat money coins left!

Suddenly! Kind Dog ran away with the four round and flat money coins!!!!

Then Ant and Bee asked the shop to send a message to Kind Dog . . . *that Ant and Bee were waiting in the Waiting Room.* BUT WHERE WAS KIND DOG?

Kind Dog was not in the part of the shop that sold BEDS. Kind Dog was not in the part of the shop that sold BOATS. Kind Dog was not in the part of the shop that sold BIRDS. BUT Kind Dog *was* in the part of the shop that sold BAR-GAINS.

Kind Dog came back to where Ant and Bee were waiting for him. And Kind Dog had spent the four round and flat money coins! . . . on two secret parcels!!!! Then Ant and Bee and Kind Dog went home.

AND NOTHING WAS SQUASHED.

Ant and Bee Go Shopping · 1961

FILLING THE LARDER

I'm guilty of buying too little food

1 carton milk
1 carton juice
1 half chicken
a little fruit and veg

Why can't you buy
for more than one day
at a time
my old man whines

Still blank as a zombie
I wander supermarket aisles

The chunky red odours
behind the cellophane
cannot revive
the spritely apples
the lady reluctantly urging samples

Between the bulge of the shelf
and the cast of my eye
between the nerve of my trolley
and the will of my mind
I'm always paralysed

'Shopping' · 1984

JUNG CHANG

Jung Chang tells the story of her family and the history of China in the twentieth century through three generations of women, the wild swans of her bestselling autobiography.

As Party officials, my parents also had special food coupons. I used to go with my grandmother to a special store outside the compound to buy food with them. My mother's coupons were blue. She was entitled to five eggs, almost an ounce of soybeans, and the same amount of sugar per month. My father's coupons were yellow. He was entitled to twice as much as my mother because of his higher rank. My family pooled the food from the canteens and the other sources and ate together. The adults always gave the children more, so I did not go hungry.

*

In 1959 a sort of black market had sprung up in Chengdu selling chickens and eggs. Because the communes had taken over chickens from individual peasants, and were incapable of raising them, chickens and eggs had disappeared from the shops, which were state owned. A few peasants had somehow managed to keep one or two chickens at home under their beds, and were now surreptitiously selling them and their eggs in the back alleys at about twenty times their previous price.

Wild Swans · 1991

MRS GASKELL

Gaskell's novels are full of shops and shopkeepers: in Cranford, *the principal shopkeeper ranges 'from grocer, to cheesemonger, to man-milliner', and claims that – like the 18th-century Towseys – he goes straight to London for the seasonal fashions exhibited in his High Street rooms.*

'Run, Mary dear, just round the corner, and get some fresh eggs at Tippin's (you may get one apiece, that will be fivepence), and see if he has any nice ham cut, that he would let us have a pound of.'

'Say two pounds, missis, and don't be stingy,' chimed in the husband.

'Well, a pound and a half, Mary. And get it Cumberland ham, for Wilson comes from there-away, and it will have a sort of relish of home with it he'll like, – and Mary' (seeing the lassie fain to be off), 'you must get a pennyworth of milk and a loaf of bread – mind you get it fresh and new – and, and – that's all, Mary.'

'No, it's not all,' said her husband. 'Thou must get six pennyworth of rum, to warm the tea; thou'll get it at the "Grapes."'

Mary Barton · 1903

BEATRIX POTTER

In this classic children's story, there is an alarming surprise for both host and hostess at tea.

Ribby put on her shawl and bonnet and went out again with a basket, to the village shop to buy a packet of tea, a pound of lump sugar, and a pot of marmalade . . .

Ribby went into the shop and bought what she required, and came out, after a pleasant gossip with Cousin Tabitha Twitchit.

Cousin Tabitha was disdainful afterwards in conversation—

'A little *dog* indeed! Just as if there were no CATS in Sawrey! And a *pie* for afternoon tea! The very idea!' said Cousin Tabitha Twitchit.

Ribby went on to Timothy Baker's and bought the muffins. Then she went home.

The Tale of the Pie and the Patty Pan · 1905

SOPHIE VON LA ROCHE

A pastry-cook's attracted our attention for some time, as it is surrounded, like a large spacious room, by glass cases, in which all kinds of preserved fruits and jellies are exhibited in handsome glass jars; in the middle of the shop, however, there stood a big table with a white cover containing pyramids of small pastries and tartlets and some larger pastries and sweetmeats; wine-glasses of all sizes, with lids to them, and full of liqueurs of every conceivable brand, colour and taste were attractively set out in between, as might be expected, at a large and very elegant table. What we women liked best of all though, was a large but delightful covering made of gauze, which hid nothing from view and at the same time kept the flies off. Indeed we promised ourselves a breakfast in this shop after our visit to Sir Ashton.

Sophie in London · 1786

SARAH FELL

From the Ulverston estate of her father, Judge Fell, Sarah sent to Ulverston's weekly market on Thursday or to Dalton's on Saturday, but for manufactured goods or luxuries she had to cast her net much wider, to Kendal or Lancaster. Her shopping list for a family member in London included a cask of wine 'for we have none, only some old cider and March beer bottled up. Also anchovies, olives, two larding needles, lemons, oranges and what else you think fit'.

June ye 25°. by m° pd for Ih of Salt her acct. 000 00 02
          by m° pd for 5½ li of swt buttr
          her acct 000 01 03
          by m° pd for Eggs her acct. 000 00 01
          by m° pd for strawberries her acct. . . . 000 00 04
          by m° pd for 8: chickens her acct 000 01 04
   26°.   by m° pd for Cinamon water to Jane Gregg
          for sistr Lower 000 02 06

The Household Account Book of Sarah Fell of Swarthmoor
Hall · 1674

KATHERINE MANSFIELD

J.M. Murry, or Jack, was Mansfield's husband. The second letter
refers to Ida Baker, a former schoolmate who became Mansfield's
devoted companion in later years.

To J. M. Murry   *11 January 1918*
In the morning when I opened the persiennes it was so lovely
outside, I stayed in bed till lunch. *Ma grande malle* really did
turn up. Then I got up, and after lunch went into the town . . .
The tabac woman did not know me and had no tobacco.
Nobody remembered me at all. I bought writing things and a
few bull's-eyes – about a penny for two, they were – and suddenly I met Ma'am Gamel . . . I went with her to the shop
which is just the same and saw the old mother who was most
tender about you. I bought a tiny pot of cherry jam and came
home . . .

12 October 1919
On her last but one journey to San Remo she bought *one*
hecto of coffee for 4.50 from '*such* a funny little shop' and

when I protested she thought 'the parcel was small for the money, but the beans felt very tightly packed'.

Letters and Journals · 1918, 1919

Anonymous

An unnamed journalist kept a written record for three months following the Soviet invasion of Berlin.

Sunday, 22 April 1945

They're handing out what are officially called advance rations – meat, sausage, processed foods, sugar, canned goods and ersatz coffee. I took my place in line and waited in the rain for two hours before finally getting 250 grams of coarse-ground grain, 250 grams of oatmeal, 2 pounds of sugar, 100 grams of coffee substitute and a can of kohlrabi. There still isn't any meat or sausage or real coffee. A crowd is milling about the corner butcher's, an endless queue on both sides, people standing four abreast in the pouring rain. What a mess!

Monday, 23 April, 1945

People are still taking care of business. Just before the shops closed I managed to get another 150 grams of coarse grain. Suddenly I heard excited screams around the corner, and the sound of running feet: a wagon was being unloaded near Bolle's, barrels of butter – all rancid – were being carried into the building for distribution. One pound per person, and – here's what's frightening – for free! All you have to do is get your card stamped. Is this the first sign of panic or is it the voice of reason speaking from beyond the bureaucratic files?

Tuesday, 24 April 1945

No news. We're completely cut off. Some gas but no water. Looking out of the window I see throngs of people outside the stores. They're still fighting over the rancid butter – they're still giving it away, but now it's down to a quarter of a pound per ration card. The Schutzpolizei are just now getting things under control – I see four of them. And on top of that it's raining.

At the moment I'm sitting on the window seat in the widow's apartment. She just stormed in, all worked up. A shell hit outside Hefter's meat market, right in the middle of the queue. Three dead and ten wounded, but they're already queuing up again. The widow demonstrated how people were using their sleeves to wipe the blood off their meat coupons . . .

Still, I'm astounded at how the sight of a few beef quarters and hog jowls is enough to get the frailest grandmother to hold her ground. The same people who used to run for shelter if three fighter planes were spotted somewhere over central Germany are now standing in the meat line as solid as walls. At most they'll plop a bucket on their head or perhaps a helmet. Queuing is a family business, with every member on shift for a couple of hours before being relieved. But the line for meat is too long for me; I'm not yet ready to give it a go. Besides, meat has to be eaten right away; it won't keep for more than a meal. I think they're all dreaming of eating their fill one last time, a final meal before the execution.

Thursday, 26 April, 1945
[T]he two of us go off to see whether there's any pudding powder left at the corner store that was hit yesterday. It turns out there are still a few customers, and yes, they're still selling. There's a price printed on the powder – 38 pfennigs, I think. The person selling, who also owns the store and lives right there, insisted on giving every customer exact change, so he kept running up and down the queue asking

who had small coins and could help him. And that while under fire! Only here. We'll be counting our change right into the grave.

A Woman in Berlin · 1954

AN INTERVIEW WITH A LANCASHIRE GIRL

I think dole money was about 27s. 6d. for the family. I do not know how much [my father] got for Lloyd George [sickness benefit]. Rent was 7s. 6d. a week . . . Food was largely bread and potatoes . . . Once a week mother queued at the butcher and came home if lucky with two-pennyworth of bacon bones, and made pea-soup for midday for all six. Eaten with or without bread. Hotpot and potato pie were favourite dishes . . . The chief difference between then and now [1968] is that one looked at every penny before spending it, and decided what was really essential. Milk was delivered in a churn in a horse-trap, and ladled out of the churn into a jug with a measure. The housewife had to go out to the cart every morning and buy as much as she needed, rather than leave a standing order . . . Newspaper was a favourite wrapping, and nothing was sealed. Sugar and flour were sold loose from the sacks. Butter was cut off a huge piece (56 lbs) and slapped with butter pats. Lard also came in bulk. Shopping was slow as everything had to be weighed.

English Homes and Housekeeping · 1920s

FAITH POPCORN

In 1991 Faith Popcorn, a trend forecaster, published her thoughts on the future of a variety of consumer practices. Today the book can be read as an economist's 1984 – though with less perspicacity.

COCOONING

Is there anything about the supermarket industry that brings to mind the serenity of the cocoon? No. People would rather be at home. The daunting size and glaring lights, not to mention the clash of shopping chariots, make supermarkets about as far from the cocoon as you can get. Off-trend.

FANTASY ADVENTURE

Food is one of the all-time great fantasy adventures, but supermarkets kill the fantasy. The average American supermarket has no excitement beyond the occasional chip-and-dip sampling table or parking lot clown; there's no sensuality or magic. Supermarkets are mundane. Off-trend.

SMALL INDULGENCES

You may be able to *find* some here, but the supermarket itself is hardly a Small Indulgence. More like a Big Burden. You deserve a trip to the supermarket today? Hardly. Off-trend.

EGONOMICS

What's personal about a supermarket? By definition, it's a mass market. You join the nameless, exhausted hordes wading through an endless array of products. There's very little service: no babysitting, no one to help, no recognition of your individual needs.

LIVES

Will we ever really trust those electronic-eye code-reading checkouts? Supermarket shopping is a hassle, right down to the exhausting ritual of wheeling your cart to your car, unloading it alone, then struggling back to return the cart (or just driving off). (Not to mention *urban* supermarkets, where, unless your store delivers, you buy only as much as you can carry.) Supermarkets could be so *on-trend*. But they are off-trend.

The Popcorn Report · 1991

ELIZABETH PUREFOY

Mr Willson,   6 February
1747
I desire you will send mee
One pound of the best Bohea Tea
Half a pound of the best Green Tea
Two pounds of the best Coffeeberries
A quarter of a pound of nutmegs
Two ounces of mace
A quarter of an hundred of the best treble refined loaf sugar
A quarter of an hundred of Household sugar about 6 pence a
pound
Half a quarter of an hundred of Rice

Send these by ye Buckingham carrier . . . send your Bill with
them and will order you payment. The last Bohea tea was so
ordinary I could not drink it, my neighbours had as good for six
shillings a pound. The last hundredweight of Raisins you send
were so bad they spoiled the Liquor they were made on. I hope
you will send no more bad Goods, I have had no reason to
complain until now, tho' I have dealt at yr shop these forty
years and am
                              Your humble serft

                                                              E.P.
P.S. If you can't conveniently send them on Tuesday Mr Jones
ye carrier sets out of London on Saturday mornings early.
                              The Purefoy Letters · 1747

JO SHAPCOTT

I approved of it heartily, the multiway underwired bra
from the Pearls Collection in lots of nonstandard sizes.
I took it to try. Next groceries, and maybe a plant or two,

something green and exotic enough to refresh my system,
to help me imagine the place off-shore
where I recently stashed my savings. You could
exchange it too, the multiway bra, if it didn't fit:
a serious life or time consideration. I am mostly
vegetarian and skitter up the supermarket aisles
pursuing my health. What goes in that basket is
   important.
I like it to be from the country, something that had a
   green
and happy life once, that knew hope and had a generous
and juicy nature. You can't make deals with your stomach
about the future. I try to avoid this craze and that craze
but if you're going to delay death and stay in your prime
week in and week out you have to make the hard choices
of the supermarket. Salivating over the loin chops
in the freezer and still passing by equates with goodness·
or at least good sense which is the nearest we can get to it
at this time, halving the odds on immediate decay,
   keeping
a firm straight back well into middle age, the signal
that you want something badly or want something badly
   not
to happen, because should it happen you're never ready
these days, days of oils, marks and time.

'Shopping' · 1992

BOOK-BUYING

CHARLOTTE BRONTË

The next day was the first of March, and when I awoke, rose, and opened my curtain, I saw the risen sun struggling through fog. Above my head, above the house-tops, co-elevate almost with the clouds, I saw a solemn, orbed mass, dark blue and dim – THE DOME. While I looked, my inner self moved; my spirit shook its always-fettered wings half loose; I had a sudden feeling as if I, who never yet truly lived, were at last about to taste life. In that morning my soul grew as fast as Jonah's gourd . . .

The street on which my little sitting-room window looked was narrow, perfectly quiet, and not dirty: the few passengers were just such as one sees in provincial towns: here was nothing formidable; I felt sure I might venture out alone. Having breakfasted, out I went. Elation and pleasure were in my heart: to walk alone in London seemed of itself an adventure. Presently I found myself in Paternoster Row – classic ground this. I entered a bookseller's shop, kept by one Jones: I bought a little book – a piece of extravagance I could ill afford; but I thought I would one day give or send it to Mrs. Barrett. Mr. Jones, a dried-in man of business, stood behind his desk: he seemed one of the greatest, and I one of the happiest of beings.

Villette · 1853

HELENE HANFF

Helene Hanff began a twenty-year correspondence with the staff of a London bookshop when she wrote from New York looking for second-hand volumes in 1949. Despite her best intentions, she never managed to visit before the shop closed down; the second letter from her actress friend describes it to her.

14 East 95th St.
New York City
October 5, 1949

Marks & Co.
84, Charing Cross Road
London, W.C. 2
England

Gentlemen:

Your ad in the <u>Saturday Review of Literature</u> says that you specialize in out-of-print books. The phrase 'antiquarian book-sellers' scares me somewhat, as I equate 'antique' with expensive. I am a poor writer with an antiquarian taste in books and all the things I want are impossible to get over here except in very expensive rare editions, or in Barnes & Noble's grimy, marked-up schoolboy copies.

I enclose a list of my most pressing problems. If you have clean secondhand copies of any of the books on the list, for no more than $5.00 each, will you consider this a purchase order and send them to me?

Very truly yours,
Helene Hanff
(Miss) Helene Hanff

*

Backstage
London
September 10, 1951

Dearheart—

It is the loveliest old shop straight out of Dickens, you would go absolutely out of your mind over it.

There are stalls outside and I stopped and leafed through a few things just to establish myself as a browser before wandering in. It's dim inside, you smell the shop before you see it, it's a lovely smell, I can't articulate it easily, but it combines must and dust and age, and walls of wood and floors of wood. Toward the back of the shop at the left there's a desk with a work-lamp on it, a man was sitting there, he was about fifty with a Hogarth nose, he looked up and said 'Good afternoon?' in a North Country accent and I said I just wanted to browse and he said please do.

The shelves go on forever. They go up to the ceiling and they're very old and kind of grey, like old oak that has absorbed so much dust over the years they no longer are their true color. There's a print section, or rather a long print table, with Cruikshank and Rackham and Spy and all those old wonderful English caricaturists and illustrators that I'm not smart enough to know a lot about, and there are some lovely, old, old illustrated magazines . . .

Love,
Maxine

84, Charing Cross Road · 1970

NANCY MITFORD

Another of the Mitfords, Debo, wrote to her sister Diana while she was in jail because of her fascist sympathies during the Second World War: 'I do so wish you weren't in prison. It will be vile not to have you to go shopping with.'

Twice a week Linda worked in a Red bookshop. It was run by a huge, perfectly silent comrade, called Boris. Boris liked to get drunk from Thursday afternoon, which was closing day in that district, to Monday morning, so Linda said she would

take it over on Friday and Saturday. An extraordinary trans-
formation would then occur. The books and tracts which
mouldered there month after month, getting damper and
dustier until at last they had to be thrown away, were hurried
into the background, and their place taken by Linda's own
few but well-loved favourites. Thus for *Whither British
Airways?* was substituted *Round the World in Forty Days*, *Karl
Marx, the Formative Years* was replaced by *The Making of a
Marchioness*, and *The Giant of the Kremlin* by *Diary of a
Nobody*, while *A Challenge to Coal-Owners* made way for *King
Solomon's Mines*.

Hardly would Linda have arrived in the morning on her
days there, and taken down the shutters, than the slummy
little street would fill with motor cars, headed by Lord Merlin's
electric brougham. Lord Merlin did great propaganda for the
shop, saying that Linda was the only person who had ever succeeded in finding him *Froggie's Little Brother* and *Le Père
Goriot* . . . He took a perfectly firm line with the comrades.

'How are you today?' he would say with great emphasis, and
then glower furiously at them until they left the shop.

All this had an excellent effect upon the financial side of
the business. Instead of showing, week by week, an enormous
loss, to be refunded from one could guess where, it now
became the only Red bookshop in England to make a profit.
Boris was greatly praised by his employers, the shop received a
medal . . . and the comrades all said that Linda was a good girl
and a credit to the Party.

The Pursuit of Love · 1945

JUNG CHANG

*In the middle of Chengdu was a statue of Sun Yat-sen, erected
before the Communists came to power, and around it a patch of*

ground became a plant nursery. The nursery was abandoned as a
'bourgeois decadence' when the Cultural Revolution broke out.

The commercial instinct of the Chinese is so strong that black markets, Mao's greatest capitalist *bête noire*, existed right through the crushing pressure of the Cultural Revolution . . .

When Red Guards began raiding people's houses and burning their books, a small crowd started to gather on this deserted ground to deal in the volumes which had escaped the bonfires. All manner of people were to be found there: Red Guards who wanted to make some cash from the books they had confiscated; frustrated entrepreneurs who smelled money; scholars who did not want their books to be burned but were afraid of keeping them; and book lovers. The books being traded had all been published or sanctioned under the Communist regime before the Cultural Revolution. Apart from Chinese classics, they included Shakespeare, Dickens, Byron, Shelley, Shaw, Thackeray, Tolstoy, Dostoyevsky, Turgenev, Chekhov, Ibsen, Balzac, Maupassant, Flaubert, Dumas, Zola, and many other world classics. Even Conan Doyle's Sherlock Holmes, who had been a great favorite in China.

The price of the books depended on a variety of factors. If they had a library stamp in them, most people shunned them. The Communist government had such a reputation for control and order that people did not want to risk being caught with illegally gotten state property, for which they would be severely punished. They were much happier buying privately owned books with no identification marks. Novels with erotic passages commanded the highest prices, and also carried the greatest danger. Stendhal's *Le Rouge et le Noir*, considered erotic, cost the equivalent of two weeks' wages for an average person.

[My brother] Jin-ming went to this black market every day. His initial capital came from books which he had obtained from a paper recycling shop, to which frightened citizens were selling their collections as scrap paper. Jin-ming had chatted up a shop assistant and bought a lot of these books, which he resold at much higher prices. He then bought more books at the black market, read them, sold them, and bought more.

Between the start of the Cultural Revolution and the end of 1968, at least a thousand books passed through his hands.

Wild Swans · 1991

DOROTHY DAVIS

What sort of shops were all these bookshops? It might be supposed that they bore some resemblance to their modern counterparts since, saving their dust-jackets, books are very much the same now as then. In fact, the shops must have looked very different because, until well into the eighteenth century, all their new stock was unbound, and lay about in loose sheets, looking, one must assume, like a proof-reader's Monday morning . . . If a customer liked the look of a book, he could sit down in the shop and read it on the spot. Stools were provided for the purpose. Or he could buy the loose sheets and take them home to read and get them bound privately later if he decided they were worth keeping. Or he could take a bookseller's word for it and order a book to be bound for him right away, plain or fancy 'according to the price the purchaser has to bestow on it'. Pepys mentions waiting a fortnight for this job to be done . . . The dealers in old books might have in their warehouses several rooms full of books, and they encouraged their customers to come and browse amongst them, meeting with congenial company and 'agreeable conversations' . . .

A History of Shopping · 1966

NAOMI KLEIN

Not surprisingly, it was the Walt Disney Company, the inventor of modern branding, that created the model for the branded superstore, opening the first Disney Store in 1984. There are now close to 730 outlets worldwide. Coke followed shortly after with a store sporting all manner of branded paraphernalia, from key chains to cutting boards. But if Disney and Coke paved the way, it was Barnes & Noble that created the model that would forever change the face of retailing, introducing the first superstore to its chain of bookstores in 1990. The prototype for the new construct, according to company documents, was 'old-world library ambiance and a wood and green palette' complemented by 'comfortable seating, restrooms and extended hours' – and, of course, by a little co-branding in the form of in-store Starbucks coffee shops. The formula affected not only the chain's ability to sell books but also the role it occupied in pop culture; it became a celebrity, a source of endless media controversy, and eventually the thinly veiled inspiration for a Hollywood movie, *You've Got Mail*. In less than a decade, Barnes & Noble became the first bookstore that was also a superbrand in its own right.

No Logo · 2000

JANE AUSTEN

Sunday 25 November 1798

My dear Sister

. . . The Overton Scotchman has been kind enough to rid me of some of my money, in exchange for six shifts and four pair of stockings. The Irish is not so fine as I should like it; but as I gave as much money for it as I intended, I have no reason to complain. It cost me 3*s*. 6*d*. per yard. It is rather finer, however, than our last, and not so harsh a cloth. We have got 'Fitz-Albini'; my father has bought it against my private wishes, for it does not quite satisfy my feelings that we should purchase the only one of Egerton's works of which his family are ashamed. That these scruples, however, do not at all interfere with my reading it, you will easily believe ... We have got Boswell's 'Tour to the Hebrides', and are to have his 'Life of Johnson'; and, as some money will yet remain in Burdon's hands, it is to be laid out in the purchase of Cowper's works.

Selected Letters · 1798

MARGARET H. SPUFFORD

Spufford's is a fascinating study of 17th-century chapmen, or
pedlars, and the goods inside the packs on their backs.

James Calderhead of Bristol in 1727 carried an earthen pot of snuff, and a dozen knives and forks priced at 2d each on his rounds. Even books and paper were difficult to transport uncrushed, and were therefore minor and exceptional lines to the footmen and horsemen who were not specialists in them. Even so, George Pool on foot in Cumberland carried ninepenny romances, and Thomas Hopkinson of Newark in Nottinghamshire and Cunningham and Griffin of Kent all carried books on horseback. So did John Lloyd of Norton in Radnorshire, working with horse and pack, whose basic stock in 1676 included primers. Even the remote Welsh border countryside was therefore not quite denuded of material for those who wished to learn to read.

The Great Reclothing of Rural England · 1984

GEORGE ELIOT

To Maria Lewis *June 23, 1840*

If I do not see you how shall I send the money and your Don Quixote which I hope soon to finish? I have been sadly interrupted by other books that have taken its scanty allowance of time or I should have made better haste with it. Many thanks for the trouble you have taken to get me Silvio Pellico; I will not have the other at present, but if your passage through town be altogether such as to allow of a little shopping, will you try to get me Spenser's Faery Queen? The cheapest edition with a glossary, which is quite indispensable, together with a clear and correct type. This book is of no importance whatever, so do not burden yourself with a straw's weight of inconvenience on its account. My only reason for mentioning it to you is that if I order it of Mr. Short I am almost certain to have either an inferior or a very expensive edition.

Letters · 1840

SHOPPING TRIPS

P. L. TRAVERS

Pamela Lyndon Travers was an actress and a poet. Born Helen
Lyndon Goff in Australia in 1899, she moved to England in 1924.
She was befriended by W. B. Yeats and his circle and in 1934
enjoyed her first literary success with Mary Poppins, an enchanting
children's book which spawned numerous sequels as well as a
famous film.

'But, Mary Poppins, I thought you said gingerbread—this isn't
the way to Green, Brown and Johnson's, where we always get
it—' she began, and stopped because of Mary Poppins' face.

'Am I doing the shopping or are you?' Mary Poppins
enquired.

'You,' said Jane, in a very small voice.

'Oh, really? I thought it was the other way round,' said Mary
Poppins with a scornful laugh.

She gave the perambulator a little twist with her hand
and it turned a corner and drew up suddenly. Jane and
Michael, stopping abruptly behind it, found themselves
outside the most curious shop they had ever seen. It was
very small and very dingy. Faded loops of coloured paper
hung in the windows, and on the shelves were shabby little
boxes of Sherbet, old Liquorice Sticks, and very withered,
very hard Apples-on-a-stick. There was a small dark doorway between the windows, and through this Mary Poppins
propelled the perambulator while Jane and Michael followed at her heels.

Inside the shop they could dimly see the glass-topped
counter that ran round three sides of it. And in a case under
the glass were rows and rows of dark, dry gingerbread, each slab

so studded with gilt stars that the shop itself seemed to be faintly lit by them. Jane and Michael glanced round to find out what kind of a person was to serve them, and were very surprised when Mary Poppins called out:

'Fannie! Annie! Where are you?' Her voice seemed to echo back to them from each dark wall of the shop.

And as she called, two of the largest people the children had ever seen rose from behind the counter and shook hands with Mary Poppins. The huge women then leant down over the counter and said, 'How de do?' in voices as large as themselves, and shook hands with Jane and Michael.

'How do you do, Miss—?' Michael paused, wondering which of the large ladies was which.

'Fannie's my name,' said one of them. 'My rheumatism is about the same; thank you for asking.' She spoke very mournfully, as though she were unused to such a courteous greeting.

'It's a lovely day—' began Jane politely to the other sister, who kept Jane's hand imprisoned for almost a minute in her huge clasp.

'I'm Annie,' she informed them miserably. 'And handsome is as handsome does.'

Jane and Michael thought that both the sisters had a very odd way of expressing themselves, but they had not time to be surprised for long, for Miss Fannie and Miss Annie were reaching out their long arms to the perambulator. Each shook hands solemnly with one of the Twins, who were so astonished that they began to cry.

'Now, now, now, now! What's this, what's this?' A high, thin, crackly little voice came from the back of the shop. At the sound of it the expression on the faces of Miss Fannie and Miss Annie, sad before, became even sadder. They seemed frightened and ill at ease, and somehow Jane and

Michael realised that the two huge sisters were wishing that they were much smaller and less conspicuous.

'What's all this I hear?' cried the curious high little voice, coming nearer. And presently, round the corner of the glass case the owner of it appeared. She was as small as her voice and as crackly, and to the children she seemed to be older than anything in the world, with her wispy hair and her stick-like legs and her wizened, wrinkled little face. But in spite of this she ran towards them as lightly and as gaily as though she were still a young girl.

'Now, now, now—well, I do declare! Bless me if it isn't Mary Poppins, with John and Barbara Banks. What—Jane and Michael, too? Well, isn't this a nice surprise for me? I assure you I haven't been so surprised since Christopher Columbus discovered America—truly I haven't!'

She smiled delightedly as she came to greet them, and her feet made little dancing movements inside the tiny elastic-sided boots. She ran to the perambulator and rocked it gently, crooking her thin, twisted, old fingers at John and Barbara until they stopped crying and began to laugh.

'That's better!' she said, cackling gaily. Then she did a very odd thing. She broke off two of her fingers and gave one each to John and Barbara. And the oddest part of it was that in the space left by the broken-off fingers two new ones grew at once. Jane and Michael clearly saw it happen.

'Only Barley-Sugar—can't possibly hurt 'em,' the old lady said to Mary Poppins.

'Anything *you* give them, Mrs. Corry, could only do them good,' said Mary Poppins with most surprising courtesy.

'What a pity,' Michael couldn't help saying, 'they weren't Peppermint Bars.'

'Well, they are, sometimes,' said Mrs. Corry gleefully, 'and very good they taste, too. I often nibble 'em myself, if I can't sleep at night. Splendid for the digestion.'

'What will they be next time?' asked Jane, looking at Mrs. Corry's fingers with interest.

'Aha!' said Mrs. Corry. 'That's just the question. I never know from day to day what they will be.'

Mary Poppins · 1934

MRS T.P. O'CONNOR

Mrs O'Connor's weekly 'Letter from London' appeared in the Washington Herald. *The shop she calls M.&.S. is Marshall and Snelgrove, and the jilted lover was a personal acquaintance.*

I suppose it is a rare thing for a woman with a taste for romance to enter M. & S.'s artistic shop without remembering a story connected with it. As long ago as 1864, a beautiful young girl, Lady Florence Cecilia Paget, third daughter of the Marquis of Anglesey, torn between love and duty, but with love in the ascendant, entered the shop with her fiancé, Henry Chaplin – who was then young, and, I hope, slim; now he is old and enormously fat – by the Oxford Street Entrance. She left him while she looked at the beautiful lingerie of her trousseau, and he never saw her again until he met her as the Marchioness of Hastings. She had stopped to look at the fairy-tale garments of linen and lace, but had left the shop by the Henrietta Street Entrance, been met by the Marquis of Hastings and got married that morning.

'Letter from London' · 1916

IRIS MAY BULLEN

When Churchill announced in 1940 that the Channel Islands would not be defended, Iris Bullen chose to stay on Jersey with her two

*young children. Her journal records her struggle to keep the family
going during five years of occupation and ends with the words, 'God
Save the King'.*

Teusday [sic] July 30th

The afternoon I went to town to do a lot of shopping. I have
been buying a lot of extras these weeks, as I don't know how
things will be later on, already there are some articles that are
hard to get. I went to see Valerie, and was pleased to see her
cheerful and that she had been booked for the Hospital.

Teusday October 29th

Went to town the morning, it is a sad task to venture shopping
now as it is so difficult to get anything, while lots of things
have run out altogether, Oh! for the day when we can get
those things we miss so much! we are just keeping body & soul
together now.

The War Diary of Iris May Bullen · 1940

LINDA GRANT

My mother and I are going shopping, as we have done all our
lives. 'Now Mum,' I tell her, 'don't start looking at the prices
on everything. I'm paying. If you see something you like, try it
on. You are the mother of the bride, after all.' At long last one
of her two daughters (not me) is getting married.

In recent years my mother has become a poverty shopper;
she haunts jumble sales looking for other people's cast-offs. I
don't like to think of her trying on someone else's shoes which
she does not because she is very poor but because footwear is
fixed in her mind at 1970s prices. Everything she sees in the
shops seems to cost a fortune. 'You paid £49.99 for a pair of
shoes?' she would cry. 'They saw you coming.'

'But Mu-um, that's how much shoes cost these days.'

'Yes, but where do you go looking?'

In my childhood, my mother had aspired far beyond her station to be a world-class shopper. Her role models were Grace Kelly and Princess Margaret, Ava Gardner and Elizabeth Taylor. She acquired crocodile shoes and mink stoles, an eternity ring encrusted with diamonds, handbags in burnished patent leather. In her shut-up flat in Bournemouth were three wardrobes full of beautiful, expensive garments all on wooden or satin hangers, many in their own protective linen bags – a little imitation Chanel suit from the Sixties that came back into fashion every few years; her black Persian broadtail coat with its white mink collar and her initials, RG, sewn in blue silk thread in an italic script on to the hem of the black satin lining, surrounded by a sprig of embroidered roses; her brown mink hat for high days and holidays.

And so today I want the best for her, as she and my father had always wanted the best for us. 'The best that money can buy,' my father always boasted when he bought anything. 'Only show me the best,' he told shopkeepers.

'So we're looking for a dress?' A nice dress. The sales are still raging through the summer's heat, hot shoppers toiling up and down Oxford Street. We should, I think, find something for £60 or £70. 'John Lewis is full of them,' a friend has said. She has an idea of the kind of dress someone's mother would wear, an old biddy's frock, a shapeless floral sack.

'I don't think that's her kind of thing,' I had told her, doubtfully. But then who knew what was left? Could my mother's fashion sense be so far eroded that she would have lost altogether those modes of judgement that saw that something was classic and something else merely frumpy?

'I'm not having a dress, I want a suit,' my mother says as the doors part automatically to admit the three of us, for tagging along is my nephew, her grandson, who also likes to shop.

'OK. A suit. Whatever you like.'

And now we're in the department store, our idea of a second home. My mother has never been much of a nature lover, an outdoors girl . . . has never got her hands dirty in wellingtons, bending down among the flower beds to plant her summer perennials. Or put her hands to the oars of a boat or tramped across a ploughed field in the morning frost or breasted any icy waves. She shrinks in fear from sloppy-mouthed dogs and fawning kittens. But show her new improved tights with Lycra! They never had that in my day, she says admiringly on an excursion to Sainsbury's, looking at dose-ball washing liquid.

And no outing can offer more escape from the nightmare of her present reality than shopping for clothes, the easiest means we know of becoming our fantasies and generally cheering ourselves up all round. Who needs the psychiatrist's couch when you have shopping? Who needs Prozac?

Through the handbags, gloves and scarves and utilitarian umbrellas. Not a glance at fabrics and patterns for neither my mother nor I have ever run up our own frocks at the sewing machine, shop-bought *always* being superior to home-made in our book. Why do an amateur job when you could get in a professional?

Up the escalators to the first floor where the land of dreams lies all around us, suits and dresses and coats and skirts and jackets. And where to begin? How to start? But my mother has started already.

At once a sale rack has caught her eye with three or four short navy wool crêpe jackets with nipped-in waists, the lapels and slanted pockets edged in white, three mock mother-of-pearl buttons to do it up. My mother says she thinks she is a size twelve. She tries the jacket on right then and there and it takes fifty years off her. She stands in front of the mirror as Forties Miss, dashing about London in the Blitz, on her way to her job in Top Ops. She turns to us, radiant. 'What do you think?'

'Perfect.' The sleeves are too long, but this is a small matter. We will summon the seamstress and she will take them up, her mouth full of pins. As my mother folds the sleeves under I steal a covert look at the price tag. The jacket is reduced to £49.99, and this, in anybody's book, is a bargain.

'Now I need a skirt and blouse. I've got to match the navy.' . . .

She disappears between the rails and I am anxious for it is not hard to lose sight of her, she has shrunk so in recent years . . .

She's back quickly with her selection. The navy of the skirt and blouse she has chosen match each other and the jacket exactly, which isn't the easiest thing in the world to do so that I know that her perception of colour is quite unaltered and whatever else is wrong with her, there is nothing the matter with her eyes. I take the garments from her as we walk to the changing rooms, for everything apart from the smallest and lightest of handbags is too heavy for her now. A full mug of tea is too heavy for her to pick up . . .

What she gives me to hold is a Karl Lagerfeld skirt and a Jaeger blouse, both substantially reduced, at £89.99 and £69.99, but not within the £60 budget I had estimated when the old biddy dress came to mind, like those which hang from rails ignored by my mother. She has obeyed my instruction. She has not looked at the prices. Half-submerged in whatever part of the brain contains our capacity to make aesthetic judgements, her old good taste is buried and my injunction to ignore the prices has been the key that released it. A young woman of twenty-five could attend a job interview in the outfit she has put together.

In the changing room, she undresses. I remember the body I had seen in the bath when I was growing up, the convex belly that my sister used to think was like a washing-up bowl from two Caesarean births. The one that I have now, myself. She used to hold hers in under her clothes by that rubberized garment called a roll-on, a set of sturdy elasticized knickers . . .

The pencil skirt, a size ten, is an exact fit but the blouse (also a ten) is a little too big, billowing round her hips, which is a shame for it is beautiful, in heavy matte silk with white overstitching along the button closings.

And now my mother turns to me in rage, no longer placid and obedient, not the sweet little old-age pensioner that shop assistants smile at to see her delight in her new jacket.

Fury devours her. 'I will not wear this blouse, you will not make me wear this blouse.' She bangs her fist against the wall and (she is the only person I have ever seen do this) she stamps her foot, just like a character from one of my childhood comics or a bad actress in an amateur production.

'What's the matter with it?'

She points to the collar. 'I'm not having anyone see me in this. It shows up my neck.'

I understand for the first time why, on this warm July day as well as every other, she is wearing a scarf knotted beneath her chin. I had thought her old bones were cold, but it is vanity. My mother was seventy-eight the previous week. 'Go and see if they've got it in a smaller size,' she orders.

My patient nephew is sitting beneath a mannequin outside watching the women come and go. There are very few eleven-year-old boys in the world who would spend a day of the school holidays traipsing around John Lewis with their aunt and their senile gran looking for clothes but let's face it, he has inherited the shopping gene. He's quite happy there, sizing up the grown ladies coming out of the changing rooms to say to their friends, 'What do you think? Is it too dressy?' or 'I wonder what Ray's sister will be wearing. I'll kill her if it's cream.'

'Are you all right?' He gives me the thumbs-up sign.

There is no size eight on the rack and I return empty-handed. My mother is standing in front of the mirror regarding herself: her fine grey hair, her hazel eyes, her obstinate chin, the illusory remains of girlish prettiness, not ruined or faded or decayed but withered. Some people never seem to look like grown-ups but retain their childish faces all their lives and just resemble elderly infants. My mother did become an adult once but then she went back to being young again; young with lines and grey hair. Yet when I look at her I don't see any of it. She's just my mother, unchanging, the person who tells you what to do.

'Where've you been?' she asks, turning to me. 'This blouse is too big round the neck. Go and see if they've got it in a smaller size.'

'That's what I've been doing. They haven't.'

'Oh.'

So we continue to admire the skirt and the jacket and wait for the seamstress to arrive, shut up together in our little cubicle where once, long ago, my mother would say to me: 'You're not having it and that's final. I wouldn't be seen dead with you wearing something like that. I don't care if it's all the rage. I don't care if everyone else has got one. You can't.'

My mother fingers the collar on the blouse. 'I'm not wearing this, you know. You can't make me wear it. I'm not going to the wedding if I've got to wear this blouse.'

'Nobody's going to make you wear it. We'll look for something else.'

'I've got an idea. Why don't you see if they have it in a smaller size.'

'I've looked already. There isn't one. This is the last . . .'

'Did you? I don't remember. Have I ever told you that I've been diagnosed as having a memory loss?'

'Yes.'

Now the seamstress has come. My mother shows her the blouse. 'It's too big round the neck,' she tells her. 'Can you take it in?'

'No, Mum, she's here to alter the jacket.' . . .

We pay for the jacket and the skirt which are wrapped, the jacket remaining, ready to be collected absolutely no later than the day before the wedding, which is cutting it a bit fine but what can you do? We leave John Lewis and walk a few yards to the next store which is D. H. Evans.

Up the escalator to the dress department and on a sale rack is the very Jaeger blouse! And there are plenty of them and right at the front what is there but an eight.

'Look!' I cry. 'Look what they've got and in your size.' . . .

She tries the blouse on in the changing rooms. The fit is much better. She looks at the label. 'Jaguar. I've never heard of them.' Her eyes, which could match navy, sometimes jumbled up letters.

'Not jaguar, Jaeger.'

'Jaeger! I've never had Jaeger in my life before.'

'You must be joking. You've got a wardrobe full of it.' . . .

My mother wants to take the tube home (or rather to the Home in which we have incarcerated her) for a taxi is an unnecessary extravagance. 'I'm fresh,' she says. But I am not. A moment always comes, towards the end of these outings, when I want to go into a bar and have a drink, when I wish I carried a hip flask of innocuous vodka to sip, sip, sip at throughout the day. Most of all I want it to stop, our excursion. I can't put up with any more and I fall into cruel, monosyllabic communication. 'Yes, Mum.' 'No, Mum.' 'That's right.' 'Mmm.'

Here is a taxi and do not think for a moment, Madam, that despite the many burdens of your shopping, however swollen your feet or fractious your child, that you are going to take this cab before me.

'Get in,' I order. As we drive off up Portland Place I am calculating how much her old biddy outfit has cost. It has come to £209.97 which is more than I have paid for mine and has beaten out all of us, including the bride herself, on designer labels.

'Are We Related?' · 1997

RACHEL HENNING

Rachel Henning left Bristol in 1854 to join her brother and sister, who had emigrated to Australia the year before. Her amusing descriptions of colonial life, addressed for the most part to her sister Etta, were never intended for publication.

We also made expeditions into Sydney and paid a visit to Farmer's where I fitted out myself with some new garments, which I badly wanted, not having been in Sydney for a year before. The said Farmer's is a most convenient place. It is an immense establishment divided into departments for everything; you can choose a dress, have the material sent to the dressmaking department, where it is made for you in the best fashion; go to another for a mantle, another for a bonnet, another for underclothes; another large room is for carpets and upholstery, and all the very best that can be had in Sydney. It is a wonderful save of time and trouble.

Letters · 1853–82

JACKIE COLLINS

Nicci and Saffron cruised into Fred Segal on Melrose, their favourite shopping spot. As they walked around inspecting all the new clothes, Nicci kept checking her cellphone messages.

'*Why* do you keep doing that?' Saffron asked. 'I mean, you *speak* to Evan like *seven* times a day. So what's the deal, girl?'

'I *am* getting married, you know,' Nicci reminded her.

'I *know*,' Saffron replied, tossing back her dreadlocks. 'Only it's not *him* you're checking on.'

'What *do* you mean?' Nicci said innocently, pulling a pair of studded leather pants off the rack.

'C'mon, you *know* you can't keep secrets.'

'No secrets,' Nicci said, holding the pants up for further inspection.

'Yeah?' Saffron said, giving her a knowing look.

Nicci was dying to confide in someone – but if she did, wouldn't that be incredibly disloyal to Evan?

'It's nothing,' she said vaguely. 'Evan's brother is flying in from the location, and I'm supposed to give him some papers. If I miss him, it'll piss Evan off.'

'Hmm . . .' Saffron said with a wicked grin. 'The *babe* brother?'

Nicci shot her a surprised look. 'You think Brian's a babe?'

'Oh, yeah, the dude is smokin'. Didja get an eyeful of that ass? Man! Gives "tight" a whole new meaning.'

'Brian's a major player,' Nicci said, startled that Saffron had noticed. 'He sleeps with anyone.'

'Somethin' wrong with that?' Saffron joked. 'Maybe *I* should date him.'

'Let's *not* keep it in the family,' Nicci said pointedly, throwing the leather pants down and walking off.

'Jealous?' Saffron said, right behind her.

'Are you *losing* it? Jealous – of *Brian*? He's a sleaze-bag, the kind of guy you go out of your way to avoid.'

'Uh-huh,' Saffron said knowingly. 'The girl is jealous all right.'

'I am *so not*,' Nicci said indignantly, snatching up a red T-shirt with BAD GIRL emblazoned in sequins across the front.

'What's the deal, Nic?' Saffron persisted. 'Don't tell me you like Brian too?'

Nicci shook her head vigorously. 'I *so do not* appreciate this conversation.'

'Check your messages again,' Saffron teased. 'Maybe he's called. And, girl, that T-shirt is *not* for you. You gotta have no boobs to carry it off.'

'Anyone ever told you you're a twenty-carat bitch?' Nicci demanded, well aware she'd been busted.

Saffron grinned and twirled her gold nose-ring. 'All the time, girl. All the time!'

Hollywood Wives · 2001

JODI DEAN

Dean teaches political theory in New York.

I missed confession at the Weblog on Friday. And, really, although this is a confession, it doesn't fit all that well. It involves shopping. I like it. Not shopping for sustenance or shopping for recreation. I don't like malls. But, I like shopping as a practice of friendship and shopping as a way of getting my bearings. Clearly, a critical assessment of the role of capital in configuring lifeworld experiences would dissect and diagnosis these practices. But, they work for me, whatever their faults.

I love shopping with another woman. Sometimes it can go wrong, but usually, if I cross this line, I know the woman well enough to know it will work. I had a great time shopping with Jane in Baltimore. She was looking for a necklace. I then decided to get one as well. I wasn't planning on it, but I wanted to, as a way of sharing in the experience. I've worn it most every day since. I was also really thrilled to find a serving plate that she liked. I got to be closer friends with my best friend, Lee, through shopping. We both collected the same kind of American art pottery, McCoy. So, whenever we went to a meeting, we would find an antique show and look for McCoys. Lee preferred white and I didn't care, so we didn't clash. What matters is the practice as a way of hanging out. I think it's interesting that this practice requires some degree of financial ease and flexibility. But, I think that women may engage in it at all sorts of different financial levels. I also like the way that, even as I was shopping with theorists, our interaction wasn't work oriented. Nor was it mediated by men or children.

Bearings: when I shop for bearings, I don't really need to purchase anything, although I usually do. It's the way I navigate a new city or space. Is this common? It must be. But, when all the shops are the same, does it work? Do the common shops provide security and familiarity, making it easier to know my way around? Or is the similiarity disorienting? Neither Rehoboth Beach nor the Baltimore inner harbor have a bunch of mall-y, typical, places, although RB has a bunch of beach like places. I wonder, what does it mean that shops provide such an orientation?

posted by Jodi @ 12:55 AM in <u>Boring stuff about me</u>, <u>Capital</u>, <u>women</u> | <u>Permalink</u> on July 11, 2006

Mrs Elizabeth Bonhote

'The Print Shop'

A print shop is a place which has generally a numerous set of visitors. — We saw a very good one, and stopped to take a view of the prints which were placed against the windows.

'The Undertaker's Shop'

These windows had attracted none to stop and take a view of them. — They were furnished with terrifying rather than with entertaining goods.

'The Milliner's Shop'

''Tis a genteel ribbon,' said I, – 'and I will buy it for my Julia: – nor is that the only treasure I shall have purchased in my ramble – for I shall carry home more wisdom than I brought out.' – I went into the shop – the mistress of it was drest out much finer than any of her dolls, – and nearly represented that curious one in the possession of Mr George Alexander Stevens. – 'Cut me five yards of this ribbon,' said I – She sent a pretty girl, who was her apprentice, to serve me.

'The Toyshop'

'I will step into this toyshop,' said I, 'and buy my boy Charles a pretty "fellow".' – I did so – and soon made a purchase of the young gentleman. The toyshop was an emblem of the world. – 'The world is indeed a larger toyshop than this,' said I, looking round; 'but we daily see its inhabitants employed after just such trifles as this contains in miniature. Here are fine ladies – fine gentlemen – and pretty fellows – here are watches – rings – birds and bird-cages – coaches – horses – and wheelbarrows.' But the master of the shop was as great a curiosity as any it contained.

The Rambles of Mr Frankly, published by his sister · 1776

LADY MARY CAMPBELL COKE

– I am not well enough to take my intended walk into the City. I cou'd not eat my breakfast, but have been out all the morning working in my Garden. The weather is not pleasant, tho' warmer then [*sic*] it has been. Last night I had a fire, but I still hope to leave it off, & that the weather will mend before it grows worse: all this is very unentertaining; but what can I do, when I see nobody to tell me the news of the Town? Did I mention to you the result of the Duchess of Manchester's private Audience? The fear of repeating what I have already told you makes me sometimes guilty of ommissions [*sic*]. After dinner, finding myself better, I order'd my Coach, & Jane & I went in it as far as the Strand; there we got out & proceeded on foot to the Exeter Exchange, where I bought two garden knives, Ld Anson's Voyage, & the last addition of Thomson's Works; left them in the shop, & went farther up the Strand; Cheapen'd a bird cage, but not getting it for my price, left it, & went on to a seed Shop, where I bought two enormous Narcissus roots, which I hope to shew you next spring in my garden; from thence we walked to Temple bar, where, at the great fishmonger's, I bought three whittings & some shrimps for my supper; left them in the Shop & went up fleet street [*sic*], but bought nothing; & observing the light decline apace, return'd back, calling at all the shops where I had made purchases, & carried them with me to the Coach, getting home just before it was dark. I eat one of my

Whittings for supper, & found it fresh and good. To night it grew much warmer. I left off my fire.

Diary of Lady Mary Campbell Coke · 1768

ELIZABETH MISSING SEWELL

I had some shopping to do, and therefore set forth boldly by myself to what is called the Goldsmith's Street, which was not far from the hotel. It is a narrow street with small shops on each side, filled with silver, and gold, and coral orna-ments, most beautifully worked, for which Genoa is famous. I suppose I must have spent an hour or more in this street, looking at the different things, and choosing what I wanted; and at last I finished by finding my way to another street, and purchasing a bright blue umbrella; such a lovely colour, that it almost made me wish for rain for the pleasure of using it!

'Memoir of Elizabeth Missing Sewell' · 1852

LADY GREGORY

In 1904 Lady Augusta Gregory founded the Abbey Theatre with W.B. Yeats. She wrote many plays herself, and her home in Coole Park, County Galway, was the centre of the Irish Literary Revival.

I found my little man in his tiny room, looking cool & com-fortable in loose grey trousers & a blue coat – He had been a little lonely at first – the only new boy in the House & rather 'out of it' – feeling in the way in their games – but is beginning to settle down – We went out shopping & got a little clock & some plants & a blotter & stuff for a new curtain & the room looked much more homelike when we had arranged it & taken down some of the fans – We also proceeded to a grocer for some supplies – as if you spend 7/6 you get a book of American views! This however was rather a fraud – however we cut out the best ones & stuck them up.

Lady Gregory's Diaries · 1892–1902

CLARA ASPINALL

Clara was the sister of a Melbourne barrister and she spent three years with him from 1858 to 1861, noting the prices of food and clothes as well as the cost of transport.

Collins Street is to Melbourne what Regent Street is to London. As compared with the other shopping streets, it is decidedly very attractive. Ladies may walk in Collins Street and find pleasant variety, irrespective of the excitement of buying a new dress or hat. No lady ever ventures into the other streets, excepting on urgent business. There is an American, go-a-head spirit pervading them, very objectionable to the well-regulated minds of our sex. Everybody appears to be in a hurry; and if we are not equally so, our dresses, perhaps, are trodden on, or we get unceremoniously jostled; not that people are intentionally rude, but everybody is on business bent.

How different is Collins Street! Here all things are conducted calmly, quietly, harmoniously. Beautiful ladies may be seen gliding out of one shop into another, bright with the hope of meeting some of their fair friends, who like themselves, have come in from the suburbs with shopping intentions; but they are, nevertheless, resigned to the chance of encountering a whole army of admirers . . .

Three Years in Melbourne · 1862

JANE AUSTEN

Marianne rose the next morning with recovered spirits and happy looks. The disappointment of the evening before seemed forgotten in the expectation of what was to happen that day. They had not long finished their breakfast before Mrs Palmer's barouche stopt at the door, and in a few minutes she came laughing into the room; so delighted to see them all, that it was hard to say whether she received most pleasure from meeting her mother or the Miss Dashwoods again. So surprised at their coming to town, though it was what she had rather expected all along; so angry at their accepting her mother's invitation after having declined her own, though at the same time she would never have forgiven them if they had not come!

'Mr Palmer will be so happy to see you,' said she; 'what do you think he said when he heard of your coming with mama? I forget what it was now, but it was something so droll!'

After an hour or two spent in what her mother called comfortable chat, or in other words, in every variety of inquiry concerning all their acquaintance on Mrs Jennings's side, and in laughter without cause on Mrs Palmer's, it was proposed by the latter that they should all accompany her to some shops where she had business that morning, to which Mrs Jennings and Elinor readily consented, as having likewise some purchases to make themselves; and Marianne, though declining it at first, was induced to go likewise.

Wherever they went, she was evidently always on the watch. In Bond-street especially, where much of their business lay, her eyes were in constant inquiry; and in whatever shop the party were engaged, her mind was equally abstracted from every thing actually before them, from all that interested and occupied the others. Restless and dissatisfied every where, her sister could never obtain her opinion of any article of purchase, however it might equally concern them both; she received no pleasure from any thing; was only impatient to be at home again, and could with difficulty govern her vexation at the tediousness of Mrs Palmer, whose eye was caught by every thing pretty, expensive, or new; who was wild to buy all, could determine on none, and dawdled away her time in rapture and indecision.

Sense and Sensibility · 1811

TRANSFORMATIONS

I am clearly a chameleon when it comes to shopping. My personality changes radically depending on which shop I am in. Argos apparently turns me into a thug while in Sainsbury's Homebase I am wan and vague and attempt to look like Mia Farrow, in the hope that someone in apple-green dungarees will take pity and direct me to the rawlplugs.

In Russell & Bromley I am a posh thug, a bossy woman from Gloucestershire. I am overbearing, which is my way of railing against the fact that I am now old enough to buy most of my shoes from a shop that has many branches in Middle England.

In Prada, where I occasionally go, but never alone, to laugh at the prices and teeny-weeny Mrs Beckham sizes, my friend and I behave like sniggering sixth-formers; and in the butcher I am brusque and efficient and endeavour to say things like 'half a pound of best of neck and some chitterlings, please'.

'City Lives' · 2006

Jess Cartner-Morley

Unlike almost every other woman I know, I love communal changing rooms. Not because of any exhibitionist tendencies, nor Sapphic ones. I am not interested in seeing my fellow changees without their clothes on, but rather in watching their reactions when they try on their chosen wares.

Specifically, I love watching the moment when a woman tries on something and loves it. Because the same thing always happens: she starts to flirt with herself in the mirror. Often, she will shift her weight slightly onto one hip, unconsciously adopting the figure-flattering pose beloved of Liz Hurley and her fellow paparazzi princesses; frequently she will hook her thumbs into her hip pockets, pushing the breasts forward a little. If barefoot, she will usually lift her heels, adopting the Barbie pose of being high-heeled even when naked. And, in 99% of cases, she will fluff her hair and pout a bit. This is fashion's version of sexual chemistry; suddenly, the stale fug of air freshener (or worse) is pierced by the new scent of possibility.

'Communal Changing Rooms' · 2006

HELEN FIELDING

Saturday 11 February
8st 13, alcohol units 4, cigarettes 18, calories 1467 (but burnt off by shopping).

Saturday 6 May: VE Day
9st 1, alcohol units 6, cigarettes 25, calories 3800 (but celebrating anniversary of end of rationing), correct lottery numbers 0 (poor) . . .

7 p.m. The heat has made my body double in size, I swear. I am never going in a communal changing room again. I got a dress stuck under my arms in Warehouse while trying to lift it off and ended up lurching around with inside-out fabric instead of a head, tugging at it with my arms in the air, rippling stomach and thighs on full display to the assembled sniggering fifteen-year-olds. When I tried to pull the stupid dress down and get out of it the other way it got stuck on my hips.

I hate communal changing rooms. Everyone stares sneakily at each other's bodies, but no one ever meets anyone's eye.

There are always girls who know that they look fantastic in everything and dance around beaming, swinging their hair and doing model poses in the mirror saying, 'Does it make me look fat?' to their obligatory obese friend, who looks like a water buffalo in everything.

It was a disaster of a trip, anyway. The answer to shopping, I know, is simply to buy a few choice items from Nicole Farhi, Whistles and Joseph but the prices so terrify me that I go scuttling back to Warehouse and Miss Selfridge, rejoicing in a host of dresses at £34.99, get them stuck on my head, then buy things from Marks and Spencer because I don't have to try them on, and at least I've bought something.

I have come home with four things, all of them unsuitable and unflattering. One will be left behind the bedroom chair in an M&S bag for two years. The other three will be exchanged for credit notes from Boules, Warehouse, etc., which I will then lose. I have thus wasted £119, which would have been enough to buy something really nice from Nicole Farhi, like a very small T-shirt.

It is all a punishment, I realize, for being obsessed by shopping in a shallow, materialistic way instead of wearing the same rayon frock all summer and painting a line down the back of my legs . . .

Bridget Jones's Diary · 1996

MARIA DYER DAVIES

Maria Dyer Davies came from a prosperous family in the Deep South before the Civil War.

3 June

'Had the blues. I bought me a dress.'

The Diary of Maria Dyer Davies · 1852

FRANCES HODGSON BURNETT

'. . . We must go to shops and theatres. It will be good for you to go to shops and theatres, Rosy.'

'I have nothing but rags to wear,' answered Lady Anstruthers, reddening.

'Then before we go we will have things sent down. People can be sent from the shops to arrange what we want.'

The magic of the name, standing for great wealth, could, it was true, bring to them, not only the contents of shops, but the people who showed them, and were ready to carry out any orders. The name of Vanderpoel already stood, in London, for inexhaustible resource. Yes, it was simple enough to send for politely subservient saleswomen to bring what one wanted.

The being reminded in every-day matters of the still real existence of the power of this magic was the first step in the rebuilding of Lady Anstruthers. To realise that the wonderful and yet simple necromancy was gradually encircling her again, had its parallel in the taking of a tonic, whose effect was cumulative. She herself did not realise the working of it. But Betty regarded it with interest. She saw it was good for her, merely to look on at the unpacking of the New York boxes, which the maid, sent for from London, brought down with her.

As the woman removed, from tray after tray, the tissue-paper-enfolded layers of garments, Lady Anstruthers sat and watched her with normal, simply feminine interest growing in her eyes. The things were made with the absence of any limit in expenditure, the freedom with delicate stuffs and priceless laces which belonged only to her faint memories of a lost past.

Nothing had limited the time spent in the embroidering of this apparently simple linen frock and coat; nothing had restrained the hand holding the scissors which had cut into the lace which adorned in *appliques* and filmy frills this exquisitely charming ball dress.

'It is looking back so far,' she said, waving her hand towards them with an odd gesture. 'To think that it was once all like – like that.'

She got up and went to the things, turning them over, and touching them with a softness, almost expressing a caress. The names of the makers stamped on bands and collars, the names of the streets in which their shops stood, moved her. She heard again the once familiar rattle of wheels, and the rush and roar of New York traffic.

The Shuttle · 1907

GILLIAN CLARKE

Clarke lives on a smallholding in Wales with her family and a flock of sheep.

Brought up with make do and mend, she wanted nice things.
Saturday shopping and afternoon tea at *The Angel*,
after haberdashery and household linen she'd move
in a trance through departments of china and glass
in the big city stores. As she moved, light sang
on the rims of tea-cups and glasses.
The shimmer stayed with her, reflecting her face
when she unpacked the parcels on the kitchen table
that stood on worn linoleum they couldn't afford to replace.

'Shopping' · 1998

MARGARETE BÖHME

The weary, careworn countenances became interested and eager, the dull eyes shone with secret longing, with delight in the mere spectacle; it was as if there were something in the air

that was like an injection of morphia in its transfiguring, glad-
dening power.

The Department Store · 1912

SARAH KENNEDY

I found myself shopping
whenever I had an afternoon free.
I should have been working,
I should have been reading,
I should have been taking care of the children.
Leaving the farm behind,
leaving the animals back there,
leaving the dirt, the endless work,
the fencing, the hay, the manure.
My half-built house, my lousy marriage,
all dissolved in the cloud of exhaust.

It felt as it did when I was going to see a lover;
the interstate empty of traffic
in the middle of the day,
just waiting for me
to get out there and drive,
the windows down, the music turned up loud,
the sky summer blue and me
driving right into it.
I went to very expensive department stores.
There, everything is beautiful
and everything's for sale.
The women working treat you like their closest friend,
and you don't have to talk to them.
You run your fingers through the silks and wools,
you look at all the rings,

you try perfume, and when you leave,
everybody smiles and waves good-bye.
Good-bye. And you don't have to buy
a thing that you don't want.
It's always like that, that time you went
to the hardware store to pick up something
you needed for the house. You looked up
and you saw it: the light display
with everything turned on high.
The thousand tiny facets of the chandeliers
all turning, soft, in the circulating air.
You forgot for just a minute
that the plumbing's clogged, that the wiring's bad,
you stood beneath the graceful golds
of the quiet lights, you felt
the warmth they always radiate, and thought, yes,
it's just what I've always wanted.

'Untitled' · 2001

HELEN SIMPSON

Simpson made up her autobiography to win a job with Vogue. *The story below brilliantly captures the breathless mystery that characterises the most thrilling of shopping trips.*

'What have you told them at work?' she asked.

'What have you told them at yours?' I countered.

'I don't need to tell them anything,' she said, looking down her long nose at me unsmilingly. 'I'm in charge.' . . .

We exchanged nods, avoiding each other's eyes. Guilt and complicity hovered in the air like creaky old stage conventions.

'So,' she said, after we had exchanged formal greetings. 'Where is this secret cavern of temptation?'

'I'm not allowed to say,' I said, truthfully. 'You'll just have to follow me.'

'That's ridiculous!' she hissed as I led her down past Fashion Street and the police station, then left into Chicksand Street. 'Ludicrous! Who do they think they are?'

I had met Isobel Marley two days before at Iddon Featherstone's reception for their corporate finance clients in Seething Lane . . .

She had been distracted; she had noticed what no man would ever notice . . . Isobel paused, then allowed herself to comment, 'That's a nice shirt.'

I was wearing a white shirt with my grey suit, boringly meek and plain. Only a member of the unofficial ocular freemasonry would have noticed that it was made of nun's veiling, with a faint grey stripe the width of a pencil lead.

'Why,' I remembered asking the sales assistant at Wurstigkeit that time, staring hard at the beautiful but after all plain shirt, 'Why, um, is it so much money, this one?'

'Ah, this one,' he had replied. 'Look, there, the stripe, you see? It is because the line is broken.'

Sure enough there were minute sugar-grain sized gaps in the fine stripe.

'Of course,' I'd said. And bought it.

'Thank you,' I now said to Isobel.

I saw her struggling with herself. She was an intensely competitive type, that much was obvious, and she would not be able to bear not to ask.

'It's nice cloth,' I taunted, almost laughing. 'Like down against the skin. And see, the line is broken.' I held out my cuff for inspection.

'So it is,' she said. 'Yes.'

She paused again, poker-faced, then could not help herself and asked, 'It's not from that shop, is it? That mad shop with the password where they won't give out their address? What's it called?'

'Wurstigkeit,' I said, blushing slightly.

'What a ludicrous idea, a shop with a password,' she scoffed.

She couldn't bear to feel excluded, it was obvious. She was used to being on every list, right at the top.

'It's eccentric,' I agreed, blithely.

'Isn't it terribly expensive?' she sniffed.

'Not to someone in the updraught,' I said. 'Surely.'

It was far too expensive for me now, but I wasn't going to tell *her* that. Since I first visited, Wurstigkeit's prices had quintupled, sextupled, rising by at least a hundred per cent each year. Market forces!

Five years ago I had met a man from Shibui Investments for lunch in a restaurant near Liverpool Street. He had been summoned by his mobile to an emergency deal-breaker before we had finished the amuse-gueules and so, finding myself with a rare uncharted hour, I had allowed myself to drift outside mapless into the dusty sun . . .

Anyway, it was during this window-like hour at a less than euphoric stage in my life that, by chance, I stumbled into Wurstigkeit, which had opened only that week. It was like stepping into the fabled wardrobe and finding yourself in another country. The point was, it was an experience in weightlessness. It subtracted your centre of gravity . . .

We turned from Chicksand Street into Frostric Walk, then down a villainous urinous alley so narrow that where a moment before there had been enough blue sky above to cut out a pair of sailor's trousers, now there was nothing but a forget-me-not ribbon.

'Are you *quite* sure you know where we're going?' asked Isobel with some asperity as she picked her well-shod way between various noisome puddles.

We took a twist at the end here, then on to one last dark paved lane, and we had arrived.

'You must be joking,' said Isobel flatly, staring at the scuffed and numberless portal with the blacked-out picture window beside it.

She glanced at her watch with irritation, then at me.

'Wait a moment,' I said.

On the wall at the level where a doorbell should have been was the bas-relief head of a satyr, and into the ancient whorled ear of this creature I whispered the password. Then I stepped back and waited.

The door opened slowly on backward hinges, and we followed. Inside, it was the hall of the Mountain King filled with the trousseau of his robber bride. I caught my breath, and started to feel bouncy and oxygenated, airy and greedy. My eyes lusted around all over the place. The colours teased and tingled and clashed like music, while the walls receded into velvety darkness. I tried to keep some semblance of indifference but the smiles kept crossing my lips, and soon I was cooing and clucking and gasping as I moved from rail to rail. Isobel riffled through this rack and that, pursing her lips. I saw the stuff through her eyes, as when I'd looked in for the first time five years ago. What a load of tat, I'd thought. What a heap of magpie rubbish, little bright bits of rubbish.

Then I'd suddenly got caught. Was it a corsair's slanted stripes down the front of a structured cardigan? I'd thought, how *can* they charge more than a fiver for this nonsense; and, a second later, the scales had fallen from my eyes. I'd understood that here was something indefensible at work, and had reached for my chequebook. It was the story of the Emperor's new clothes, but backwards.

Now Isobel was reaching for the price tags and huffing and puffing and casting stuff aside with a curled lip.

'Don't look at the price tags,' I advised. 'Look at the clothes.'

I took a long viridian garment fom its hanger and held it out behind her. Instinctively she slid her arms back into the sleeves and shrugged it on. We looked at her guarded face in the long mirror, and at the grande dame opera coat whose plaited, puffy, serpentine collar she had drawn superbly up to her chin.

'No,' she said, casting it aside. 'I'd never wear it. *When* would I wear it?'

'That's not the point,' I started to say, but decided to wait.

Perhaps after all she was merely status-seeking, an acquisitive label-conscious shopper. If so, I had misjudged, and this was a waste of time . . .

'There is nothing here that I could wear to work,' she said. 'There is nothing here that I could wear at home. Family life. What's the point?'

'But it's *you*, that coat. You can see that,' I declared. 'Apotheosis clothes, that's what this place is for.' . . .

Then Isobel caved in. Her defences crumbled, reason fled. She didn't care about the money any more, she stopped looking at the little tickets and their prices. Instead she narrowed her eyes and started to hunt down the most fantastical, the most artfully bizarre. I knew I hadn't been mistaken. I knew she had an eye. We were two of a kind when it came to this. She'd caught on. She was caught in. From now on she was a driven woman.

Soon we had amassed enough between us to start trying

on. In the little side lavatory off the showroom – Wurstigkeit had nothing as utilitarian as a changing room – with silks and velvets over the rusted old wash basin, elbows in each other's faces, we struggled into mad dresses, lunatic ensembles. I barely knew this woman, I'd only met her once before, yet here we were taking off our clothes together in a rusty cubicle . . .

I looked away. I hoped she wouldn't appraise what she saw of me with that merciless female regard which is so chilling. You must have seen the way women look at each other in dressing rooms or at the gym – furtive, assessing, without lust or kindness, hypercritically alert to any sign of age or deterioration . . .

Isobel's mobile phone sang out in muffled urgency from her bag. It was buried beneath a heap of bias-cut frangipani-petalled skirts and pinstriped peignoirs, pink plush toreador pants and a richly ribboned peajacket.

It rang and rang.

She looked at the heap of clothes as though it cradled a howling baby. She scowled, and the frown line between her brows was like a fault-line running clean through her.

'Leave it,' I said. 'I can't even hear it.'

'It might be important,' she said.

I shrugged.

It stopped after a while.

Both of us ought to have been somewhere else. Both of us had too much to do . . .

As for Isobel, she had accumulated a heap of finery and was now standing frowning by the till while they totted up how much it would cost. She looked like a baffled monarch, unable to believe that she was preparing to hand over vast sums to these illusionists.

'I think these things are right for you,' said the salesgirl consolingly. She smiled and nodded her head and wandered back to her patch . . .

I wandered off while she paid. When I returned she sat sprawled on a chair, flushed and exhausted and leaden-eyed.

Our salesgirl approached with a little tray holding a crystal noggin of eau-de-vie and a few frail sugar biscuits. These Isobel wolfed down.

Then she said crossly, 'What are they *for*.'

We turned and watched as a pair of cowry-trimmed chaperejos was wrapped in silver tissue paper.

'They are smart but casual,' pronounced the beautiful boy who was wrapping them.

'Yeah, yeah,' said Isobel rudely.

Back in her work clothes, the spell was wearing off. She glanced at her watch and clicked her tongue impatiently.

'You can wear them anywhere,' he insisted, looking up from under raven's wing brows.

'Like where?' snapped Isobel.

He shrugged superbly.

'You can do the gardening in them,' he said.

'Oh yes of *course*,' said Isobel. 'The gardening!'

And at last she capitulated. She was positively wreathed in smiles. I barely recognised her. Amusement played on her face and made it appear like floating quicksilver. She was transmogrified; she had literally lightened up.

'I can offer you a five per cent discount,' said the boy, superbly magnanimous.

'Well,' she gurgled, 'that might just tip me over the edge.'

I glanced at my watch. Good grief, was that the time? It was.

Things started to move fast. Her five per cent was restored in a hurry, the crackling carrier bags were handed across like hot cakes, and we were out in the real world again, turfed out onto the pavement with the numberless door closed firmly behind us.

'Where are you going next?' she asked.

'Eastcheap.'

'We can share a cab,' she said. 'Do you know, I've got eight hundred pages to read before four o'clock.'

We were walking fast towards the main road, almost skipping. Her strong face was alive with pleasure and sweetness, silvery and flickering with smiles like water in the sun.

'And I've got to go and interview the Head of Sales.' I laughed. 'Guilty as hell. Out on his ear!'

'That reminds me,' she said, slowing down for a moment. 'Now I've paid, I want the password.'

'Fair enough,' I said.

We stopped, she stooped down, and I stood on tiptoe to whisper it into her ear.

She laughed aloud.

'Wurstigkeit' · 2000

Index of Authors

ACKNOWLEDGEMENTS

I would like to thank Boris Bradley-Kramer, Malcolm Bull, Ann Colcord, Donna Coonan, Elise Dillsworth, Lennie Goodings, Christine Jones, Michelle Lovric, Vanessa Neuling and Andrew Wille for their suggestions.

Every effort has been made to trace the copyright-holders of the copyright material in this book and to provide correct details of copyright. Virago regrets any oversight and upon written notification will rectify any omission in future reprints or editions.

When Ladies Go A-Thieving: Middle-Class Shoplifters in the Victorian Department Store by Elaine Abelson, published by Oxford University Press, Inc, reprinted by permission of the publishers. Copyright © 1989 Elaine S. Abelson.

'Shopping Lists' from *Green Resistance: New and Selected Poems* by Anna Adams, published by Enitharmon Press, reprinted by permission of the publishers. Copyright © 1996 Anna Adams.

The Letters of Rachel Henning, edited by David Adams, published by Angus & Robertson Ltd, reprinted by permission of HarperCollins Publishers Australia.

'Consider the Red Cloak' from *The Love of Clothes and Nakedness* by Karen Alkalay-Gut, published by the Israel Federation of Writers Unions, Tel Aviv, reprinted by permission of the author. Copyright © 1999 Karen Alkalay-Gut.

A Woman in Berlin (anonymous), published by Virago Press, reprinted by permission of the publishers. Copyright © 2002 Hannelore Marke, English translation copyright © 2004 Philip Boehm.

'Men, Women have similar rates of compulsive buying, Stanford Study Shows' by Michelle Brandt, first published on www.eurekalert.org in September 2006, reprinted by permission of the Stanford University School of Medicine.

I Love a Sunburnt Country: The Diaries of Dorothea Mackellar, edited by Jyoti Brundon, published by Angus & Robertson Ltd, reprinted by permission of the Dorothea Mackellar Estate, care of Curtis Brown (Australia) Pty Ltd.

The War Diary of Iris M. Bullen from *A Record or Diary of an Anxious and Eventful Period in My Life*, published in *British and Irish Women's Letters and Diaries* by Alexander Street Press (2004).

Excerpt from *Manhattan, When I Was Young* by Mary Cantwell. Copyright © 1995 Mary Cantwell. Originally published in *Manhattan, When I Was Young*. Reprinted by permission of the estate of the author.

Five Months Fine Weather in Canada, Western U.S., and Mexico by Lady Mary Rhodes Carbutt (1889), from Early Canadiana Online, produced by Canadiana.org. CIHM number 03839.

The Magic Toyshop by Angela Carter, published by Virago Press, reprinted by permission of the Estate of Angela Carter c/o Rogers, Coleridge & White Ltd. Copyright © 1979 Angela Carter.

Articles by Jess Cartner-Morley and Rahila Gupta from the *Guardian*, articles by Lynn Barber and Lucy Siegle and an extract from an interview with Lisa Snowdon from the *Observer*, reprinted by permission of Guardian News and Media Ltd. Copyright © 2006 Guardian News and Media Ltd.

Wild Swans by Jung Chang, published by HarperCollins Publishers Ltd, reprinted by permission of the publishers. Copyright © 1991 Globalflair Ltd.

The Girl with a Pearl Earring by Tracy Chevalier, published by HarperCollins Publishers Ltd, reprinted by permission of the publishers. Copyright © 1999 Tracy Chevalier.

'Shopping' from *Five Fields* by Gillian Clarke, published by Carcanet,

Café Europa: Life after Communism by Slavenka Drakulić, published by Abacus, reprinted by permission of the publishers. Copyright © 1996 Slavenka Drakulić.

An American Girl in London by Sara Jeannette Duncan (1891), from Early Canadiana Online, produced by Canadiana.org. CIHM number 05290.

A Social Departure: how Orthodocia and I went round the world by ourselves (1890) by Sara Jeannette Duncan, from Early Canadiana Online, produced by Canadiana.org. CIHM number 05296.

Maria Monk's Daughter: an autobiography by L. St John Eckel (1874), from Early Canadiana Online, produced by Canadiana.org. CIHM number 06398.

The Purefoy Letters, edited by George Eland, published by Sidgwick & Jackson in 1931.

Fanny Herself by Edna Ferber, reprinted by permission of Julie Gilbert, Executor for the Estate of Edna Ferber.

Bridget Jones's Diary: a Novel by Helen Fielding, published by Picador, an imprint of Pan Macmillan, reprinted by permission of the publishers. Copyright © 1996 Helen Fielding.

Watching the English: The Hidden Rules of English Behaviour by Kate Fox, published by Hodder & Stoughton, reprinted by permission of the publishers. Copyright © 2004 Kate Fox.

Window Shopping: Cinema and the Postmodern by Anne Friedberg, published by the University of California Press, reprinted by permission of the publishers. Copyright © 1993 Anne Friedberg.

'Are We Related?' by Linda Grant, published in Granta 60: *Unbelievable*, December 1997, reprinted by permission of A.P. Watt Ltd. Copyright © 1997 Linda Grant.

The George Eliot Letters, vol 1: 1836–1851 and vol 7: 1878–1880, edited by George S. Haight, published by Yale University Press in 1954.

84, Charing Cross Road by Helene Hanff, published by Andre

Mystery Series®. Nancy Drew and all related characters and images are © registered trademarks of Simon & Schuster, Inc. All Rights Reserved.

'Shopping' by Sarah Kennedy, originally published in *Feminist Studies*, Volume 27, Number 2 (Summer 2001): 491–2, reprinted by permission of the publisher, *Feminist Studies*, Inc.

Edwardian Daughter by Sonia Keppel, published by Hamish Hamilton, an imprint of Penguin Books Ltd. Copyright © 1958 Sonia Keppel.

The Secret Dreamworld of a Shopaholic by Sophie Kinsella, published by Black Swan, reprinted by permission of the Random House Group Ltd. Copyright © 2000 Sophie Kinsella.

Spree: A Cultural History of Shopping by Pamela Klaffke, published by Arsenal Pulp Press, reprinted by permission of the publishers. Copyright © 2003 Pamela Klaffke.

No Logo by Naomi Klein, published by HarperCollins Publishers Ltd, reprinted by permission of the publishers. Copyright © 2000 Naomi Klein.

The Shops by India Knight (Viking 2003, Penguin Books Ltd 2004), reprinted by permission of the publishers. Copyright © 2003 India Knight.

Scruples by Judith Krantz, published by Weidenfeld & Nicolson, a division of the Orion Publishing Group, reprinted by permission of the publishers. Copyright © 1978 by Steve Krantz Productions.

Selected Letters of Jane Austen, edited by Deirdre Le Faye, published by Oxford University Press, reprinted by permission of the publishers. Copyright © 1995 Deirdre Le Faye.

Not Buying It: My Year Without Shopping by Judith Levine, published by Simon & Schuster, reprinted by permission of the publishers. Copyright © 2006 Judith Levine.

Autobiography of a Geisha by Sayo Masuda, published by Vintage, reprinted by permission of the Random House Group Ltd. Copyright

Cambridge University Press, reprinted by permission of the publishers. Copyright © 1947 Margaret Penn.

Lady Gregory's Diaries, 1892–1902, edited by James Pethica, published by Colin Smythe Ltd, reprinted by permission of the publishers. Copyright © 1996 Anne de Winton and Catherine Kennedy.

The Second World War Diary of Kate Phipps, published in *British and Irish Women's Letters and Diaries* by Alexander Street Press (2004). Copyright © John Davies.

Restoration London by Liza Picard, published by Weidenfeld & Nicolson, a division of the Orion Publishing Group, reprinted by permission of the publishers. Copyright © 1997 Liza Picard.

My Mother's Wedding Dress by Justine Picardie, published by Picador, an imprint of Pan Macmillan, reprinted by permission of the publishers. Copyright © 2005 Justine Picardie.

The Popcorn Report: Faith Popcorn on the Future of Your Company, Your World, Your Life by Faith Popcorn, published by Bantam Doubleday, a division of Random House, Inc, reprinted by permission of the publishers. Copyright © 1991 Faith Popcorn.

Tale of the Pie and the Patty Pan by Beatrix Potter, published by Frederick Warne & Co Ltd, reprinted by permission of the publishers. Copyright © 1905 Frederick Warne & Co Ltd.

A Glass of Blessings by Barbara Pym, reprinted by permission of Hazel Holt, Executor for the Literary Estate of Barbara Pym. Copyright © 1958 The Estate of Barbara Pym.

Just Ask a Woman: Cracking the Code of What Women Want and How They Buy by Mary Lou Quinlan, published by J. Wiley & Sons, Inc, reprinted by permission of the publishers. Copyright © 2003 Mary Lou Quinlan.

Round About a Pound a Week by Maud Pember Reeves, published by Virago Press, reprinted by permission of the publishers. Copyright © 1913 The Estate of Mrs Pember Reeves.

published in *British and Irish Women's Letters and Diaries* by Alexander Street Press (2004). Copyright © Simon Strange.

Selected Letters of Alessandra Strozzi, translated with an introduction and notes by Heather Gregory, published by University of California Press, reprinted by permission of the publishers. Copyright © 1997 The Regents of the University of California.

Mrs Miniver by Jan Struther, published by Virago Press, reprinted by permission of the publishers. Copyright © 1939 The Estate of Jan Struther.

Bergdorf Blondes by Plum Sykes (Viking 2004, Penguin Books Ltd 2005), reprinted by permission of the publishers. Copyright © 2004 Plum Sykes.

The Secret History by Donna Tartt (Viking 1992, Penguin Books Ltd 1993, Penguin Red Classics 2006), reprinted by permission of the publishers. Copyright © 1992 Donna Tartt.

Pillion Riders by Elisabeth Russell Taylor, published by Virago Press, reprinted by permission of the publishers. Copyright © 1993 Elisabeth Russell Taylor.

'A Perfect Entente' by Elisabeth Russell Taylor, copyright © 2007 Elisabeth Russell Taylor.

'Peddler Jenny', an unpublished story by Mari Tomasi, reprinted by permission of the Library of Congress, Manuscript Division, WPA Federal Writers' Project Collection.

The Secret Diary of Adrian Mole, Aged 13¾ by Sue Townsend, published by Methuen, reprinted by permission of the Random House Group Ltd. Copyright © 1985 Sue Townsend.

Mary Poppins by P.L. Travers, reprinted by permission of the Trustees of the Estate of P.L. Travers. Copyright © The Estate of P.L. Travers.

The Rector's Wife by Joanna Trollope, published by Bloomsbury Publishing plc, reprinted by permission of the publishers. Copyright © 1991 Joanna Trollope.

Nicola Silver by Ethel Turner, published by Ward Lock, a division of

Point of Purchase: How Shopping Changed American Culture by Sharon Zukin, published by Routledge, a division of Taylor & Francis Group, reprinted by permission of the publishers. Copyright © 2004, 2005 Sharon Zukin.

FURTHER READING

Abelson, Elaine S.

When Ladies Go A-Thieving: Middle-class Shoplifters in the Victorian Department Store, © 1989 Elaine S. Abelson, New York: Oxford University Press

Adburgham, Alison

Shops and Shopping 1800–1914: Where, and in What Manner the Well-dressed Englishwoman Bought her Clothes, © 1964 George Allen & Unwin Ltd, London: George Allen & Unwin Ltd

Shopping in Style: London from the Restoration to Edwardian Elegance, © Alison Adburgham 1979, London: Thames and Hudson

Bowlby, Rachel

Carried Away: The Invention of Modern Shopping, © Rachel Bowlby 2000, London: Faber and Faber Ltd

Shopping with Freud, © Rachel Bowlby 1993, London: Routledge

Davis, Dorothy

A History of Shopping, © Dorothy Davis 1966, London: Routledge & Kegan Paul Ltd; Toronto: University of Toronto Press

Klaffke, Pamela

Spree: A Cultural History of Shopping, © Pamela Klaffke 2003, Vancouver: Arsenal Pulp Press

Rappaport, Erika Diane

Shopping for Pleasure: Women in the Making of London's West End, © Erika Diane Rappaport 1999, Princeton University Press

Satterthwaite, Ann

Going Shopping: Consumer Choices and Community Consequences, © 2001 Yale University Press

THE VIRAGO BOOK
OF FOOD
The Joy of Eating

Edited by Jill Foulston

'Sensual, funny and captivating . . . will delight anyone who loves to read about the pleasure of a good meal' *Good Housekeeping*

Beatrix Potter wove one of her most malicious tales around the roly-poly pudding. Dorothy Wordsworth noted her pie-making sessions in her diary and Anne Frank observed the eating habits of her companions in hiding.

Food is never written about so devotedly or voluptuously as in women's novels, letters and diaries. In this anthology, you can go on a picnic with Monica Ali, graze at Frida Kahlo's wedding feast and play the glutton with Edwidge Danticat. And why not sneak into the literary kitchens of Banana Yoshimoto, Emily Brontë and Angela Carter?

'This lip-smacking tome provides any food lover with a delightful spread of tasty morsels' *She*

'An ideal bedside book. The perfect Christmas gift' BBC *Good Food*

**You can order other Virago titles through our website: *www.virago.co.uk*
or by using the order form below**

☐ The Joy of Eating   ed. Jill Foulston   £9.99

*The prices shown above are correct at time of going to press. However, the
publishers reserve the right to increase prices on covers from those previously
advertised, without further notice.*

—————————————————   🍎   —————————————————

Please allow for postage and packing: **Free UK delivery.**
Europe: add 25% of retail price; Rest of World: 45% of retail price.

To order any of the above or any other Virago titles, please call our credit
card orderline or fill in this coupon and send/fax it to:

Virago, PO Box 121, Kettering, Northants NN14 4ZQ
Fax: 01832 733076   Tel: 01832 737526
Email: aspenhouse@FSBDial.co.uk

☐ I enclose a UK bank cheque made payable to Virago for £ . . . .
☐ Please charge £ . . . . . . to my Visa/Delta/Maestro

Expiry Date | | | | | Maestro Issue No. | | |

NAME (BLOCK LETTERS please) . . . .
ADDRESS . . . .
. . . .
. . . .
Postcode . . . . Telephone . . . .
Signature . . . .

Please allow 28 days for delivery within the UK. Offer subject to price and availability.